AF251404

Theophilus Brown

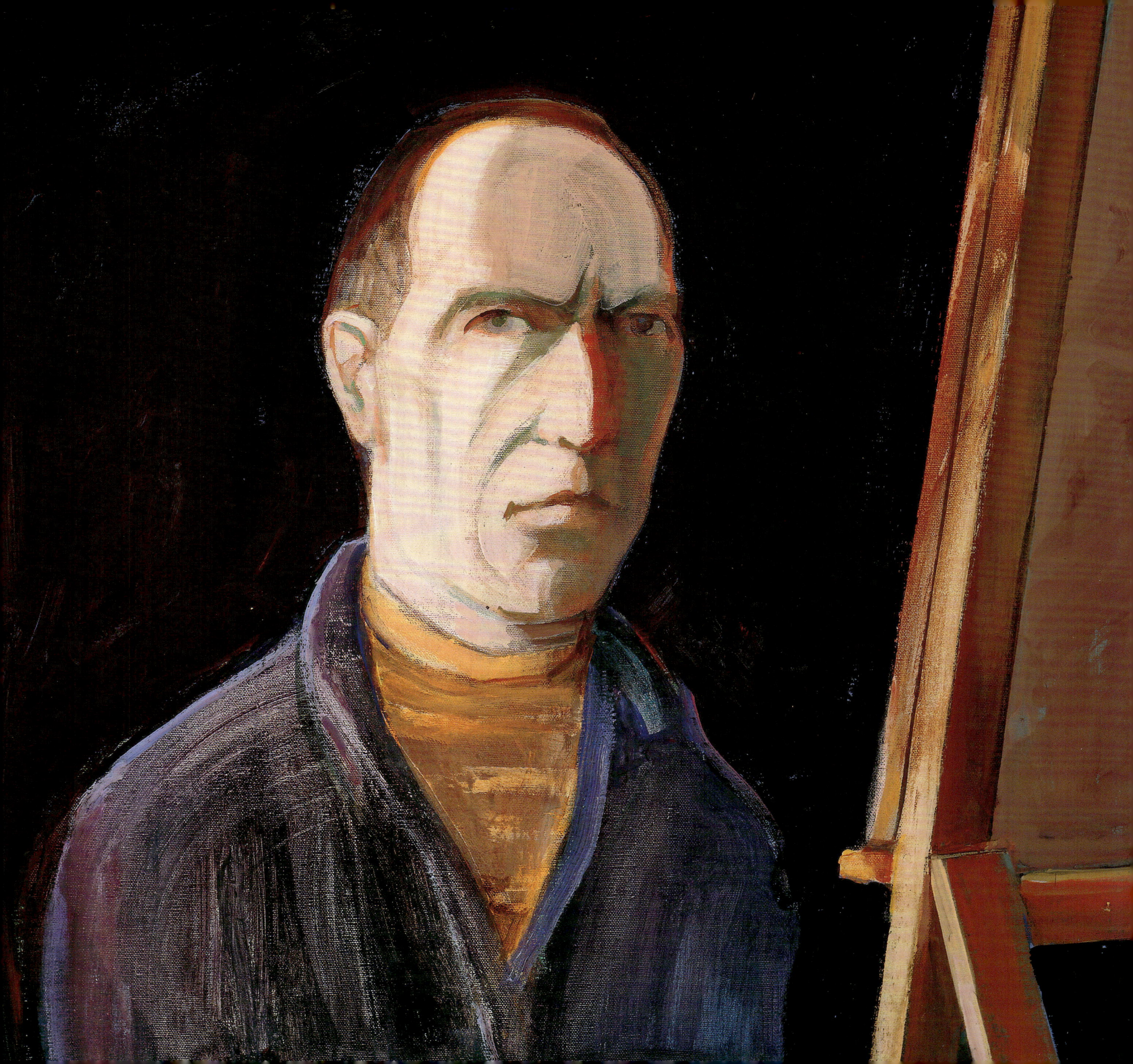

Theophilus Brown
Paintings, Collages, & Drawings

John Arthur

CHAMELEON BOOKS, MASSACHUSETTS

A CHAMELEON BOOK

Published and produced in the United States of America by
Chameleon Books
31 Smith Road
Chesterfield, MA 01012

Distributed in the United States and Canada by
Antique Collectors' Club, Ltd.
Eastworks, 116 Pleasant Street (Suite 18)
Easthampton, MA 01027

Phone: (800) 252 5231 or (413) 529 0861
Fax: (413) 529 0862
Email: orders@antiquecc.com
http://www.antiquecollectorsclub.club

13-digit ISBN: 9780915829750
10-digit ISBN: 0915829754

Printed in China

SELF-PORTRAIT 1995
acrylic on canvas, 24 x 24 inches
Courtesy of the Artist and Elins Eagles-Smith Gallery, San Francisco

For Paul Wonner

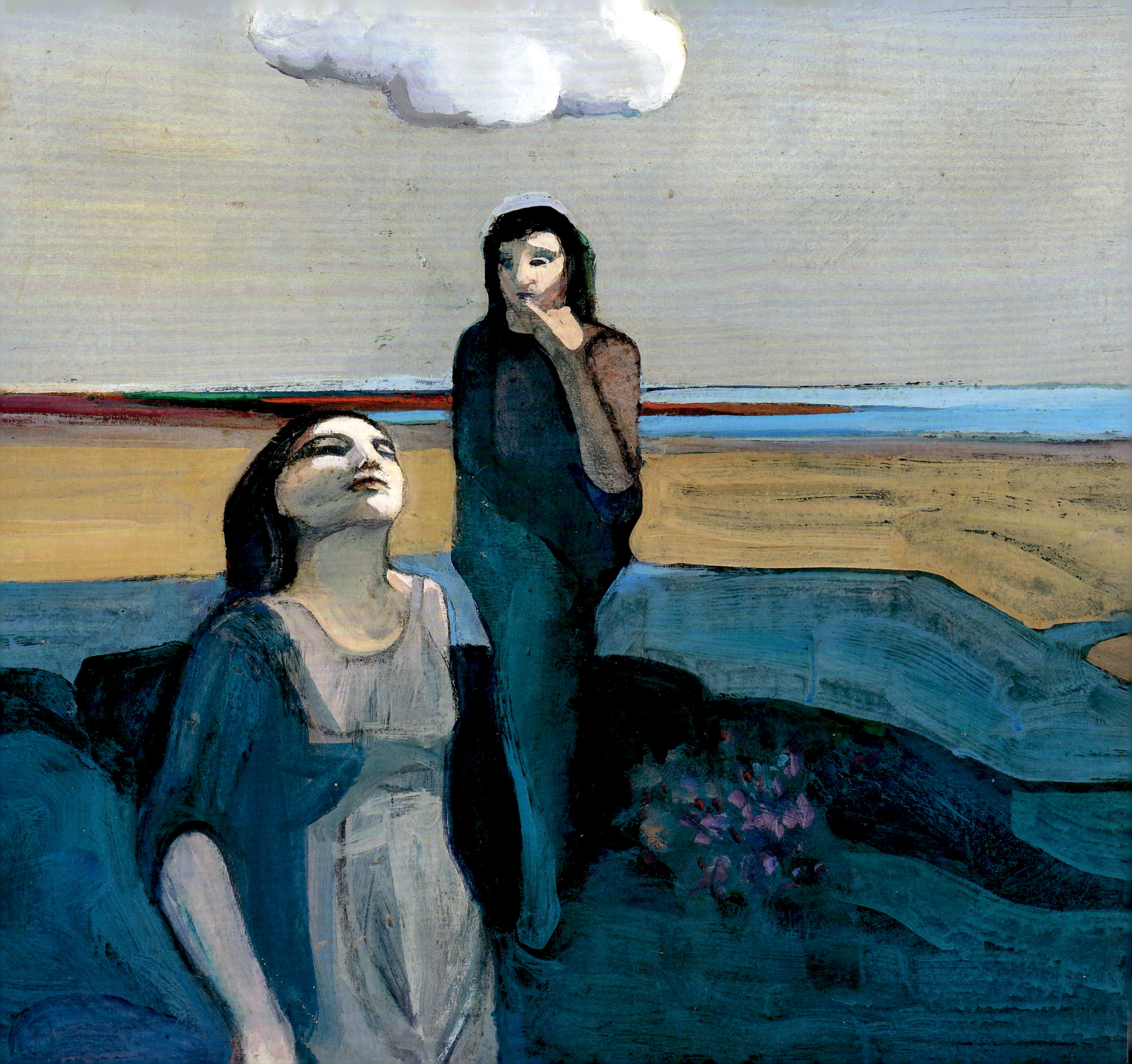

Prologue

Say what some poets will, Nature is not so much her own ever-sweet interpreter, as the mere supplier of that cunning alphabet, whereby selecting and combining as he pleases, each man reads his own peculiar lesson according to his own peculiar mind and mood.
—HERMAN MELVILLE

Me imperturbe, standing at ease in nature.
—WALT WHITMAN

WILLIAM THEOPHILUS BROWN was born in Moline, Illinois, on April 7, 1919. His father, a descendent of New England tradesmen and intellectuals, was an inventor specializing in farm implements. Accepting a position as head of the experimental department of the John Deere Company took him from New England to Moline, where he met and married Elise Koehler. He held more than one hundred and fifty patents.

The painter's great-grandfather Theophilus Brown was known as the "wit of Worcester" and was considered to be the city's "freshest and most original mind." He and Sarah Ann Brown were friends of Ralph Waldo Emerson, Henry David Thoreau, and the Concord Transcendentalists. Theophilus and Sarah's home served as the gathering place for Amos Bronson Alcott's *Conversations,* and the famous daguerreotype of Thoreau—one of the great photographic icons of American art and letters—was taken in their home.

This rich lineage, which Brown wears lightly and rarely mentions, is indicative of the abundant gifts he inherited. He is an erudite intellectual with an inventive mind, a multifaceted curiosity, and a restless spirit.

Brown's diverse abilities were clearly demonstrated when he entered Yale University. Dissatisfied with its somewhat archaic painting program, he immediately changed his major to music. In addition to his aptitude as a painter, he is a very fine pianist with a great passion for music, and he continues to play on a regular schedule.

Both Brown's career and his personal life have been marked by the deep and lasting friendships that he has so easily made and carefully maintained over the decades. To have done so is both a gift and a skill that requires loyalty, respect, and diplomacy, in addition to the bonds of mutual interests, endeavors, and principles.

While at Yale he developed close ties with the composer Paul Hindemith, fellow student Thomas Hess, and the poet May Sarton, whom he met in 1939 on the *Normandie* en route to Europe for his first summer abroad. He and Sarton corresponded throughout the war and stayed in touch until her death in 1995.

Soon after graduating from Yale in 1941, Brown was drafted into the army and served in the Signal Corps during World War II. He survived the Battle of the Bulge—from its first inglorious day to the last battle—and was among the first Allies to cross into the German mainland.

Following his discharge he moved restlessly between New York and Paris, using the GI Bill ostensibly to study painting, though it served more as a means of livelihood. While he did not often attend the ateliers, he was painting during this period.

Prior to World War II, a diverse group of immigrant artists and intellectuals—Marcel Duchamp, Francis Picabia, Arshile Gorky, Willem de Kooning, Matta, and others—had settled in New York. The art, literature, music, and film of these émigrés produced major upheavals in American culture and in the decades following the war the center of the art world gradually shifted from Paris to Manhattan.

Paris attracted such American expatriates as Ernest Hemingway, John Dos Possos, Gertrude Stein, Dorothy Parker, F. Scott Fitzgerald, Henry Miller, and Berenice Abbott before World War II was emerging from the pall of German occupation and regaining its luster. By the close of the war Picasso, Braque, and Matisse were legendary figures. Intellectual thought was heavily tinged by the Existentialism of Jean Paul-Sartre and the literature of Albert Camus. Through the criticism of *Cahiers du Cinéma* there was a gradual move from their pre-war, Hollywood-inspired pap toward the neo-realism of Jean-Luc Godard, François Truffaut, Claude Chabrol, and the postwar generation of *auteurs.*

Brown met Willem and Elaine de Kooning and Mark and Mell Rothko in New York through Thomas Hess. During his various sojourns in Paris, Brown struck up a casual friendship with Picasso and visited the studios of Braque, Giacometti, Balthus, and other modern masters. In addition, camaraderies with the composers Francis Poulenc and Samuel Barber developed. He first met Igor and Vera Stravinsky in Santa Fe in 1951. Brown's friendship with them developed in Europe and continued in Southern California.

He enrolled in the graduate studio program at the University of California, Berkeley, in 1952 at the age of thirty-three. Four years later he achieved national attention in a *Life* magazine article on his football paintings. By the late fifties he had found his center as a painter. Always a figurative artist, Brown's sensibility crystallized through the cross-pollination of de Kooning's earlier mentoring and his heady rapport with Richard Diebenkorn, David Park, Elmer Bischoff, Paul Wonner, James Weeks, and Nathan Oliveira. Of major significance was the emotional stability provided by his deepening relationship with Paul Wonner, who was also in the graduate painting program at UC Berkeley.

In 1961 Wonner accepted a teaching position at the University of California, Los Angeles, which was also the year Brown had his first solo exhibit. During this time he and Wonner lived near the beach in Santa Monica and Malibu. Wonner later accepted a teaching position in Santa Barbara, and they moved to Montecito. The years in Southern California were halcyon for Brown and Wonner. Not only was it an extremely productive period, but important personal and creative relationships evolved during that period. Their friendships with the novelist Christopher Isherwood and his companion, the portrait artist Don Bachardy, deepened. In addition, they developed close ties

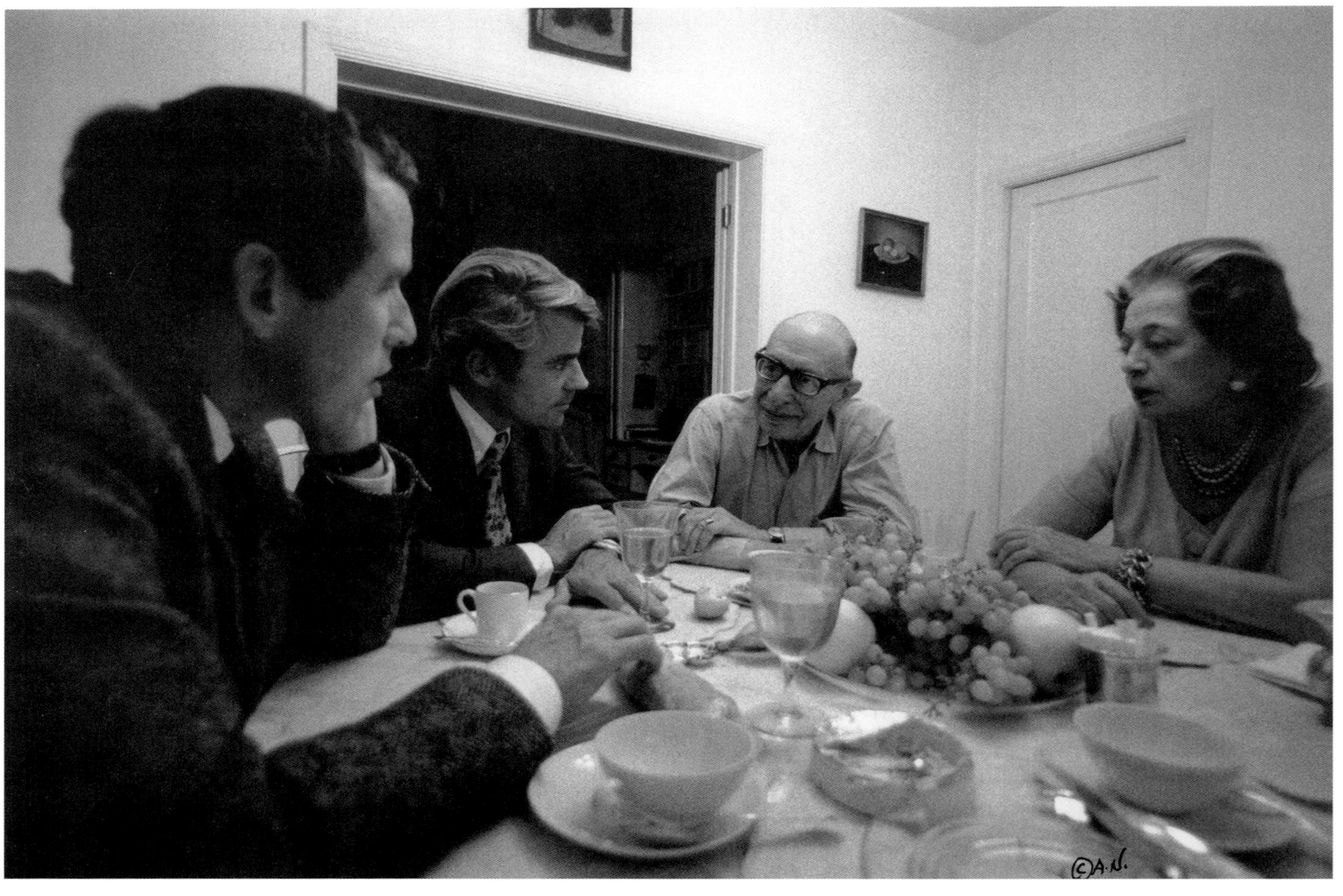

  William Theophilus Brown, Don Bachardy, Igor and Vera Stravinsky   Photograph by Arnold Newman

with the playwright William Inge; composer and conductor Andre Previn and his wife Dory; and actress Eva Marie Saint and her husband, the director Jeffrey Hayden. For a brief and very intense period the New Zealand writer Janet Frame lived with Brown and Wonner. Brown had met her earlier at the McDowell Colony in New Hampshire.

Over the decades—in Berkeley, Southern California, and San Francisco—Brown has worked from the model in weekly studio sessions. At various times, this drawing group has included David Park, Richard Diebenkorn, Paul Wonner, Elmer Bischoff, James Weeks, Don Bachardy, Gordon Cook, Beth Van Hoesen, Mark Adams, and Wayne Thiebaud.

Now in his eighties, Brown still drives to the studio almost daily and continues to paint and draw. He is a voracious reader and plays piano sonatas accompanied by a violinist once a week.

Theophilus Brown—more than any painter this writer has encountered over the past three decades—deserves a full and carefully researched biography, an endeavor unfortunately outside the parameters of a monograph and beyond the means of this writer. Without Brown's account, too much of his rich personal history and the numerous delightful and vivid details about his friends and associates—many of them key figures in the arts and literature of the twentieth century—will simply disappear, and this will be a loss to the intellectual and cultural history of our time. Such revealing incidents are never buried; instead they are lost in bits and pieces.

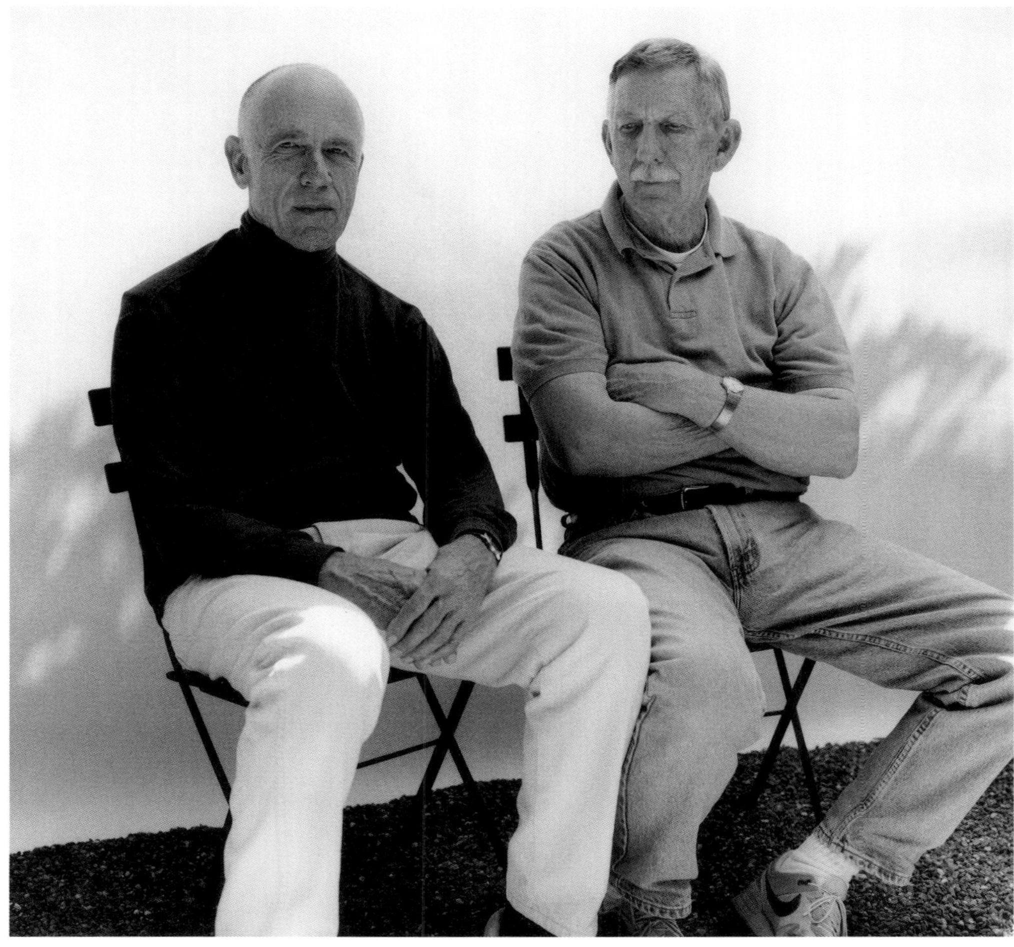

Theophilus (Bill) Brown and Paul Wonner   Photograph by Ira Shank

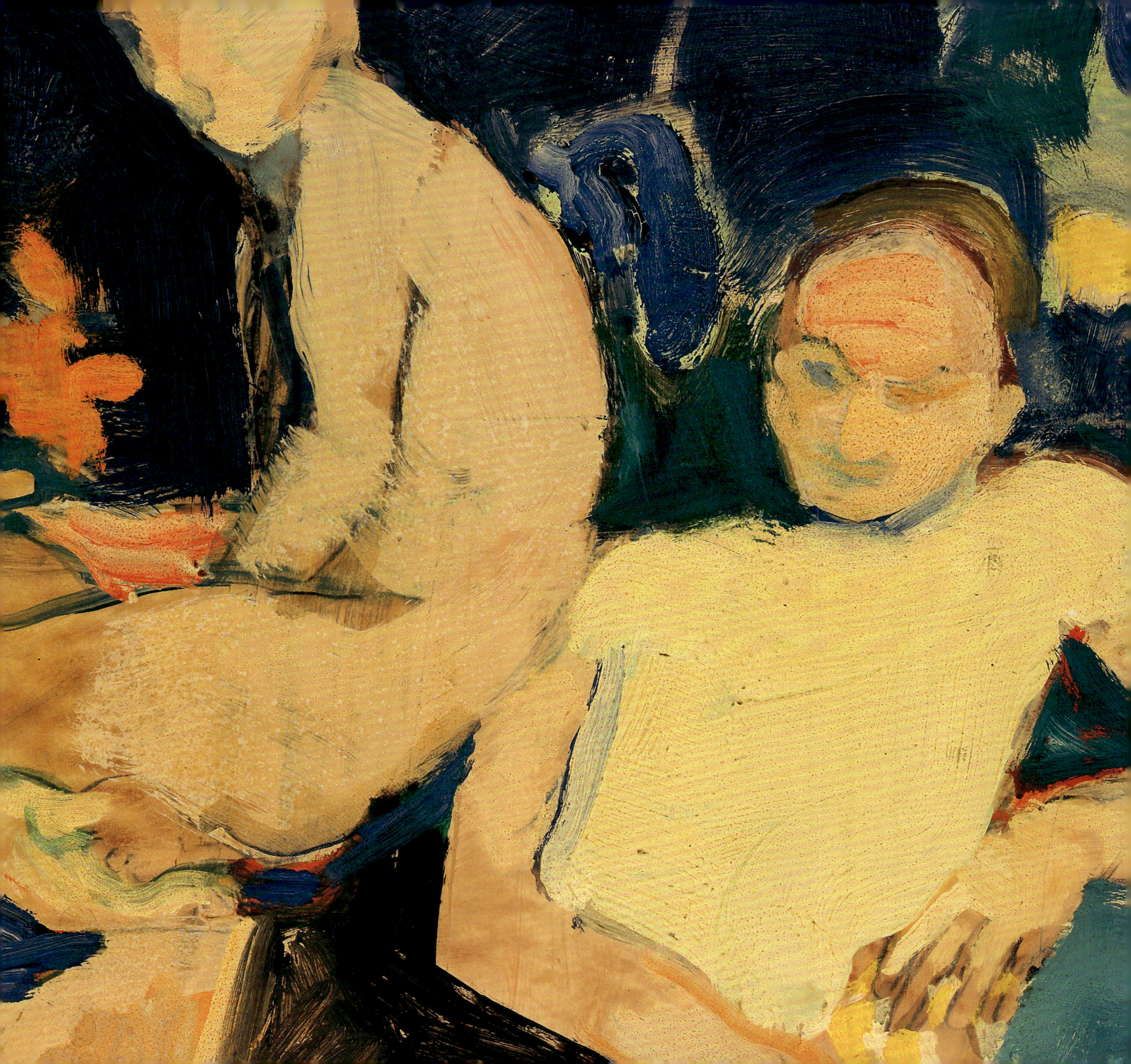

Theophilus Brown and Bay Area Figurative Painting

Experience, and experience alone, tells me that representational painting and sculpture have rarely achieved more than minor quality in recent years, and that major quality gravitates more and more toward the nonrepresentational.
—CLEMENT GREENBERG, *Art and Culture,* 1961

He [Greenberg] wants to be my boss but without pay.
—WILLEM DE KOONING

The American mainstream has fanned out into a delta in which the traditional idea of the avant-garde has drowned. Thus in defiance of the dogma that realist painting was killed by abstract art and photography, realism has come back in as many forms as there are painters.
—ROBERT HUGHES, "The Realist as a Corn God"
Time, JANUARY 31, 1972

BY THE EARLY FIFTIES Abstract Expressionism had changed all of the equations in contemporary painting and sculpture. Before the decade closed, its monumental influence was apparent in every aspect of the visual arts, including photography and film. Edward Hopper, Rockwell Kent, Charles Burchfield, Georgia O'Keeffe, and Edwin Dickinson were at their creative zenith during this same period, but having been born in the late nineteenth century, their sensibilities were nearer to the generation of Marsden Hartley, Charles Demuth Arthur Dove, and the Modernists of the Stieglitz circle. Figurative painters such as John Koch, Paul Cadmus, Fairfield Porter, and Alice Neel—their visual descriptions ranging from Koch's eloquently painted autobiographical incidents to Cadmus's masterfully rendered homoerotic narratives and allegories, Porter's form of painterly realism based on empirical observation and plein air painting, and Neel's psychologically probing and frequently savage portraits—were all roughly the same age as Willem de Kooning, Mark Rothko, Jackson Pollock, and Franz Kline.

Unfortunately, the importance of these distinct and care-fully nuanced figurative parallels in American art of the fifties has been largely ignored in most accounts of the period. Perhaps having drunk too long from the cup of Formalism—a diet indubitably bad for the eyes—many art historians continually insist on a narrow, anemic program for the American art of the last half of the twentieth century that simply did not exist.

In the fifties, Willem de Kooning moved freely from his depictions of wild-eyed, fang-teethed creatures such as *Woman I* (1950–55) and *Woman as Landscape* (1955) to the raw, highly charged abstractions as *Police Gazette* (1954–55) and *Interchange* (1955). This was an act that he—in spite of Greenberg's admonishment—found to be neither misogynistic nor inconsistent. Also, the insinuation of a rift between abstract painters and figurative painters was primarily a quarrel hatched by the critics, curators, and academics. This ongoing misconception has been coupled with a widely propagated notion held by the academics that the true inheritors of the mantle of Abstract Expressionism are the Formalists, Minimalists, and Conceptualists.

In fact, the painter and critic Fairfield Porter, whose realism was rooted in the tradition of early twentieth-century French painting, was one of the earliest champions of Willem de Kooning, and Mark Rothko always spoke glowingly of the strong influence of Milton Avery, who was a close friend and a trusted mentor.

Decade after decade, such blinkered narrowness has been repeatedly demonstrated by many of our critics, museum curators, and art historians. In 1997, the Museum of Modern Art mounted *Objects of Desire: The Modern Still Life*. This incoherent, agenda-sodden survey ranging from Picasso and Matisse to Andy Warhol, Jasper Johns, and Robert Rauchenberg limped to a conclusion with the works of Cindy Sherman and Jeff Koons, and came to a numbing end with Wolfgang Laib's conceptual milk tray. However, at no point along the way was there any suggestion of the presence of the many major Modern artists who were widely heralded during the same period for their still lifes—Georgia O'Keeffe, Charles Demuth, Hyman Bloom, Edwin Dickinson, Fairfield Porter, Richard Diebenkorn, Paul Wonner, Wayne Thiebaud, William Bailey, Janet Fish, and others—in spite of the fact that they were much better known for the genre than most of their contemporaries in the exhibit. Even major Pop artists such as James Rosenquist, Tom Wesselman, and Jim

Dine inexplicably failed to make the curator's cut.

The following year, in spite of the abundance of evidence provided by Jackson Pollock's late paintings, such as *Number 27* (1951), *Black and White, No. 5* (1952), *Easter and the Totem* (1953), and the widely reproduced *Portrait and a Dream* (1953), Kirk Varnedoe skirted over Pollock's search for a means of transliterating his gestural drips and slashes into a personal form of figuration.

Pointing out these distortions is not an attempt to revise or reassess the history of the last fifty years, nor is it an apologist's defense of figurative painting in the second half of the twentieth century. Instead, it is a matter of acknowledging historical facts.

Coupled with the existential angst and loss of idealism churned up in the aftermath of World War II, the concept of subjective realities was brought into brilliant focus by Kurosawa's *Rashomon* (1950), the layered and mythic narratives of Ingmar Bergman's *Seventh Seal* (1957) and Lawrence Durrell's *Alexandrian Quartet* (1957–60), and the conflicting remembrances of places and events described in Alain Resnais's *Last Year at Marienbad* (1962).

Of key importance in recounting those heady days is the fact that many of the following generation of artists had direct contact with the Abstract Expressionists through the downtown galleries and loft parties, volatile meetings at the Club, and inebriated evenings at the Cedar Street Tavern. Almost all of them began their careers as gestural abstractionists or non-objective painters. They rejected the cornpone allegories and overworked, leathery surfaces of the Regionalists and shared a reverential interest in Picasso, Matisse, Dada, and Surrealism (embracing the automatism and accidents of Breton, Miró, Ernst, Duchamp, and De Chirico rather than the flamboyant showmanship of Dali). These connections and assimilations occurred across the esthetic spectrum—Formalism, Pop, Duchampian risk, Minimalism, Assemblage, Expressionism, Realism—and deep and lasting friendships developed, such as William de Kooning's relationship with Arshile Gorky, and Mark Rothko's familial closeness to Milton Avery.

The bridge between de Kooning's *Women,* Pollock's dripped imagery, William Baziotes' amorphous automatism, and the Realism of the mid-fifties and sixties was the gestural figuration of New York's Elaine de Kooning, George McNeil, Grace Hartigan, Jan Müller, and Larry Rivers, along with the indomitable Alice Neel and the eloquent elder statesman Edwin Dickinson. In the Midwest there were the large, politically charged works of Leon Golub and Peter Saul, the inventive figuration of James McGarrell, and the baroque allegories of Robert Barnes. The Bay Area contemporaries of these figurative expressionists and improvisational artists were David Park, Elmer Bischoff, Nathan Oliveira, Richard Diebenkorn, Theophilus Brown, Paul Wonner, and James Weeks, along with other painters, printmakers, sculptors, and ceramists. It was the charismatic Park that led the Bay Area's shift from non-objective painting toward a highly charged, psychologically nuanced return to the figure late in the forties and early fifties.

By the mid-fifties Fairfield Porter had found his footing as a painterly realist, which was concurrent with the figurative transitions of Alex Katz, Philip Pearlstein, Alfred Leslie, Nell Blaine, and other New York artists.

Beyond the superficial similarities of the East Coast realists and the Bay Area figurative painters—the gestural brushwork, slathered paint, abstract compositional devices, and other formal ploys—the differences in their attitudes and studio procedures were monumental. While this distinction is rarely mentioned in art criticism, East Coast realism centered on the European tradition of perceptual painting and that has remained a central factor over the decades. While retaining the figure with all of its intrinsic connotations and themes, the Bay Area artists tilted the emphasis toward automatism and invention—elements that were central to Abstract Expressionism, Surrealism, the improvisations of jazz, and Beat literature. Without considering these polarities, it is impossible to come to grips with the figurative painters of that period and the art that has evolved on both coasts.

After his discharge from the army in 1946 William Theophilus Brown returned to New York. He met Hedda Sterne, her husband Saul Steinberg, and Elaine and Willem de Kooning at a small dinner party given by his old Yale classmate Thomas Hess. A deep, affectionate camaraderie with the de Koonings quickly developed, and during this extended stay in New York Willem became a trusted mentor. He recalled that during one of de Kooning's visits to his studio, the painter advised him to "Just draw what you see," and then demonstrated this point by sketching the buildings beyond the window. While the rapid lines corresponded with the view, the drawing was immediately recognizable as a de Kooning. This invaluable lesson—that one does not need to strive for "style," for it is something a painter acquires with the crystallization of his or her personal vision—would be one of enduring importance for Brown.

In 1948, following the recommendation of the Abstract Expressionist sculptor Mary Callery, whom he had met after the war, and the architect Mies van der Rohe, Brown used the GI Bill to enroll in Amédée Ozenfant's atelier in New York. Ozenfant was an important theorist of the school of Paris, an exponent of Purism, and the co-publisher of *L'Esprit Nouveau*. However, Brown found his pedagogy disagreeable. After two months he left Ozenfant and returned to France for the summer.

Years earlier, while on leave in Paris during the war, Brown left a carton of American cigarettes on Georges Braque's stoop, knowing that tobacco was quite difficult to buy at that time. During his two-month sojourn in 1948 and his ten-month stay in 1949, ostensibly to study with Fernand Léger, he met Picasso, Giacometti, Braque, the Chilean surrealist Matta,

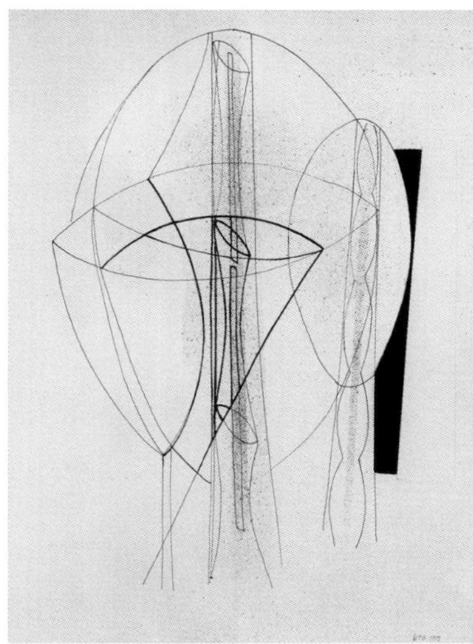

Balthus, and many other artists, often through introductions provided by the highly regarded and well connected Callery and Hess. On various occasions he visited their studios. When he showed one of his still lifes to Braque, whom he greatly admired, the painter offered the advice, "If you have the sacred fire, guard it well."

Although he enrolled in the atelier of Fernand Léger, Brown acknowledges that he rarely attended. However, the modest stipend from the education bill for returning soldiers allowed him to live in Paris during those exhilarating postwar years. On this extended stay he became involved with Francis Poulenc's biographer, and through him, Brown met the composer and other illustrious figures in the world of music.

In the spring of 1950 Brown stayed in the Rothkos' apartment while they were abroad. It was Rothko's first return to Europe since immigrating to America in 1914. During their travels Mell realized she was pregnant, and they cut short their stay after the birth of their daughter Kate in Rome. When they returned to New York Brown lived with them briefly until he found an apartment.

During these periods in Manhattan he sat in on the heated and often rowdy discussions at the Club, frequented the galleries and museums, attended concerts at Carnegie Hall, and often spent weekends with the de Koonings and other friends in the Hamptons.

Brown saw *Woman I* in progress (the painting took more than a year to complete), and witnessed the transition of Rothko's automatismic pictograms to the vaporous "multiforms." He spent winter evenings lingering over dinners filled with witty art-world gossip, career dissections, and incisive conversations about art, film, literature, and politics. And like so many of his enduring friendships, Brown remained in contact with Hess, Callery, the de Koonings, and the Rothkos over the ensuing decades. Due to his parallel avocation as a classical pianist and his voracious interest in music, literature, and poetry, he has continued his association, often through correspondence, with some of the most consequential and widely heralded musicians, composers, writers, and poets of the twentieth century.

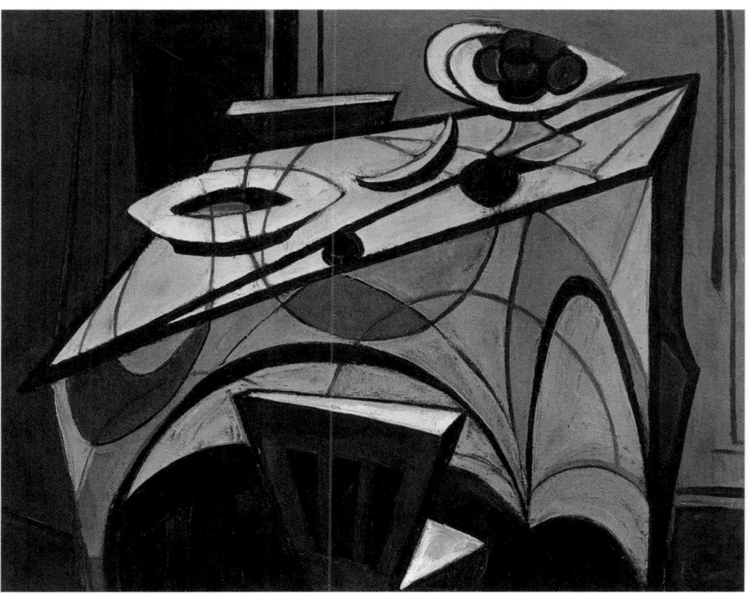

In 1951 Brown began a series of drawings and paintings that marked the first sure steps of his move toward maturation as a painter. In these works from the early fifties, the loose strands of his seemingly disassociated intellectual, esthetic, and emotional threads were woven with his personal interests and sexual inclinations as he moved toward a more idiosyncratic vision. These drawings and canvases were based on grainy, monochromatic photographs clipped from the sports pages of newspapers and magazines—cacophonous, chiaroscuro images of lunging and colliding bodies, twisting and heaving in a surreal melodrama reminiscent of Signorelli's frescoes of damnation and salvation—depicting boxing, lacrosse matches, and football games. Their spontaneity, vigorous brushwork, drips and smears, crowded perimeters, and "overall compositions" (to use Greenberg's inelegant term) reflect the strong influence of—in fact his deep familiarity with—de Kooning's abstractions and figurative paintings from the late forties and early fifties. It must be noted that Brown had no particular interest in football or any of the other competitive sports. Instead, the attraction lay closer to the dissonant jumble of patterns, the depiction of strenuous physicality, and the clutter of clashing bodies. These works take on the visual characteristics of Abstract Expressionism's non-objective character while adhering to the

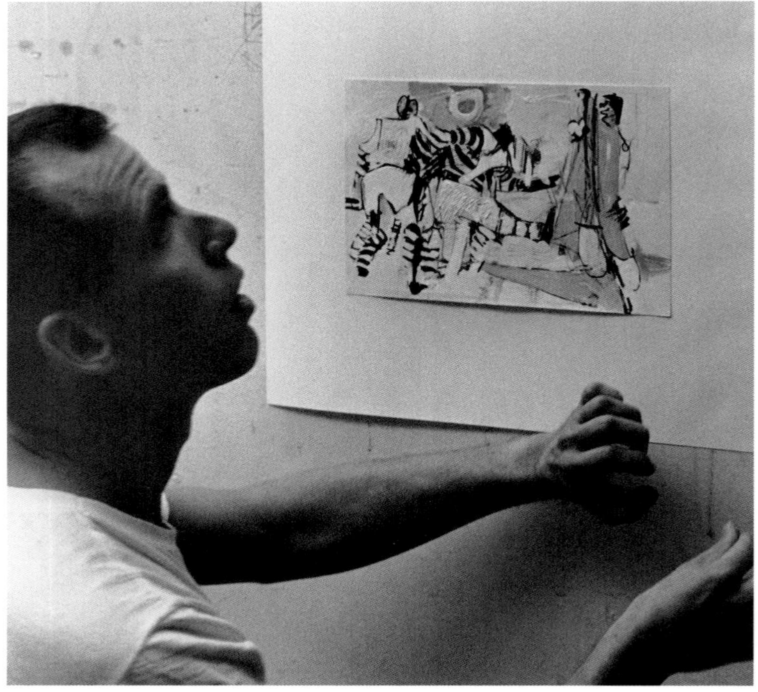

Theophilus Brown in his studio, 1956

chiaroscuro and forms of the photographs.

In the spring of 1952 Brown returned to Europe and stayed through the summer. He spent a few leisurely weeks with Poulenc and his friends in the composer's country house, and then was invited to Amsterdam by the Stravinskys for a festival honoring the composer and his music. At the end of the summer he stayed for a week with Samuel Barber in Corsica, and then returned to New York in late August.

On the advice of Reginald Neal, Brown applied to the graduate painting program at the University of California in Berkeley for the fall semester. Neal had been his high school art instructor in Moline and had remained a trusted advisor. At this time he was the head of the Cornell University art department, and though Brown applied quite late, with Neal's recommendation he was accepted. Brown immediately moved to Berkeley and, once settled, continued his series of football and sports paintings.

William Theophilus Brown was thirty-three, roughly the same age as Elmer Bischoff, Richard Diebenkorn, Paul Wonner, and James Weeks. Like him, they were using the GI Bill to study art at the university.

That first semester in Berkeley, Brown met Paul Wonner in the university painting studio, a casual encounter that ultimately proved to be of major significance in his personal life. Wonner had served a stint in the army and completed his service in 1946. After being discharged he moved to New York where he attended the Arts Students League, sat in on the lectures at Robert Motherwell's studio, and, like Brown, spent his free time in the museums and galleries. Although they were in Manhattan at the same time, they never met. In the fall of 1950 Wonner returned to California and was studying painting at Berkeley when Brown entered the program. Both Wonner and Brown completed their Master of Arts degrees in 1953. They began living together in 1954 and have been inseparable for more than half a century.

Brown was employed as a teaching assistant at UC Berkeley for three years. In 1955 he taught drawing at the California School of Fine Arts in San Francisco, commuting from Berkeley to San Francisco with Nathan Oliveira. During this period he shared a studio on Shuttuck Avenue with Wonner. Other artists, including Richard Diebenkorn, had studios in the same building. Models were hired for informal drawing sessions. From time to

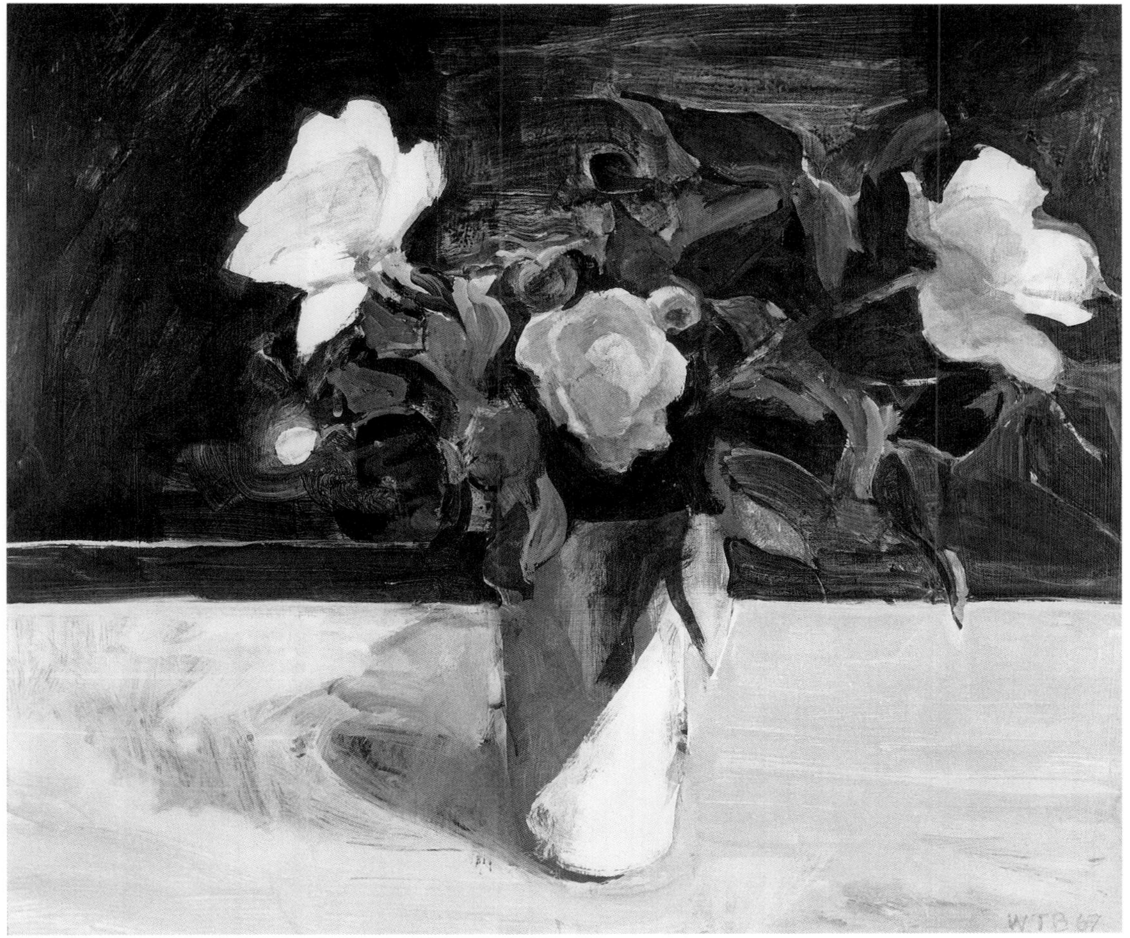

time, these sessions included Richard Diebenkorn, David Park, Elmer Bischoff, Nathan Oliveira, Brown, and Wonner. This informal and highly individualistic group—bound together by abiding friendships, meager means, common aspirations, and working facilities rather than by a shared polemic or esthetic program—formed the nucleus of what is well known today as the Bay Area figurative painters. Brown was the only one, from his early years until very late in his career, whose paintings and drawings never strayed from forms of recognizable representation.

Brown's first decade in California clearly marks the course toward his maturity as an artist. The earlier aspects of Brown's formal inventory, such as his sports paintings, would become more visually specific, more inclined toward narrative or allegorical incident, and more erotically charged. From the fifties to the present, his imagery has consistently contained an eccentric edge. Then and now, his subjects take on an enigmatic and dreamlike quality and there are ongoing references to his personal proclivities and allusions to autobiographical incidents.

A small, vigorously rendered oil of a women in bed (p. 20) pays homage to de Kooning's *Women,* whereas another canvas the same size (p. 21) depicting two nudes in a lush, green field seems to nod toward allegory. While Brown has not extensively explored the still life genre, there are beautiful examples in his oeuvre, such as *Blue Match Box* (p. 22), *Still Life with Glass* (p. 24), and *Roses,* one of many paintings that the painter has either destroyed or drastically reworked.

In the iconic *Sun and Moon* (p. 32), those ancient symbols of night and day, with their myriad connotations in every culture,

ROSES 1967, oil, 15 3/4 x 18 1/2 inches (destroyed)

hover over a stark landscape that is equally divided between their opposing effects of light and shadow. A figure with a white, reductive mask of a face stares anxiously outward, like a vignette from a medieval drama.

Like *Sun and Moon,* there are numerous small oils on hardboard, such as *Two Men in an Interior* (p. 26), which is from the same year, and various paintings depicting figures in interiors. Others, such as the 1962 canvas of a man wading in a pond (p. 27), despite their broad, gestural rendering, are clearly representations of particular individuals. Most of these are of male figures, such as the untitled oil of a seated man with his robe unabashedly open (p. 34). While steeped in the French tradition of Cézanne, Edouard Vuillard, and the Fauves, these small, masterful works are classic examples of Bay Area figurative painting. Most of these studies are begun or entirely painted from the model. They, and others, such as *Muscatine Diver* (p. 30) and *The Swing* (p. 31), are the earliest manifestations of Brown's beach scenes.

Two other untitled canvases from this period depict men with horses—an animal with endless symbolic and psychologically charged connotations. The first piece depicts a man leading a large, golden horse. Perhaps it is a racetrack vignette, for he is clad in rich indigo and violet and wears a green jockey's cap. The background and sky are reduced to Rothko-like bands of rich greens, reds, and maroons (p. 33). The second painting portrays a young man with his arm around the large animal's neck (p. 23). He is nude and the horse is without a saddle, details that tilt the subject toward allegory or myth and inevitably recall numerous equine themes, from the Parthenon frieze to Géricault and Picasso. It should be noted that Brown is not an equestrian, having ridden a horse only once in his life. Although he has no more interest in riding horses than in playing football or boxing, he has a great affection for animals and birds. Besides demonstrating his attraction to the magnificence of this particular animal, these two paintings demonstrate several other important aspects of his work. With very few exceptions, the drawings are almost always directly observed, but like the earlier sports paintings, many of the figurative compositions are open-ended constructions derived from drawings, photographs, reproductions, and the imagination. While the major paintings are rooted in the art of drawing and start with a theme or subject, they are never programmatic. It is another reminder of the lasting influence of Willem de Kooning.

Other mid-sixties paintings are connected with Wonner and Brown's close friendship with Christopher Isherwood and Don Bachardy. The oil on paper of a seated nude reflected in a mirror (p. 36) was drawn in Isherwood and Bachardy's home. During this period in Santa Monica, Bachardy, Wonner, and Brown created a group of small still life drawings and paintings around lemons, after an evening discussing "lemons" in art. Later, a party was organized around their "lemons" at Isherwood and Bachardy's. Also, while Janet Frame was living with Brown and Wonner she sat for several drawings by Bachardy.

However, the most recurrent subject in Brown's oeuvre is the classical theme of the bather and nude in the landscape. In *Muscatine Diver,* the figure is depicted just as he enters the water. As with other paintings from this period it is blocked in with ultramarine blue. Beyond the lake a road runs through a dark, wooded landscape pocked with a few scattered buildings and terminates at the high line of horizon. The composition is economically described and rendered with painterly vigor, but again there are traces of shifts and revisions.

David Park, who looms over all accounts of Bay Area figurative painting, died in 1960 at the age of forty-nine. His powerfully expressive paintings and watercolors were at their zenith at the time of his death, and though he has been widely recognized, his influence has never been fully acknowledged. While Bischoff and Diebenkorn continued drawing from the figure, both returned to non-representational painting in the late sixties. Following a different course, the drawings and paintings of Weeks, Wonner, Oliveira, and Brown would evolve into a more distinctly personal means of painterly articulation while remaining rooted in the European and American figurative tradition.

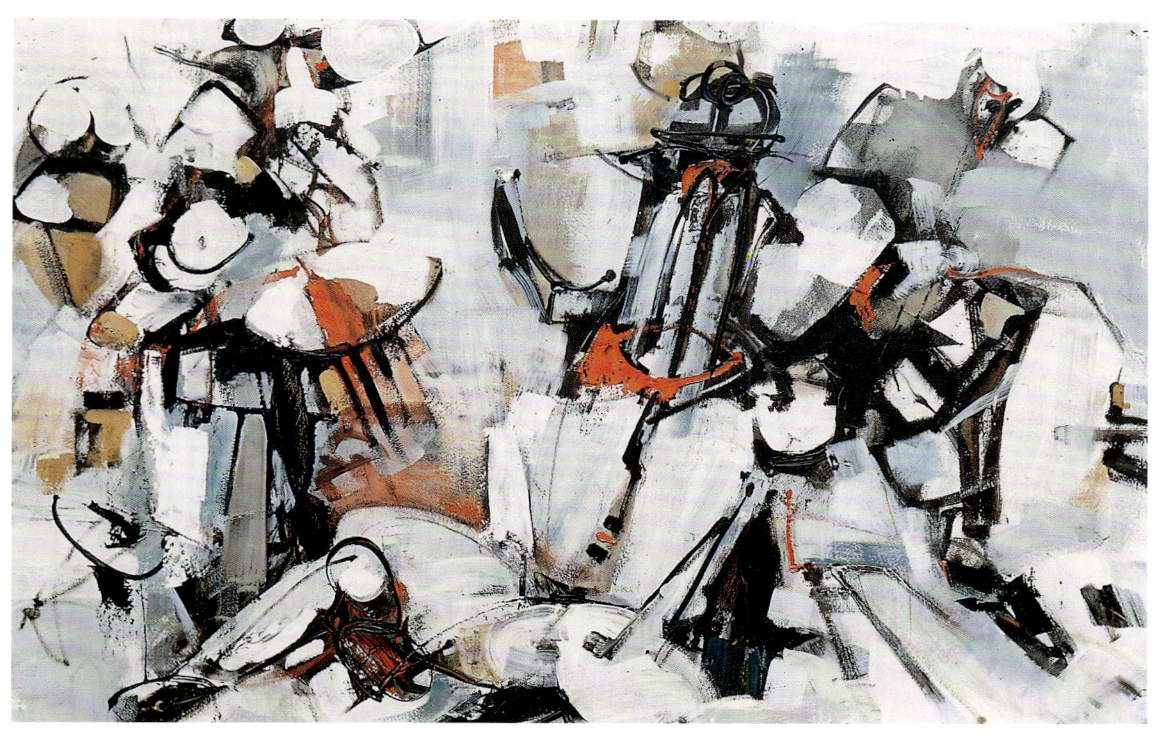

FOOTBALL 1952, oil on board, 18 x 24 inches
Collection of Elise Cade, Hinsdale, Illinois

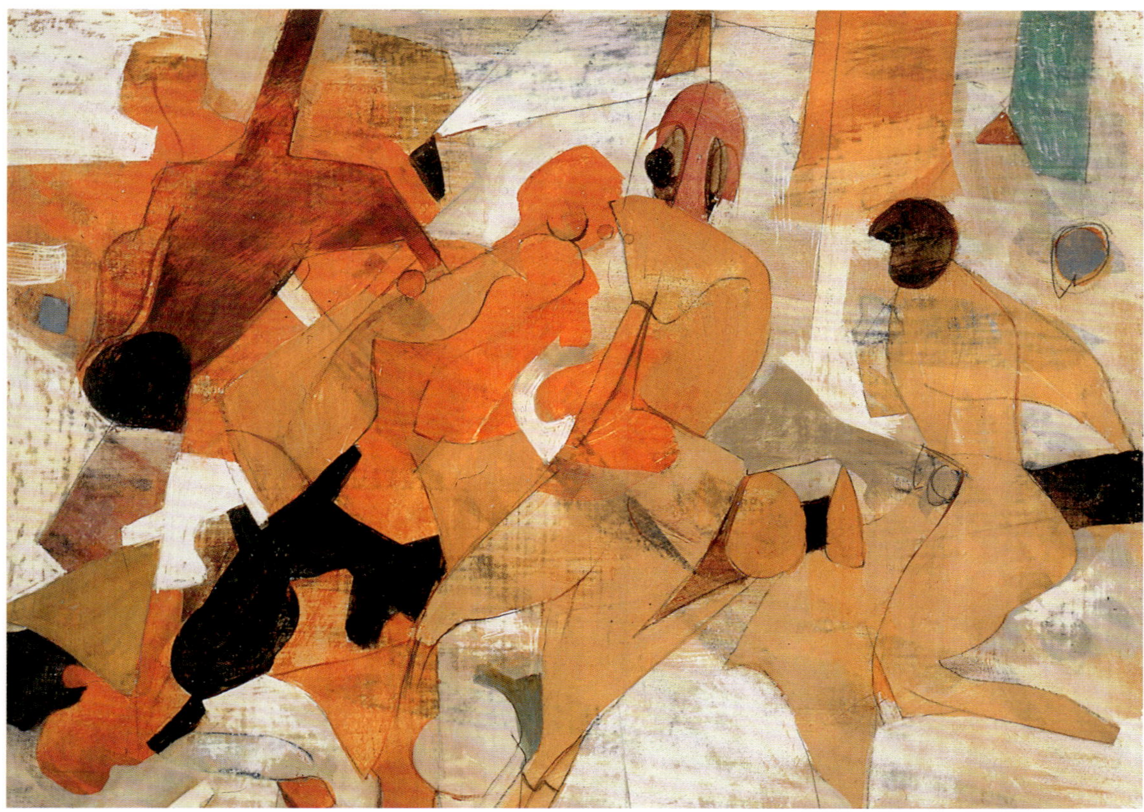

UNTITLED 1953, tempera on panel, 14 x 18 inches
Private Collection

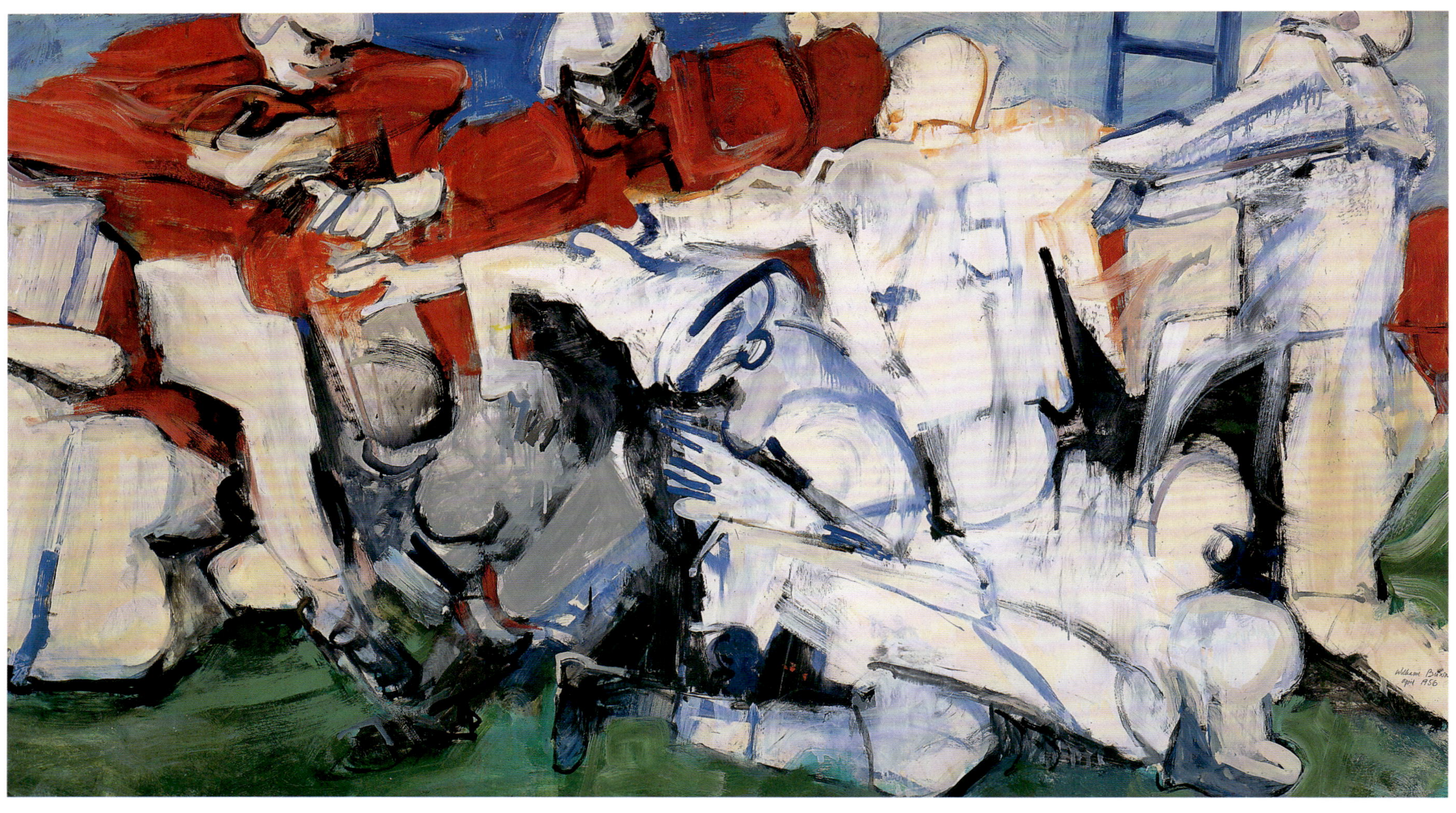

UNTITLED (FOOTBALL) 1955, oil on paper, 36 x 50 inches. Santa Barbara Museum of Art, California. Gift of Paul Wonner

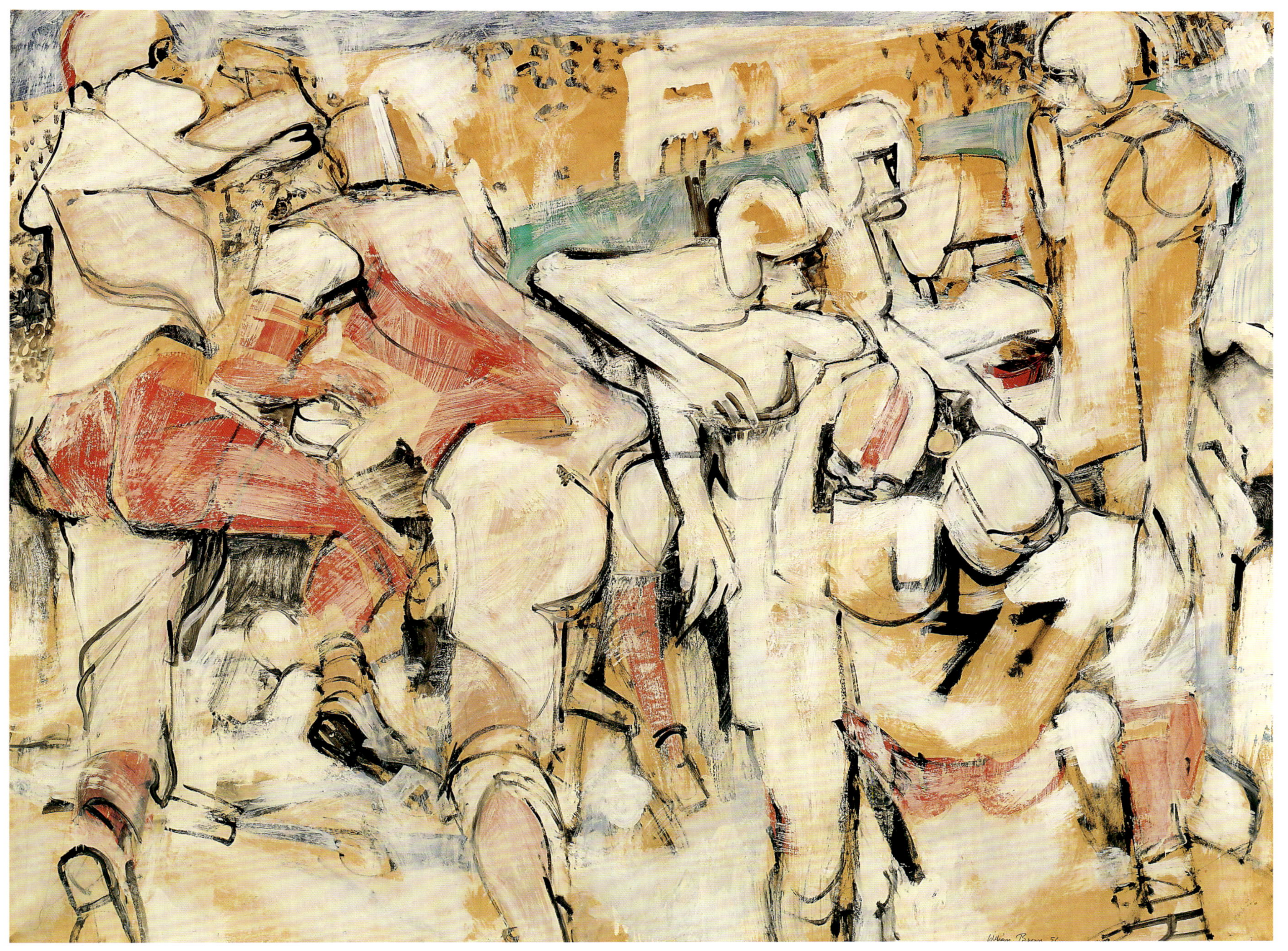

UNTITLED (FOOTBALL) 1956, oil and graphite on paper, 42 1/2 x 56 inches. Elins Eagles-Smith Gallery, San Francisco

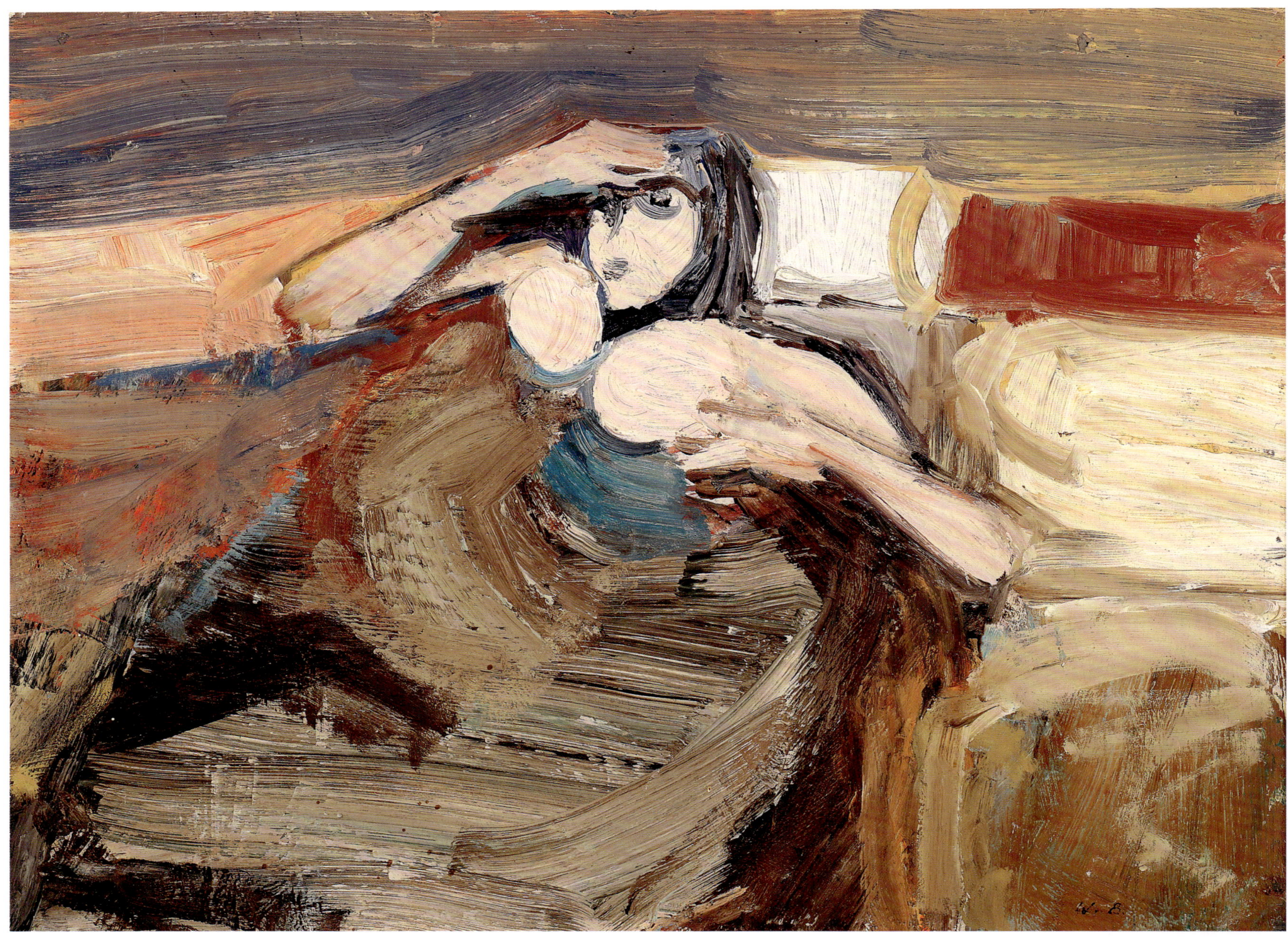

 UNTITLED 1957, oil on canvas mounted on masonite, 9 x 12 inches. Private Collection

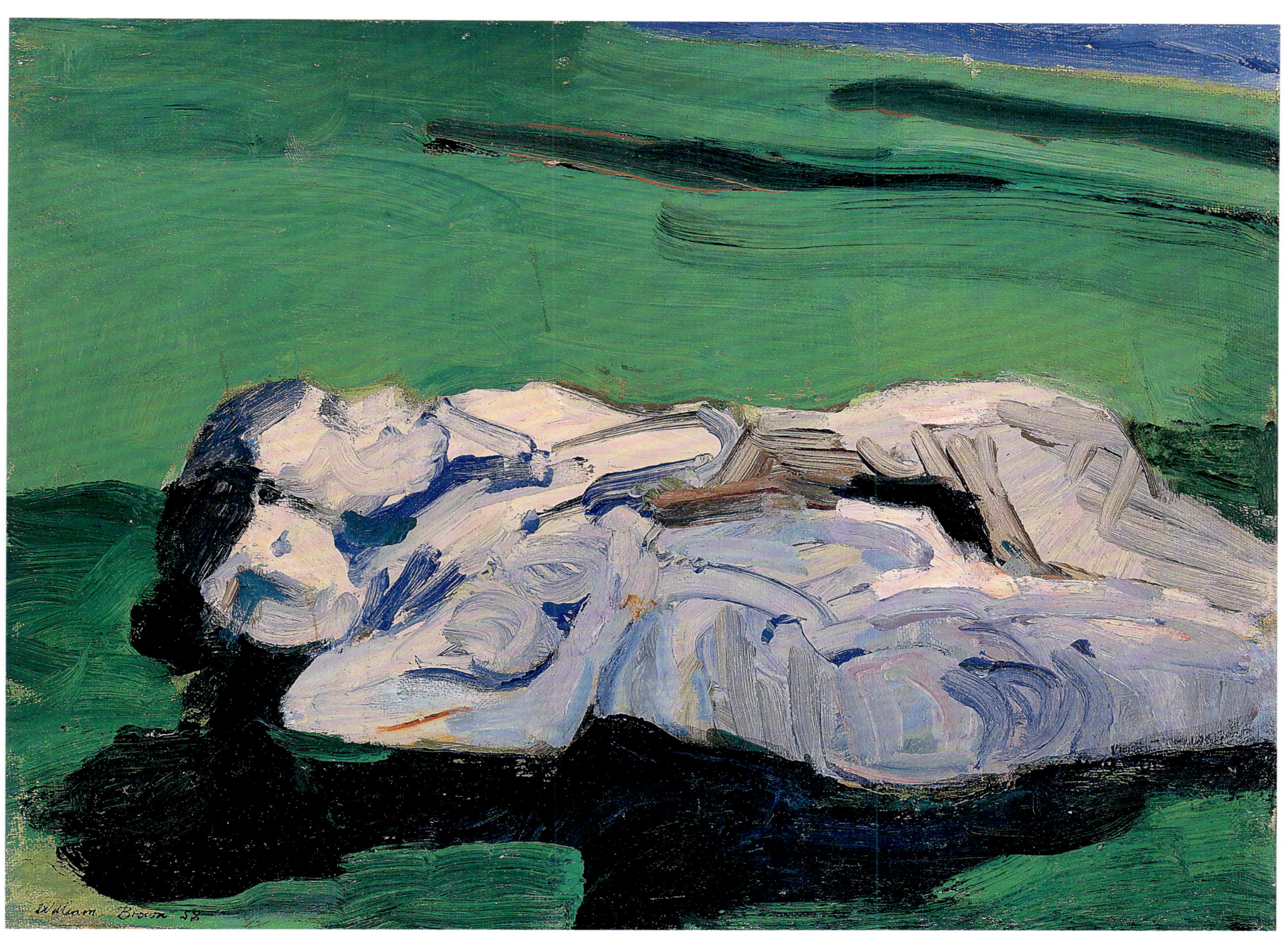

UNTITLED 1958, oil on canvas mounted on masonite, 9 x 12 inches. Private Collection

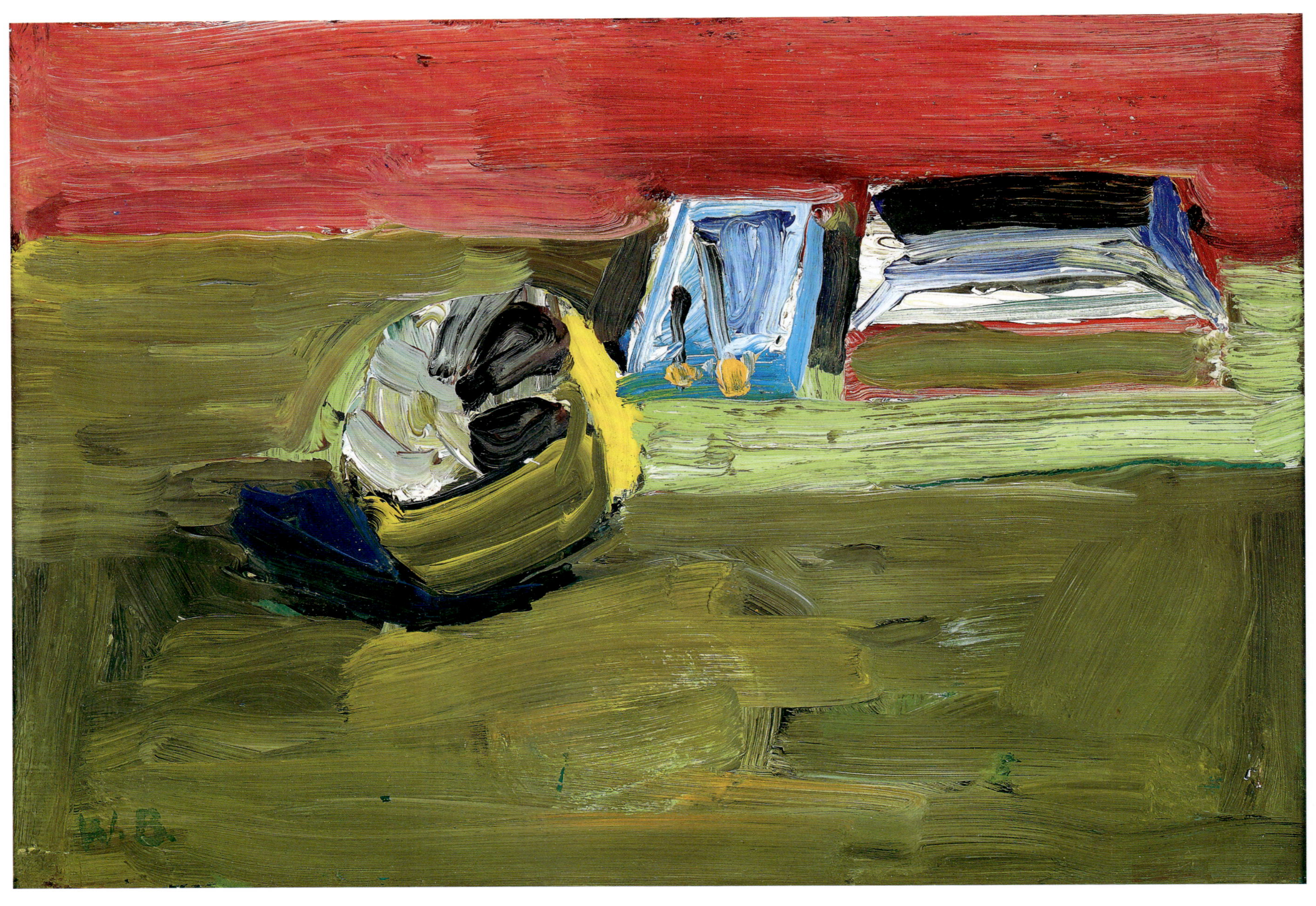

BLUE MATCH BOX 1960, oil on masonite, 8 1/2 x 12 inches. Collection of John Modell, Sar Francisco

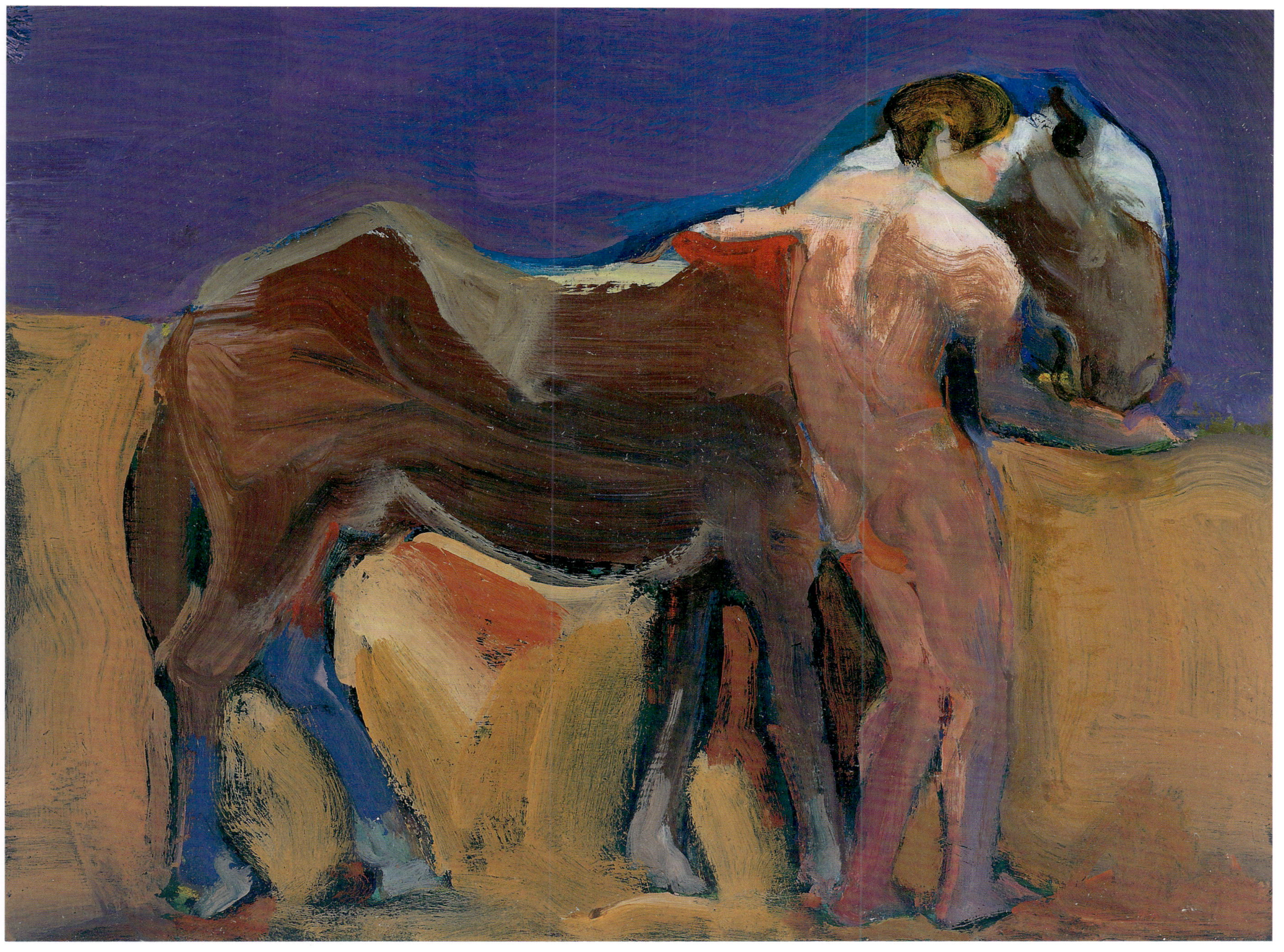

UNTITLED 1964, oil on masonite, 9 x 12 inches. Collection of Byron Meyer, San Francisco

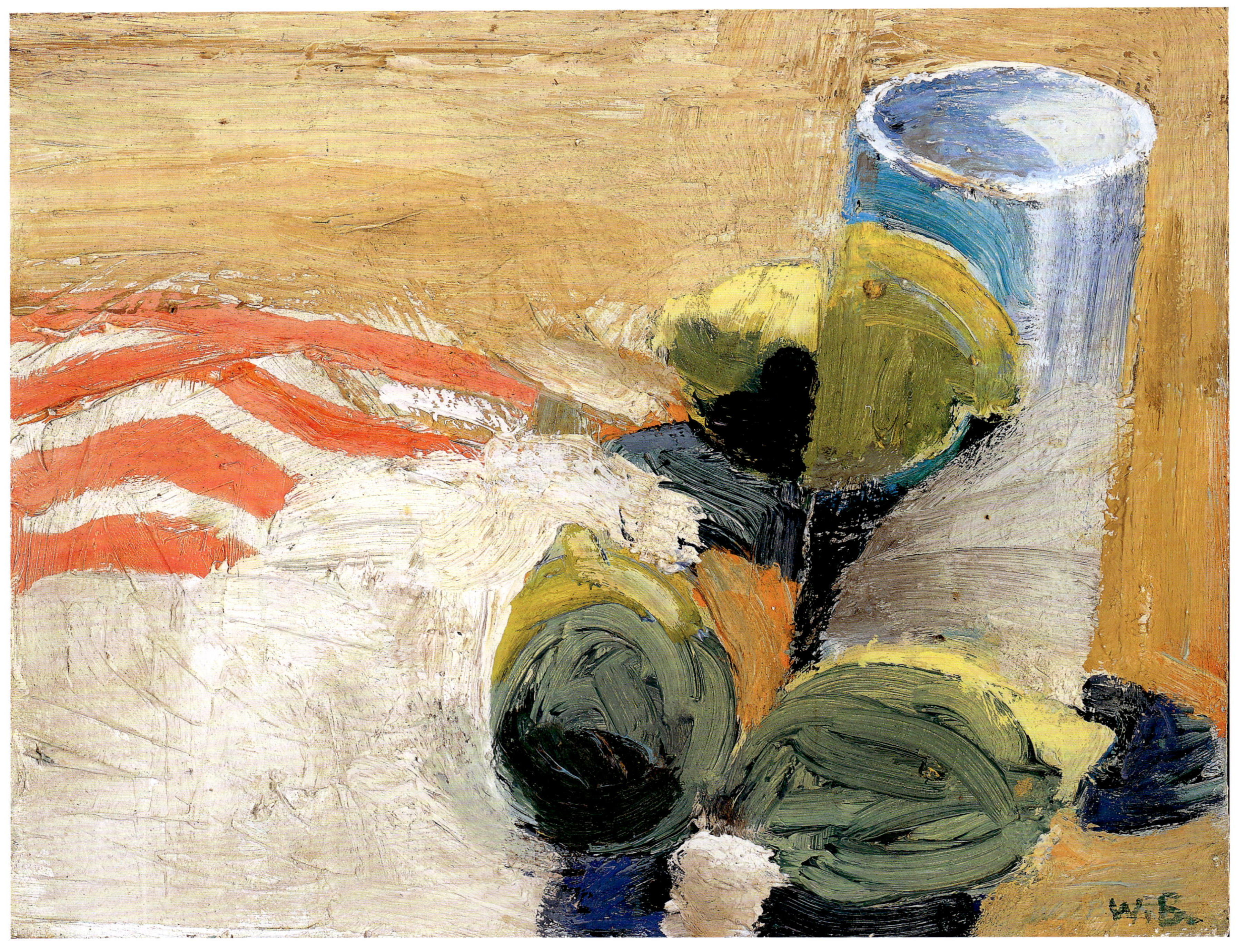

24   *STILL LIFE WITH GLASS* 1958, oil on canvas mounted on wood, 8 x 10 inches. Private Collection

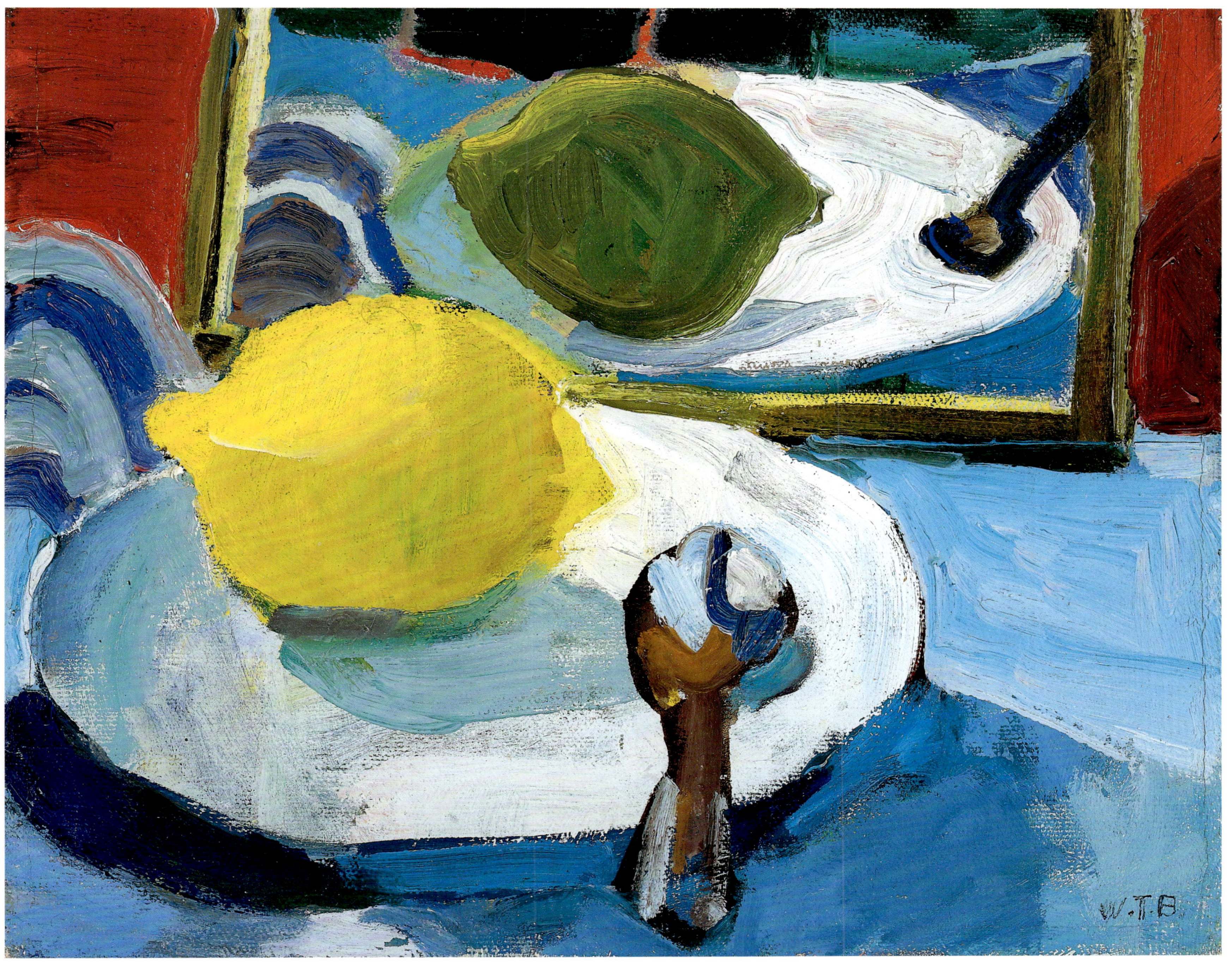

UNTITLED c. 1964, oil on masonite, 8 x 10 inches. Private Collection

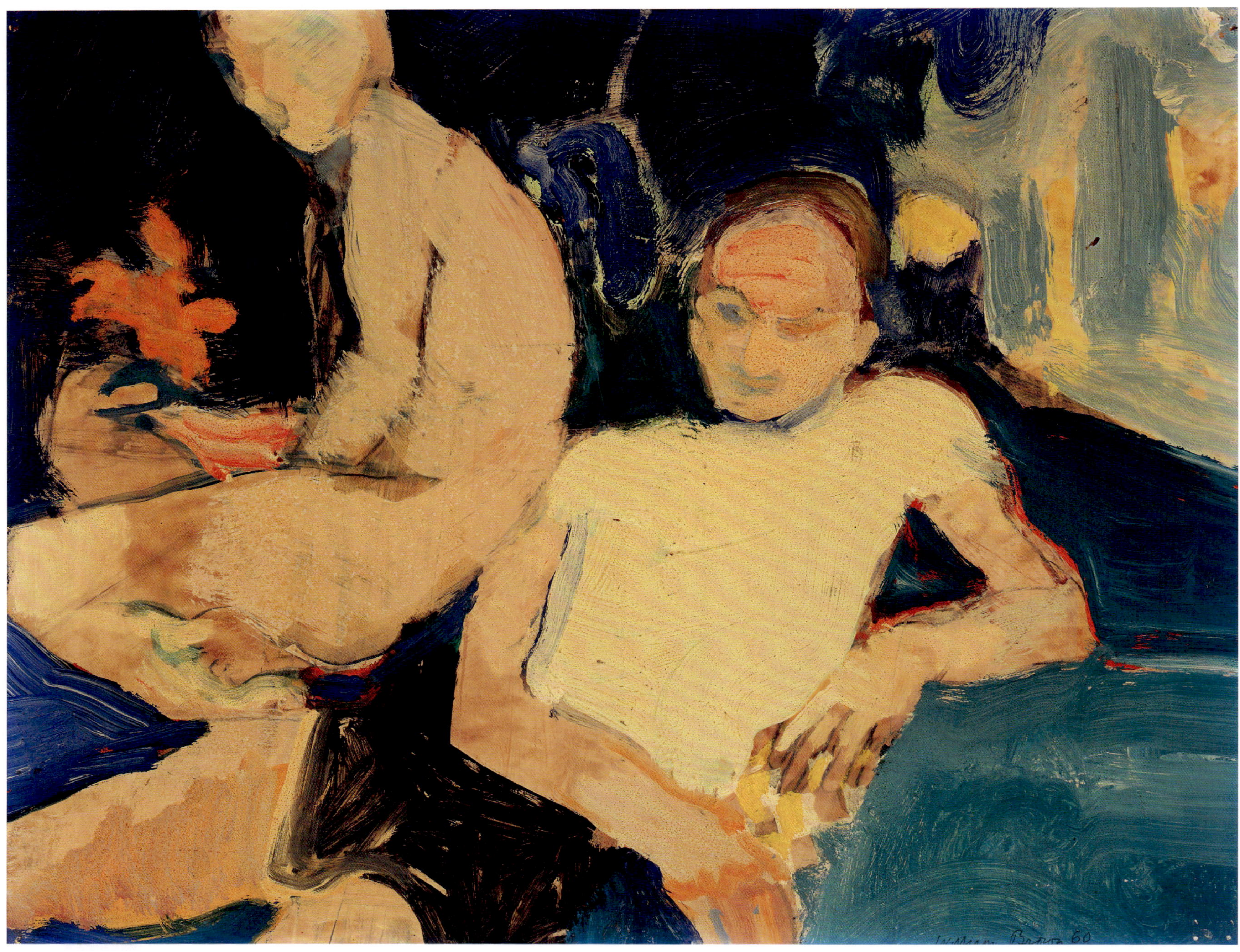

 TWO MEN IN AN INTERIOR 1960, oil on masonite, 111/4 x 141/2 inches. Private Collection

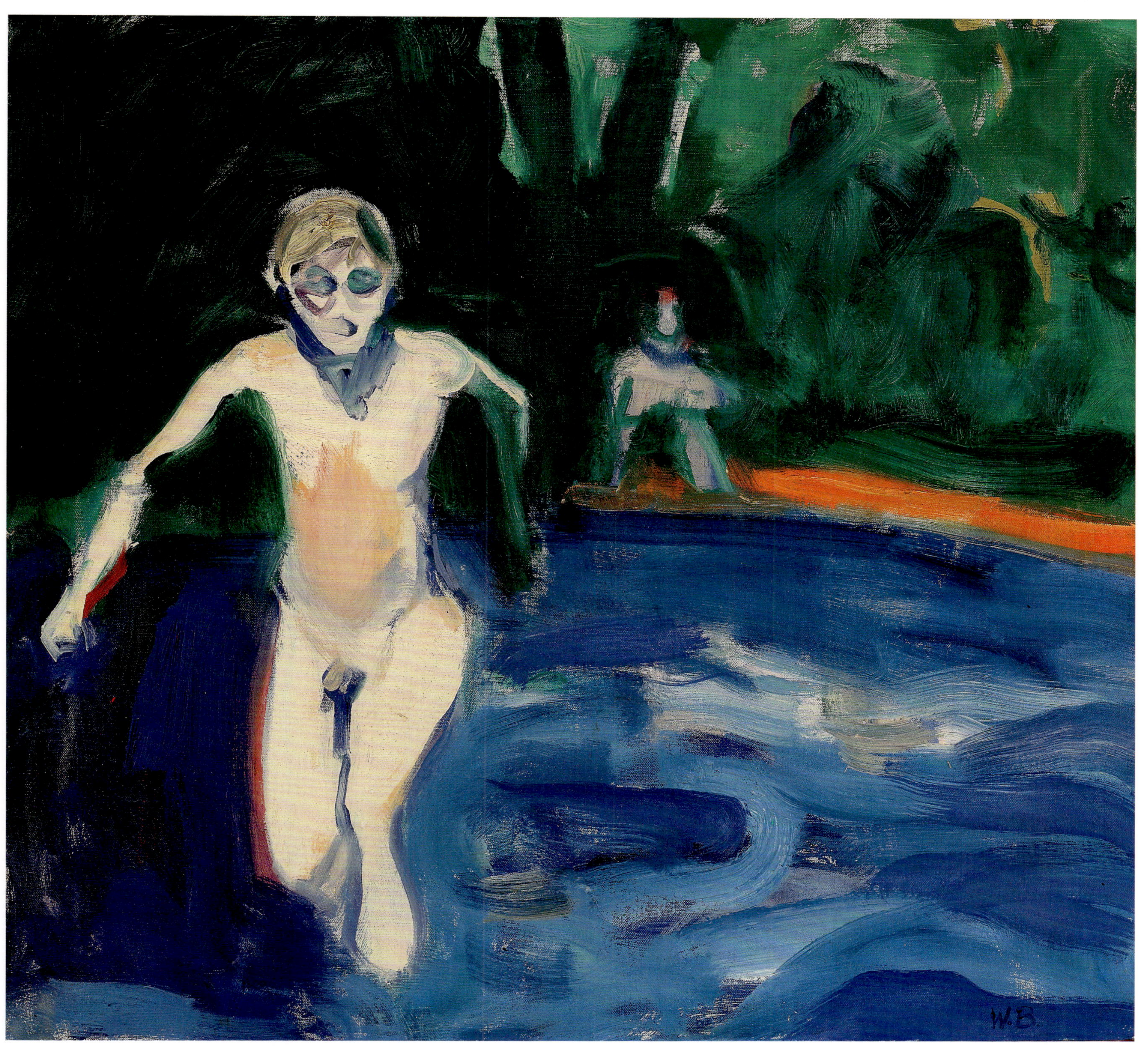

UNTITLED 1962, oil on canvas, 22 x 24 inches. Collection of John Modell, San Francisco

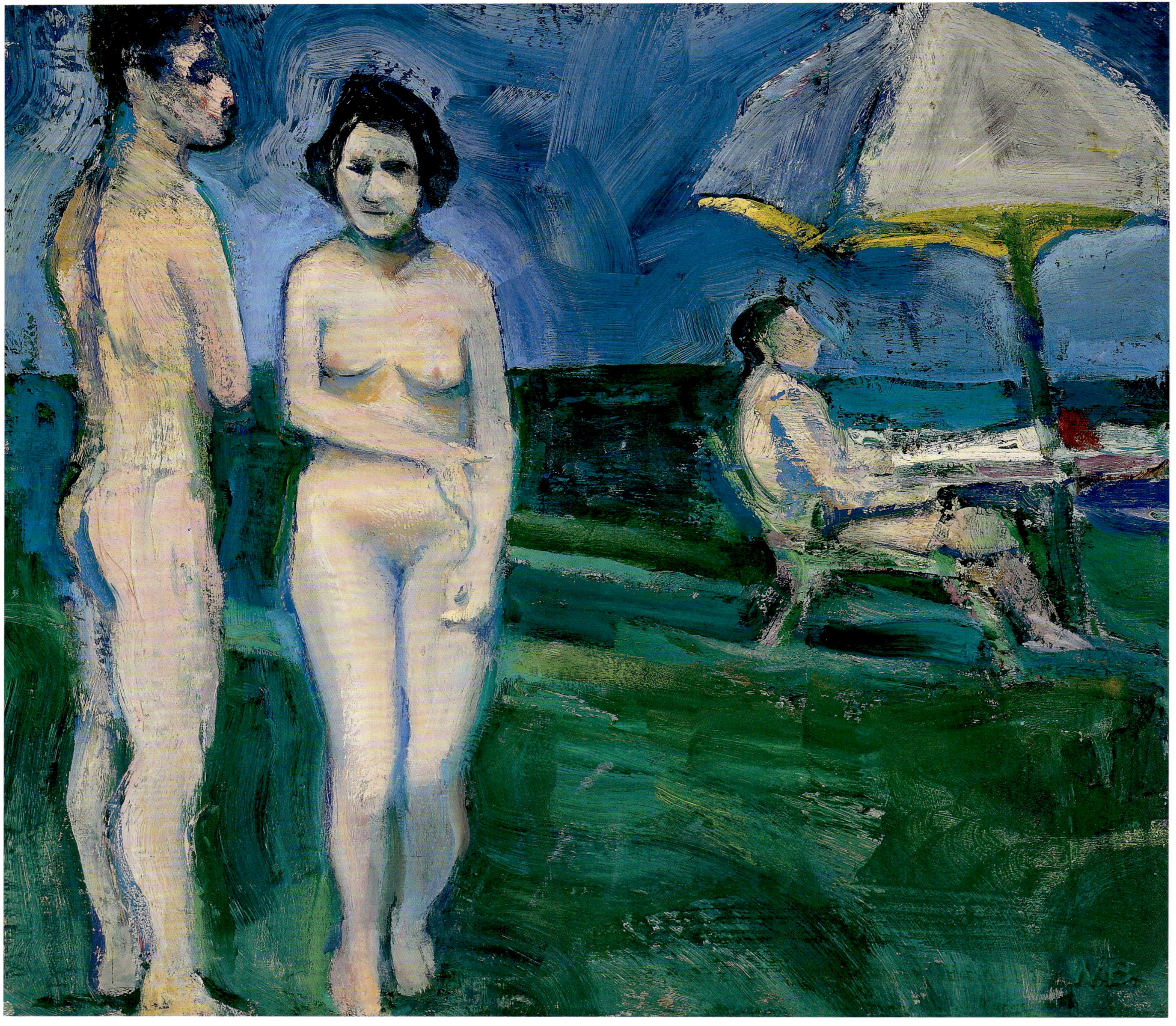

   UNTITLED 1961, oil on canvas, 16 x 18 inches. Collection of the Artist

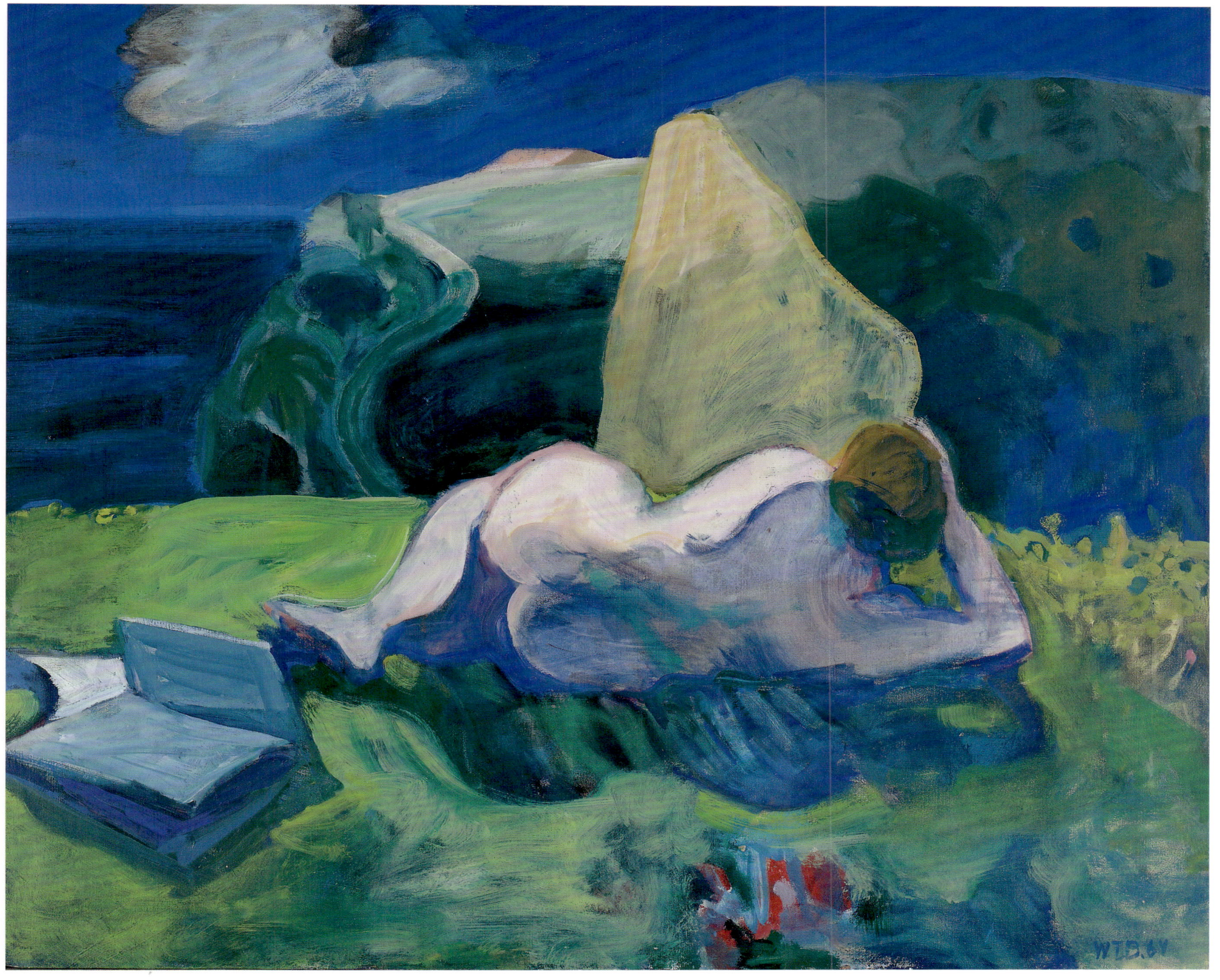

UNTITLED 1964, oil on canvas, 40 x 48 inches. Private Collection

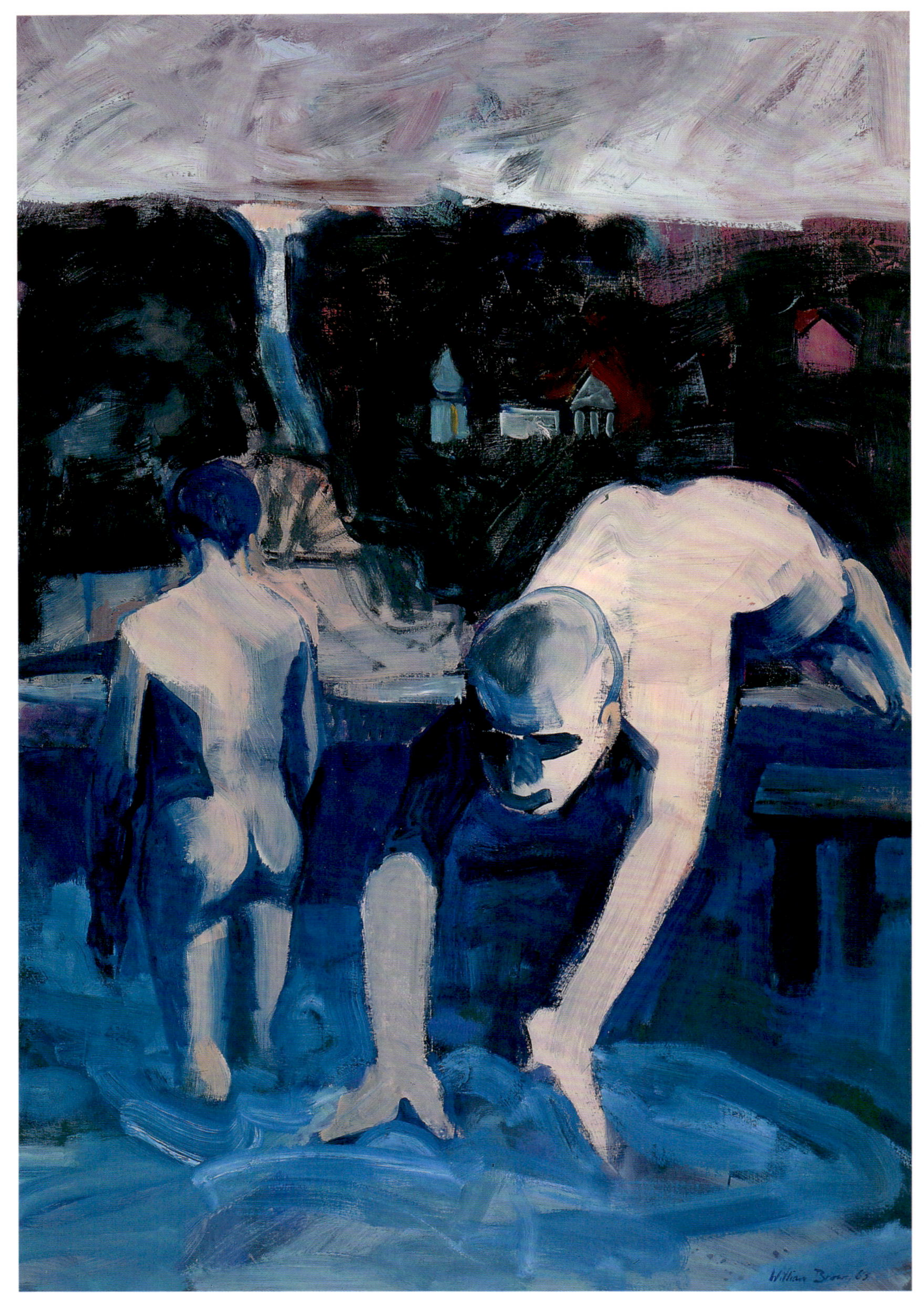

MUSCATINE DIVER 1962–63, oil on canvas, 60 x 401/4 inches
Oakland Museum of California, Gift of the Artist

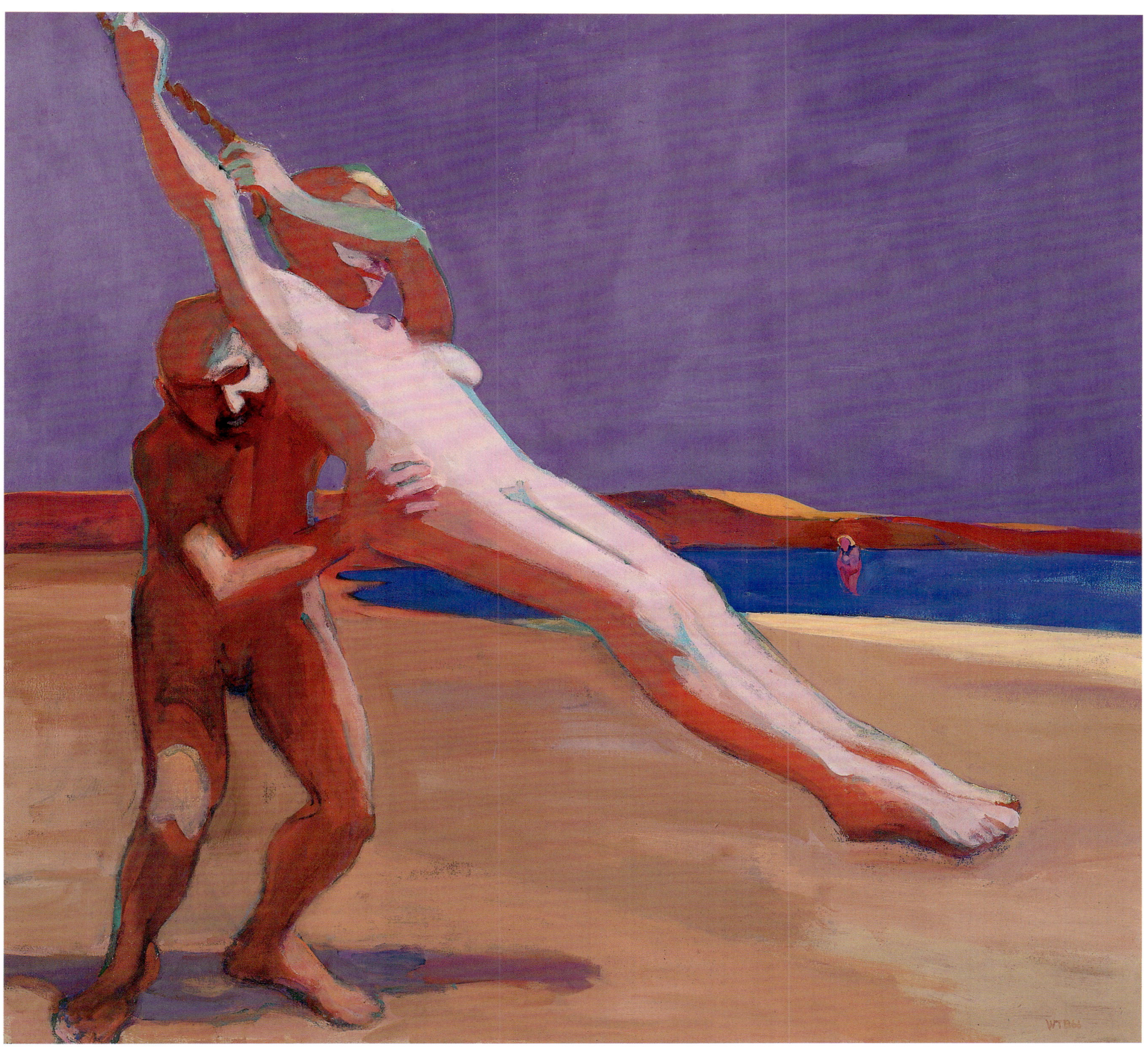

THE SWING 1966, acrylic on canvas, 52 x 56 inches. Collection of Daniel & Virginia Mardesich, San Raphael, California

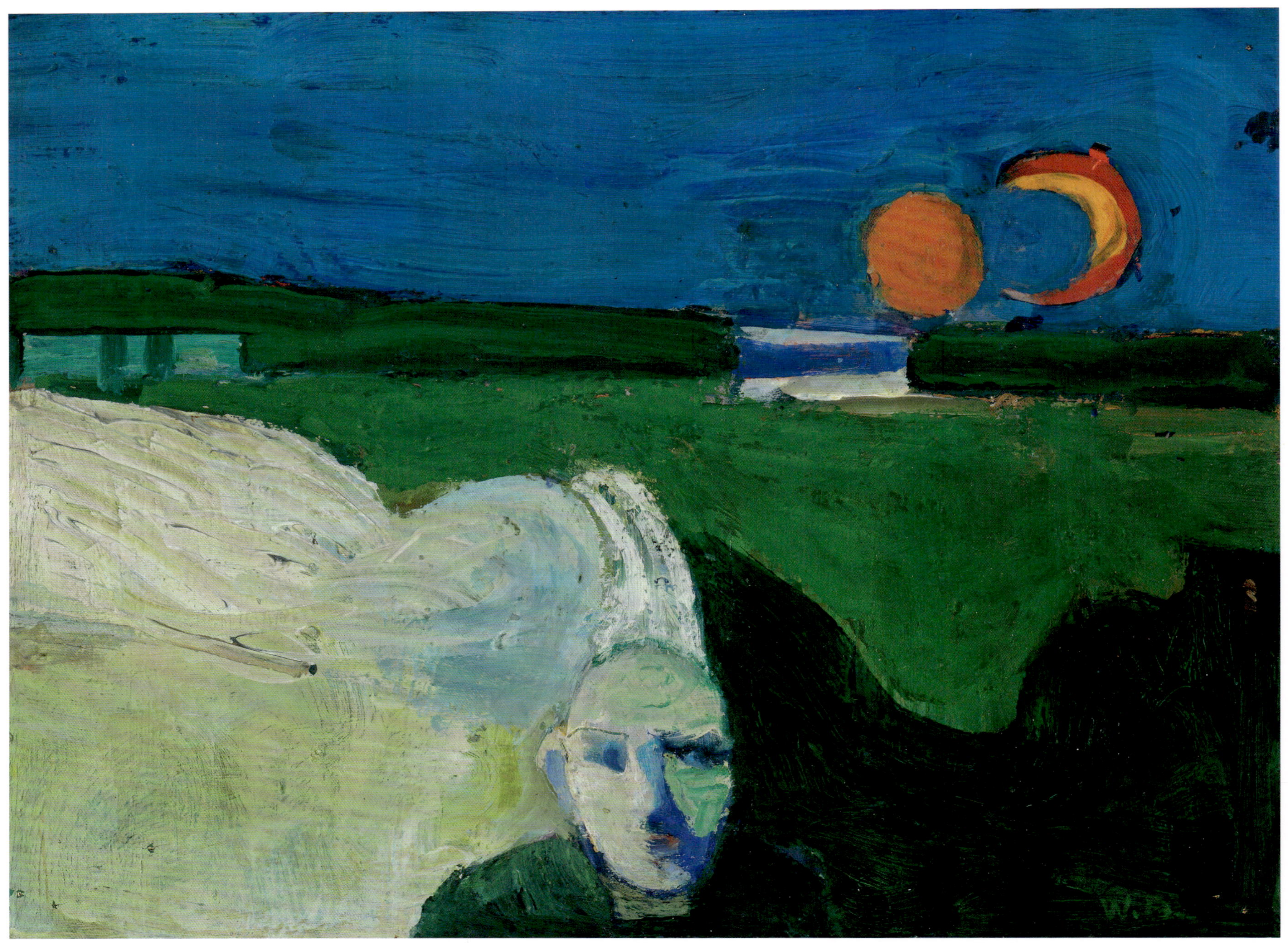

 SUN AND MOON 1960, oil on plywood panel, 9 1/4 x 12 1/2 inches. Collection of Glenna & Charles Campbell, San Francisco

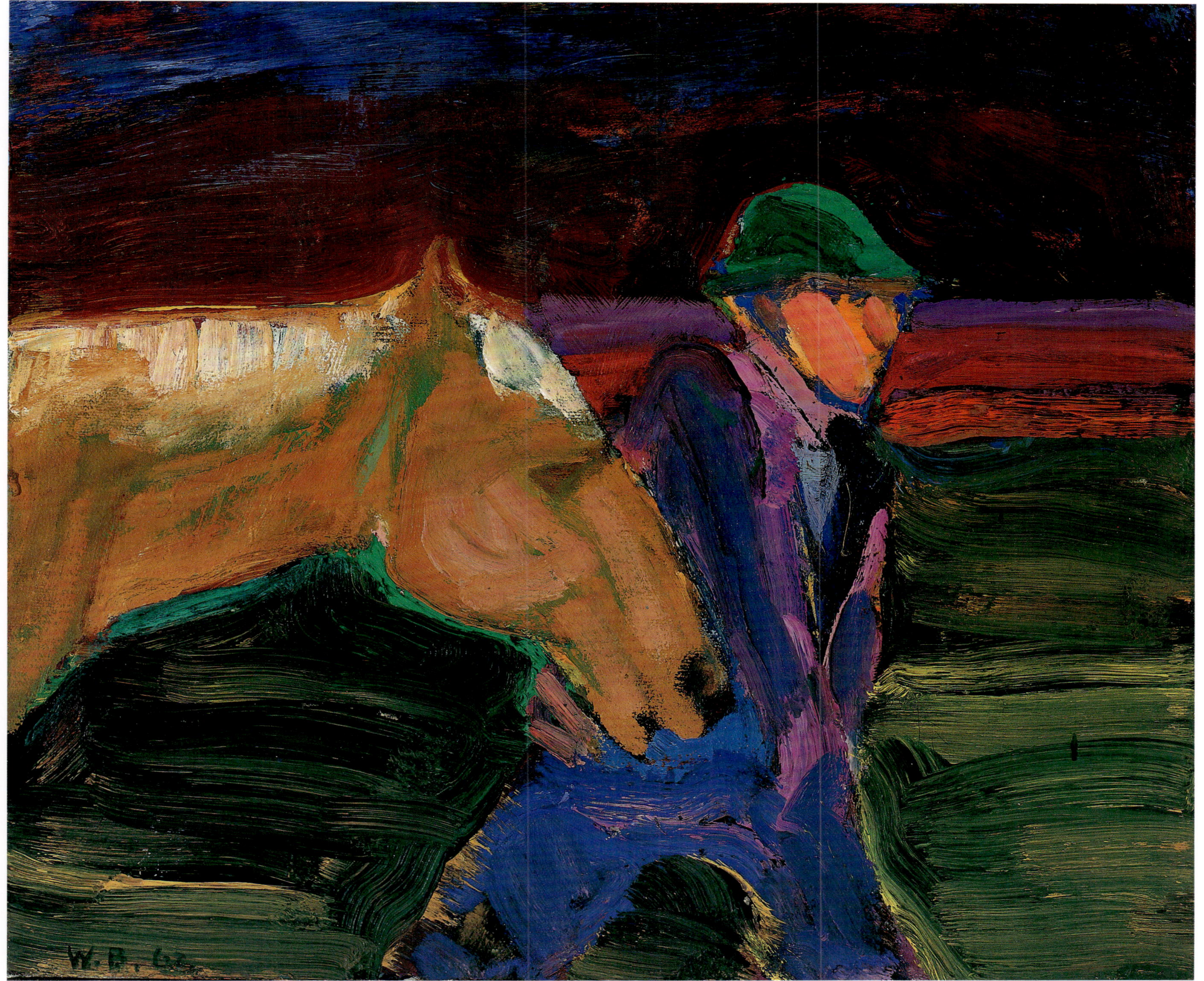

UNTITLED 1964, oil on masonite, 9 x 12 inches. Collection of Stephen Deitsch, Los Angeles

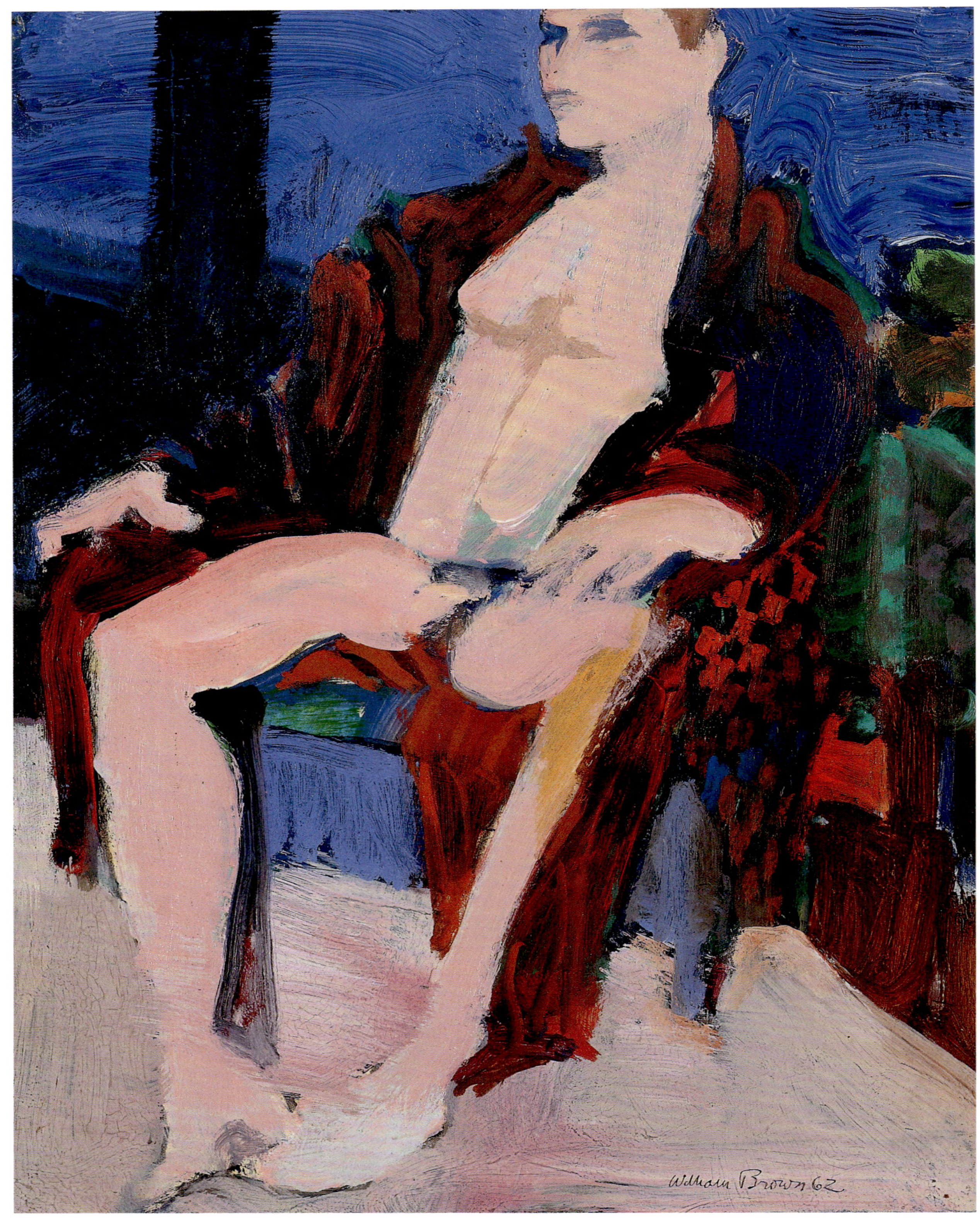

UNTITLED 1962, oil on paper, 11 1/2 x 14 1/2 inches. Private Collection

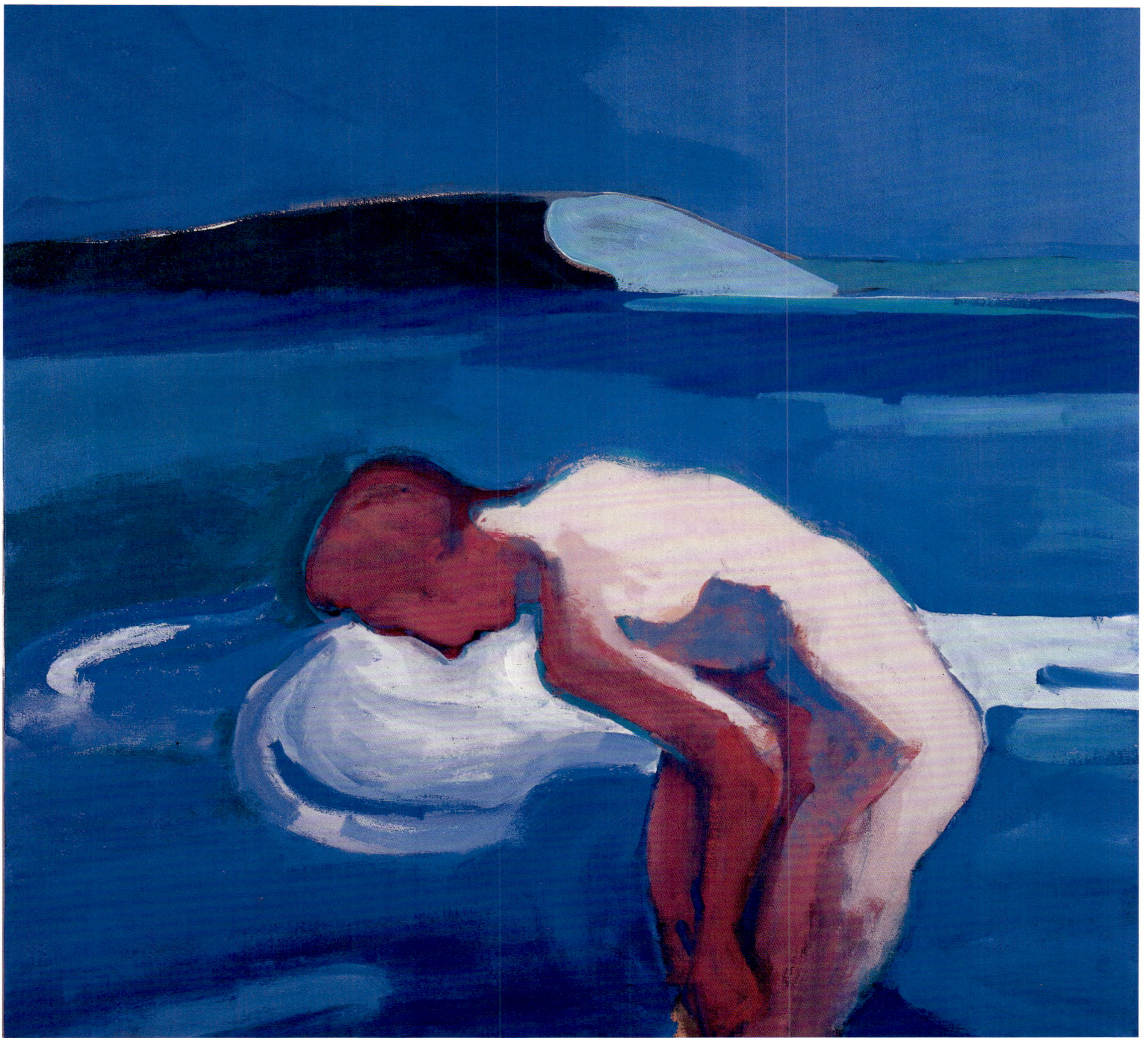

UNTITLED 1966, oil on canvas, 48 x 48 inches. Private Collection

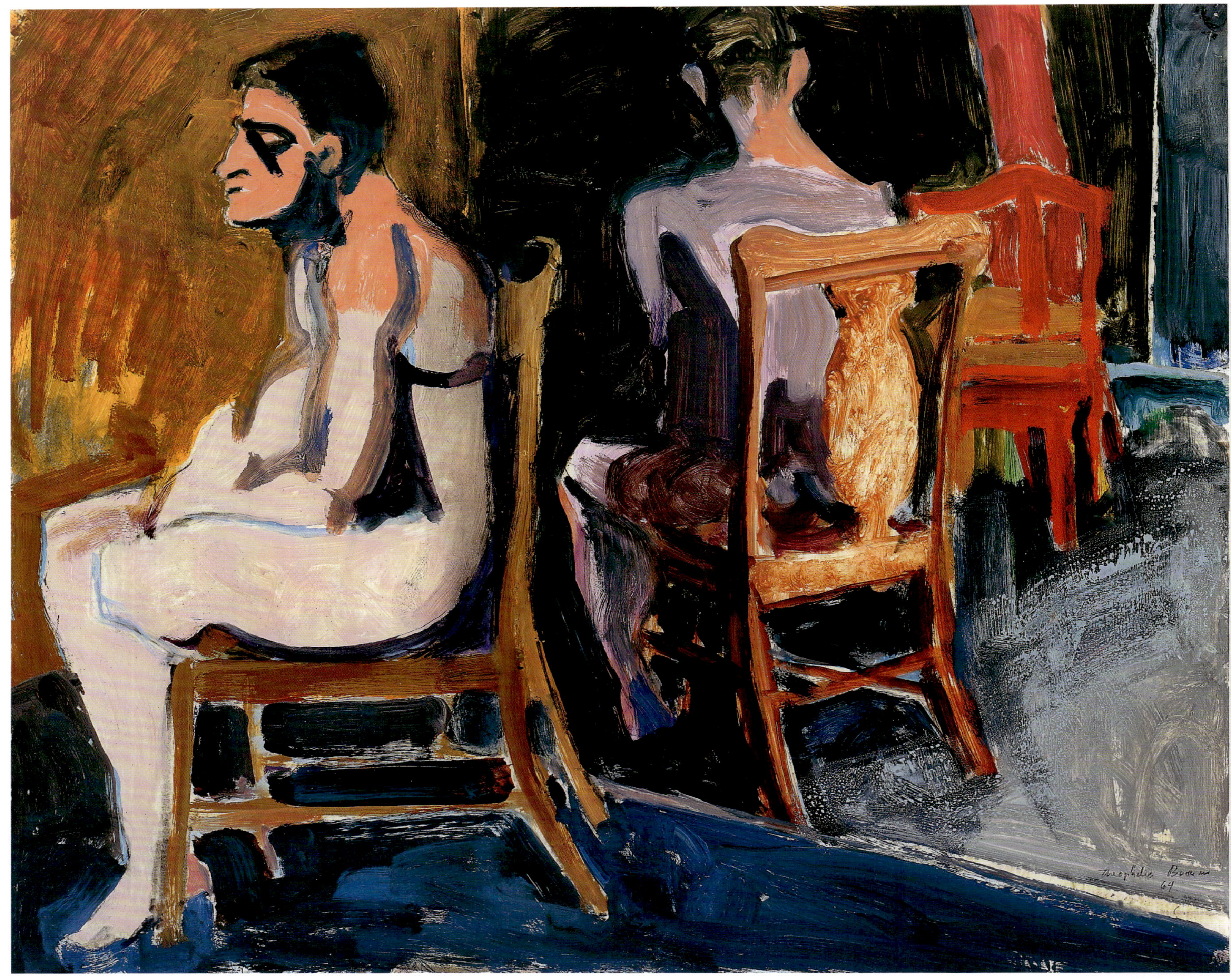

  UNTITLED 1964, oil on paper, 14 x 17 inches. Private Collection

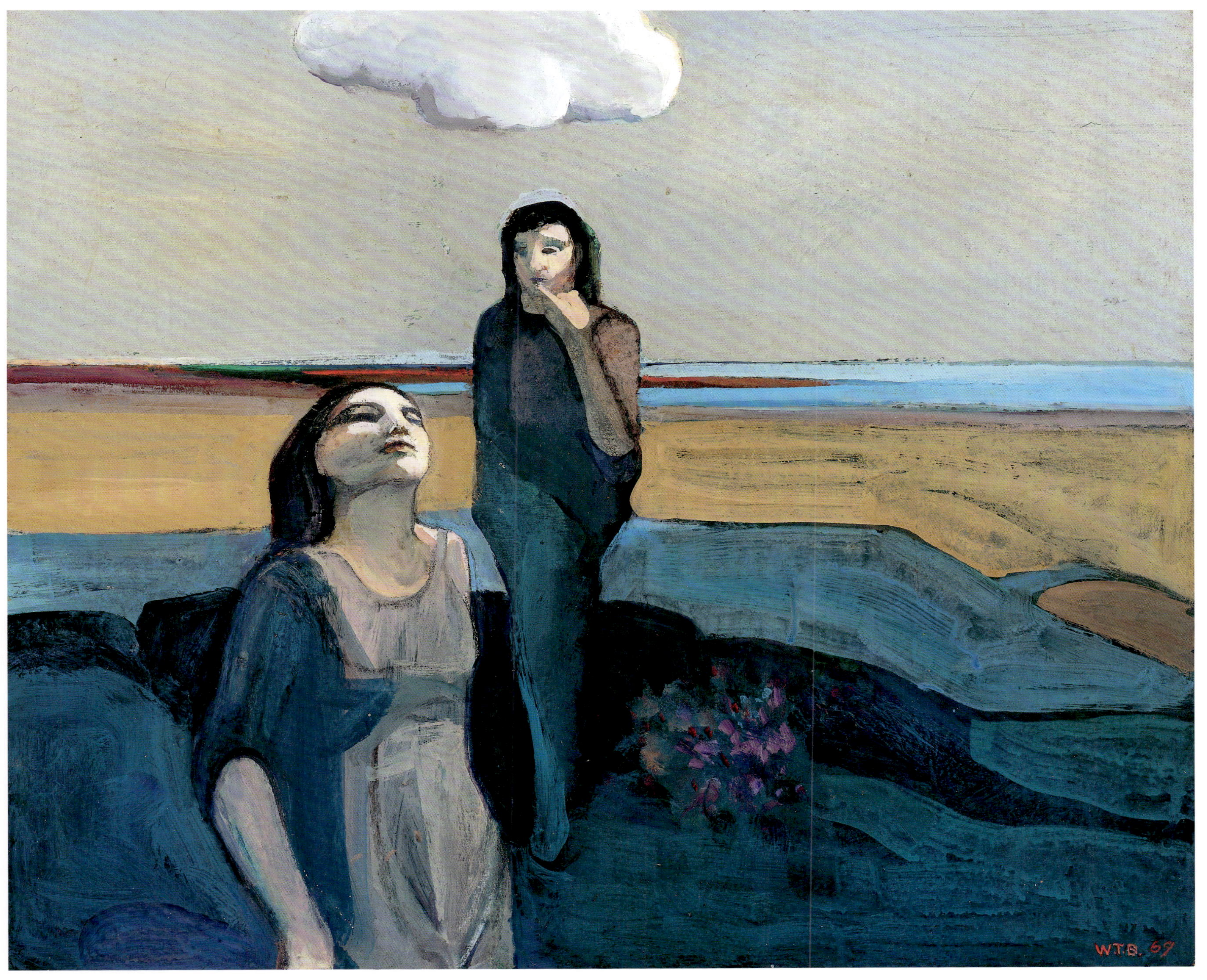

UNTITLED 1968, acrylic on hardboard, 16 1/4 x 19 inches. Collection of John Modell, San Francisco

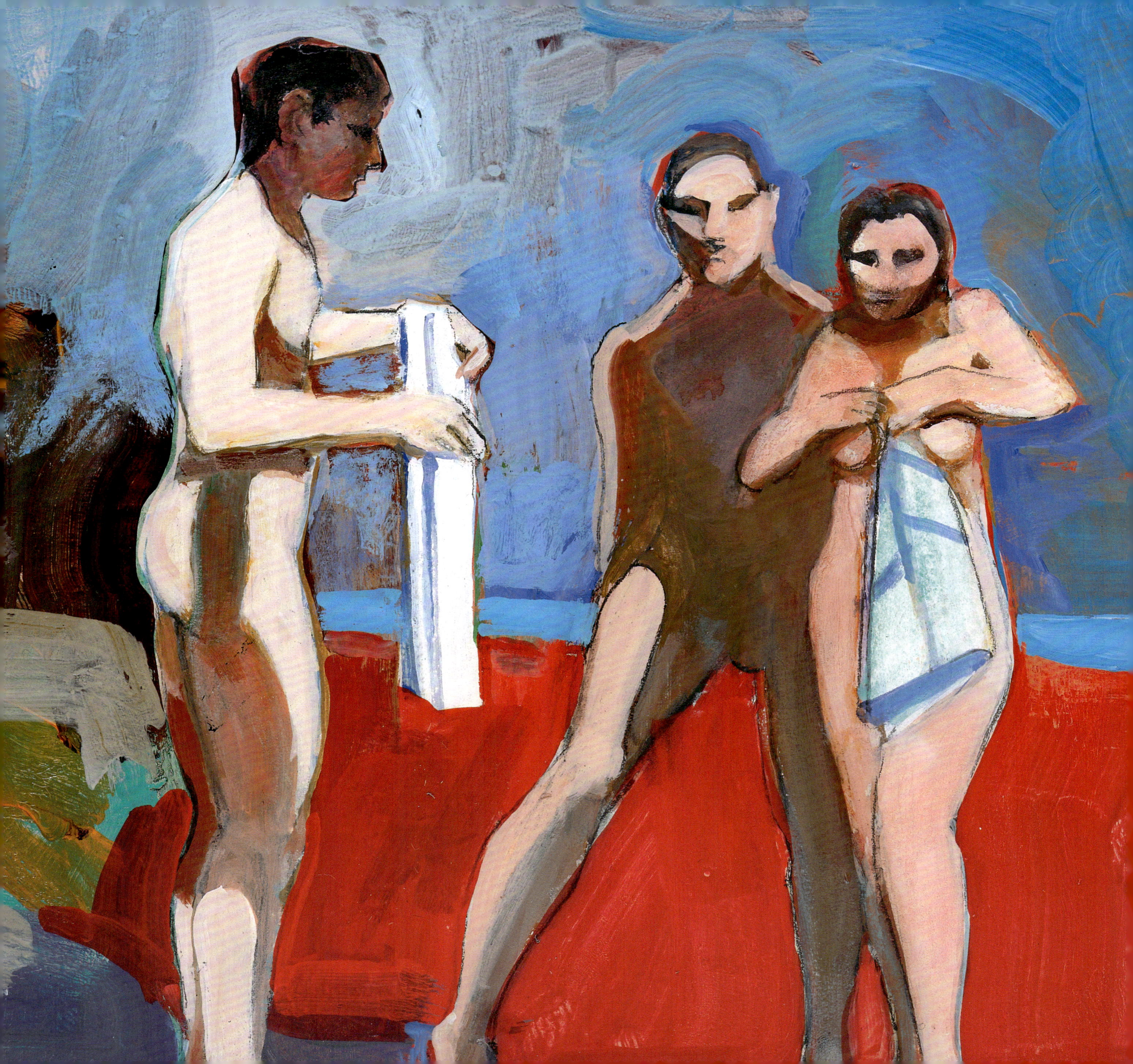

Quiet Beaches and
Other Reveries

*We must fasten these images to some reality in our
secret experience, or we shall see nothing.*
—RALPH WALDO EMERSON

*So many painters today have forgotten poetry in
their paintings—and it is the most important thing:
poetry.*   —PABLO PICASSO

*I do not know which to prefer,
The beauty of inflections
Or the beauty of innuendoes,
The blackbird whistling
Or just after.*

—WALLACE STEVENS

BETWEEN THE MID-SIXTIES and the late seventies Theophilus
Brown's oeuvre expanded to a wide variety of compositions of figures on the beach. These paintings and works on
paper consist predominantly of men absorbed in a variety of acti-
vities—swimming, sunbathing, boating, conversing—and accompanied by women, dogs, and horses. Like the animals, the men
and women are completely at ease with their nakedness.

Such unabashed depictions of the nude in art connect with
many centuries of our Western tradition. On the classical side
of the equation, these range from the idealism of the Greeks;
the realism of the Romans; and the early Christian depictions
of scrawny, pale-skinned Adams and potbellied Eves, fragilely
protected by leafy sprigs; to the pale, doughy odalisques of
Ingres and the stolid Cubist figures of Cézanne.

However, the character of Brown's nudes more closely parallels the unabashed sexuality that floats to the surface of
Asian and Western art—from the jewel-like Mughal miniatures
of elegant, turbaned men and dark eyed, full bosomed
women; the élan of Japan's ukiyo-e and their deliciously cari-
catured manga; to the haunting femmes of Eduard Munch; the
flaunted eroticism of Klimt and Schiele's worldly, seasoned
women; Bonnard's perpetually youthful wife; Balthus's nubile
seductresses; and Picasso's raunchy, rollicking ladies of the
night—which provide a discursive and widely divergent map of
our carnal desires.

For example, a painting of male bathers from 1968 (p. 45)
depicts a cluster of five nudes gathered on a broad sandy beach.
A short distance away another man watches the group. Each of
the individuals is distinctly and convincingly summarized, down
to the somewhat belligerent stance of the solitary figure, in
the sharp clarity of the midday light. It is a tableaux of sexual
tensions; a remembered incident.

The specificity of the moment clearly demonstrates Brown's
skill as a draftsman and, at this point, his deftness at carefully
edited descriptive painting. The sexual undercurrent in this work
is a characteristic that will inhabit his beach paintings, studio
nudes, drawings, as well as many of his portraits. Brown is quite
open in acknowledging such self-gratifying and voyeuristic
attractions.

Two other canvases from 1966, *Woman and Deer* (p. 42)
and *The Red Hills* (p. 43), are remarkable demonstrations of the
open-ended means that lie beneath Brown's evocative images.
In the first painting a woman stands awkwardly with her fin-
gers in her mouth. Just beyond her a deer grazes. This inexplicable tableau is set in a landscape that, with the exception of a
large red mound beyond the figure, seems to be primarily real-
istic, but the composition is clearly constructed from drawings,
photographs, and other sources. *Woman and Deer* was continually repainted and eventually destroyed. Brown had witnessed such procedures—in both the act of reworking and the

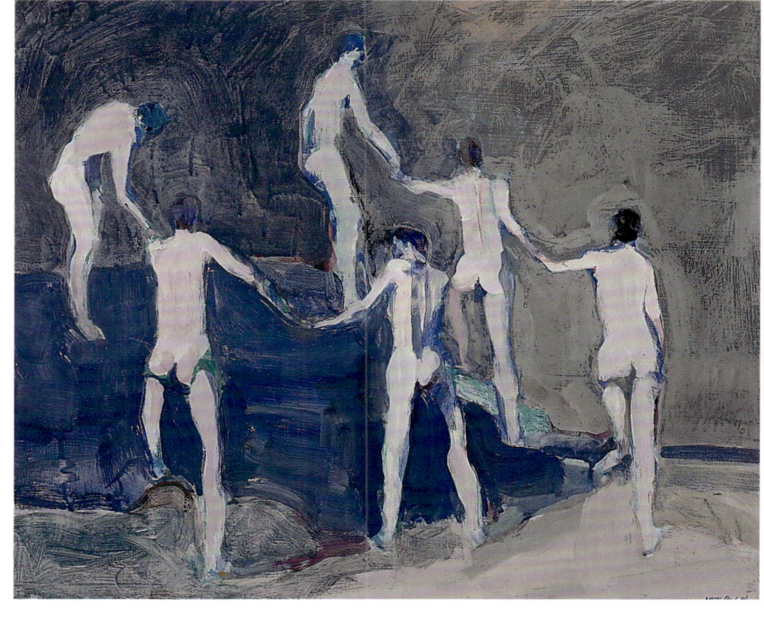

UNTITLED 1968, acrylic on board, 14 x 19 inches
Collection of Don Bachardy

numerous adjustments and refinements—in the studios of Picasso, a few of the French Moderns, and Abstract Expressionists such as de Kooning and Rothko, and adapted them to his own means. While an avoidance of the programmatic is characteristic of Bay Area figurative painting, very few witnessed the improvisational bravura of the Abstract Expressionists firsthand. The effects of that early experience on Brown, coupled with sharing AE's avoidance of formal and pictorial ingratiation, lies at the heart of his experience.

This unfortunately lost work is one of Brown's earliest depictions of animals. Horses, elephants, and a variety of dogs—including a shorthaired mongrel—birds of various species, and a menagerie of cats have populated his paintings from the sixties to the present. Usually they accompany bathers at the beach or sitters in the studio.

Unbridled horses appear recurrently on the beach, being stroked, led, or ridden bareback. A pale mongrel often escorts the nudists to the beach in an assortment of large and small canvases, and mingles with them in a variety of remarkable acrylics on paper. In another small study, a man flees from a large angry bird (p. 54).

Pedestrian Crossing (p. 67) is one of Brown's earliest moves

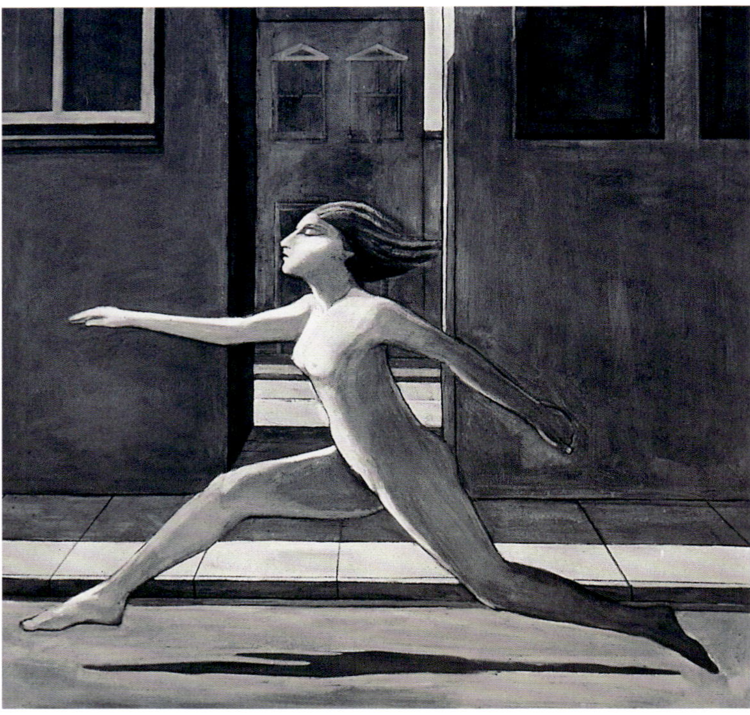

toward incorporating urban elements with the landscape; an aspect that will later become one of his recurrent subjects. In this enigmatic image, the principal elements of the composition—landscape, bridge, shadow, and figure—are stripped to their essentials. A close examination shows that each part was repeatedly nudged and reworked. In its final stage there is no hint of the roadway below the crossing, which leaves the monolithic structure as a completely intangible architectural form. This emphasis on the abstract and somewhat peculiar qualities of urban and industrial structures later becomes central to Brown's architectural themes.

In the 1971 painting, *The Chase,* a woman dashes through a room. Her movement is momentarily suspended but her graceful flight is closer to a dancer's *grand jete* than the stride of a runner. Further, the interior is parallel to the picture plane and reminiscent of a stage set. On the far right the protruding mask-like profile of a man watches her flight. This theatrical tableau—perhaps implying a sexual game—is intentionally erotic, but its meaning remains elusive and dreamlike. A fragment. Another painting incorporates the same figure, but shifts her flight to the street. The sidewalk, passageway to a courtyard, and the façade beyond form a recessional space as does the set-like interior in the other painting. However, the

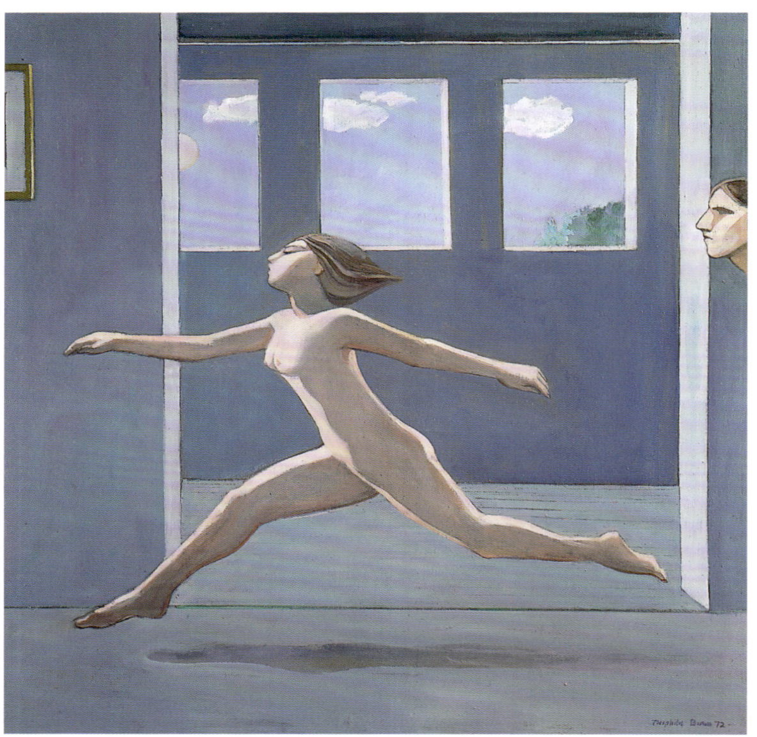

THE CHASE 1971, acrylic on canvas, 48 x 48 inches
Collection of Mr. & Mrs. Kevin Kearney, Sabastopol, California

UNTITLED 1972, acrylic on canvas, 48 x 48 inches. Private Collection

shift to an urban exterior recalls our disconcerting dreams of public nakedness.

His repeated use of certain figures can be seen in the variations of a standing man and woman with a towel, which appear in the beach paintings *Untitled* (p. 60) and *Race* (p. 61).

Brown also uses the same compositional device in *The Empty Room* (back of jacket). At its center the interior opens into a corridor that leads to several shallow rooms and through an open door. Beyond the window a crescent moon hangs in an early morning sky. In spite of its emptiness, the dreamlike character of the interior alludes to a human presence and recalls the heightened reality of the imagined piazzas of de Chirico.

Brown's reworking of his paintings and works on paper is somewhat different from the more metamorphic procedure of Diebenkorn, Bischoff, and Wonner, in which trails of their frequently radical revisions—such as painting out entire figures and objects or perspectival shifts—can often be traced by the ridges beneath the surface paint and palimpsest of underlying colors. Instead, his works follow a path of continual distillation and refinement. At times Brown continues to alter a canvas or work on paper over a period of years, and, unfortunately, some of these works are eventually destroyed with little or no record of their existence.

This evolution is clearly illustrated in the changes made to a small acrylic on paper depicting two nudes on a beach (pp. 126–127). The drawing of the figurative elements are firmly established in the earliest version—a male with his arms crossed; a female hoeing with a small shovel; and, in the water beyond, a rowboat—but the colorful and vigorously painted background is not defined. In its subsequent reworking, the sky is repainted with a flat color, the land mass shifts to a more clearly defined diagonal line, and the boat now sits on the shore. The woman now appears to be digging with an oar. In its final version, the colors are much more muted and close keyed. The beach takes on a hue somewhere between the color of sand and flesh, the water and sky are changed to pale blues, and the torso of the figure with the oar has been more carefully delineated. Her small breasts have disappeared, making her more sexually ambiguous. Either a woman or a man.

While not at all imitative, the pale gray-greens, faded blues, powdery pinks, and distilled drawing are reminiscent of Picasso's circus performers and Saltinbanques from his early years in Paris as well as his monumental Roman goddesses and nymphs of the twenties. The awkward stance of the heavily outlined youth and the sparse account of the landscape in *Boy Leading a Horse* (1905–06), as well as the sculptural, thick-limbed young men in *Pipes of Pan* (1923), provide an assortment of clues, for like those evocative images Brown's beach inhabitants are timeless and undecipherable mixtures of memories, dreams, and fictions.

Rather than working through the stylistic entablature of Picasso and Synthetic Cubism, as did Gorky, Park, and hundreds of other meritorious pre-WWII painters, Brown turned toward the allegorical substance employed by Picasso, Giacometti, de Chirico, Balthus, and other European painters. It is this facet of figurative painting that lies at the center of his work, and it is the primal allusions beneath these mixtures of past moments and poetic excursions that linger on in the memory. Perhaps Lafcadio Hearn summed up these qualities best:

Assuredly those impressions which longest haunt recollection are the most transitory: we remember many more instants than minutes, more minutes than hours; and who remembers an entire day? The sum of the remembered happiness of a lifetime is the creation of seconds. What is more fugitive than a smile? yet when does the memory of a vanished smile expire? or the soft regret which that memory may evoke?

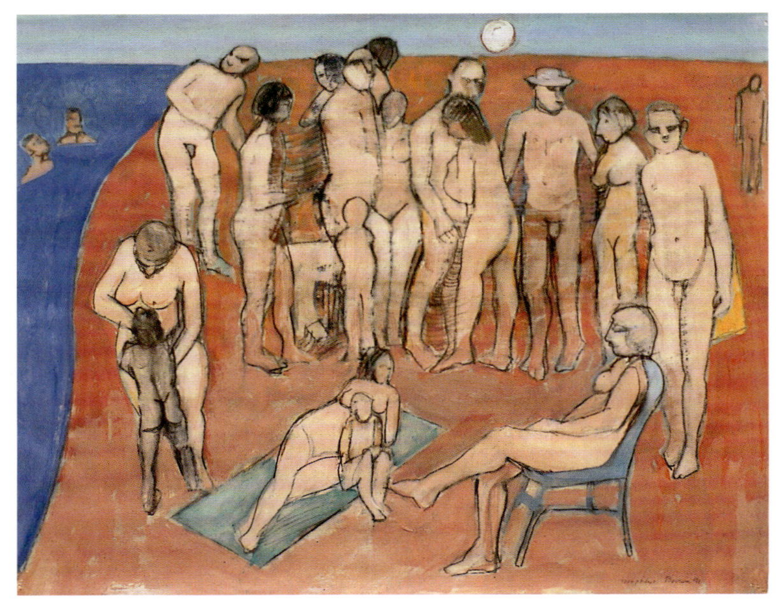

UNTITLED 1993, pencil and acrylic on paper
11 1/2 x 14 1/2 inches. Private Collection

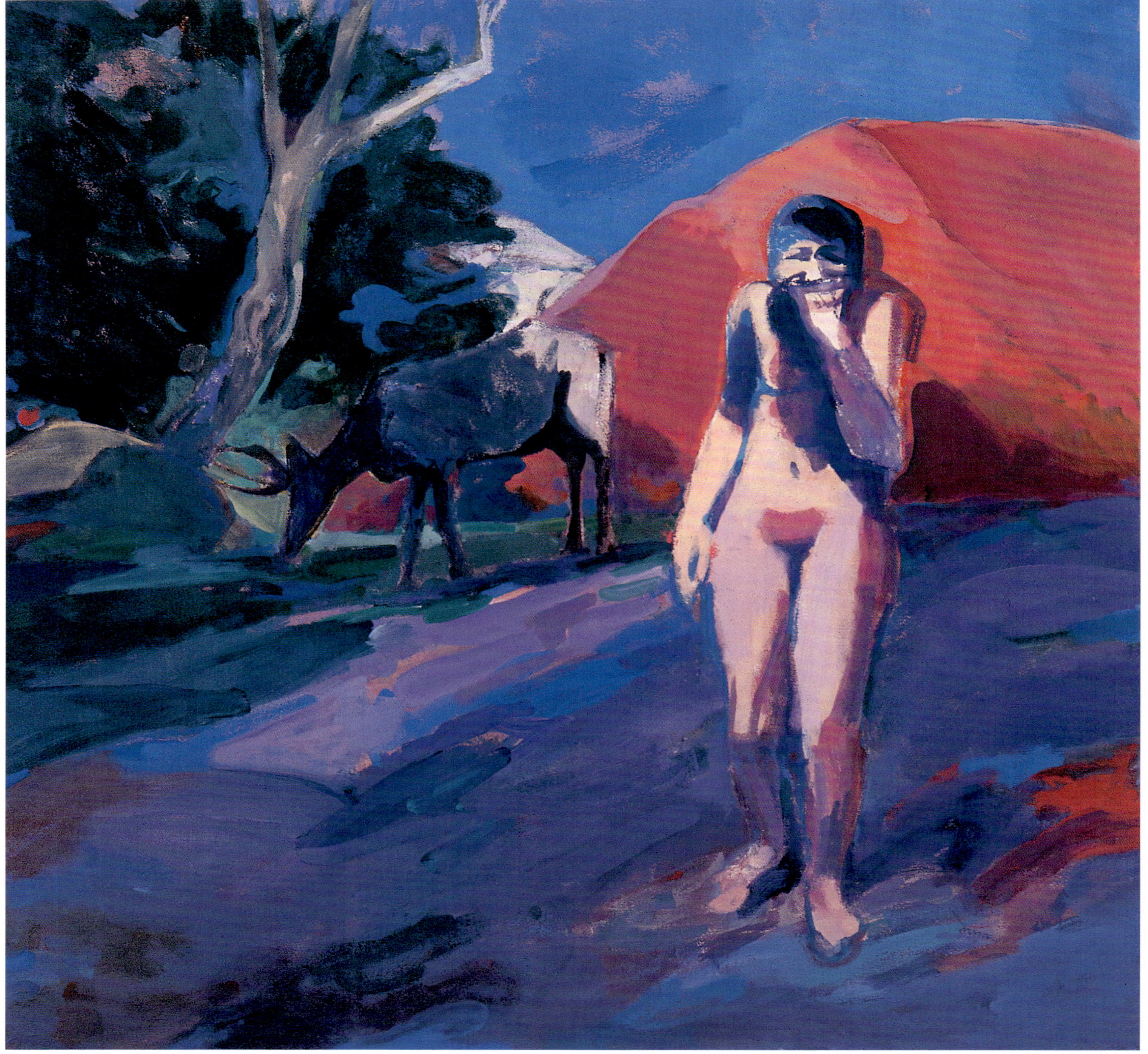

WOMAN AND DEER 1966, oil on canvas, 40 x 42 inches (destroyed)

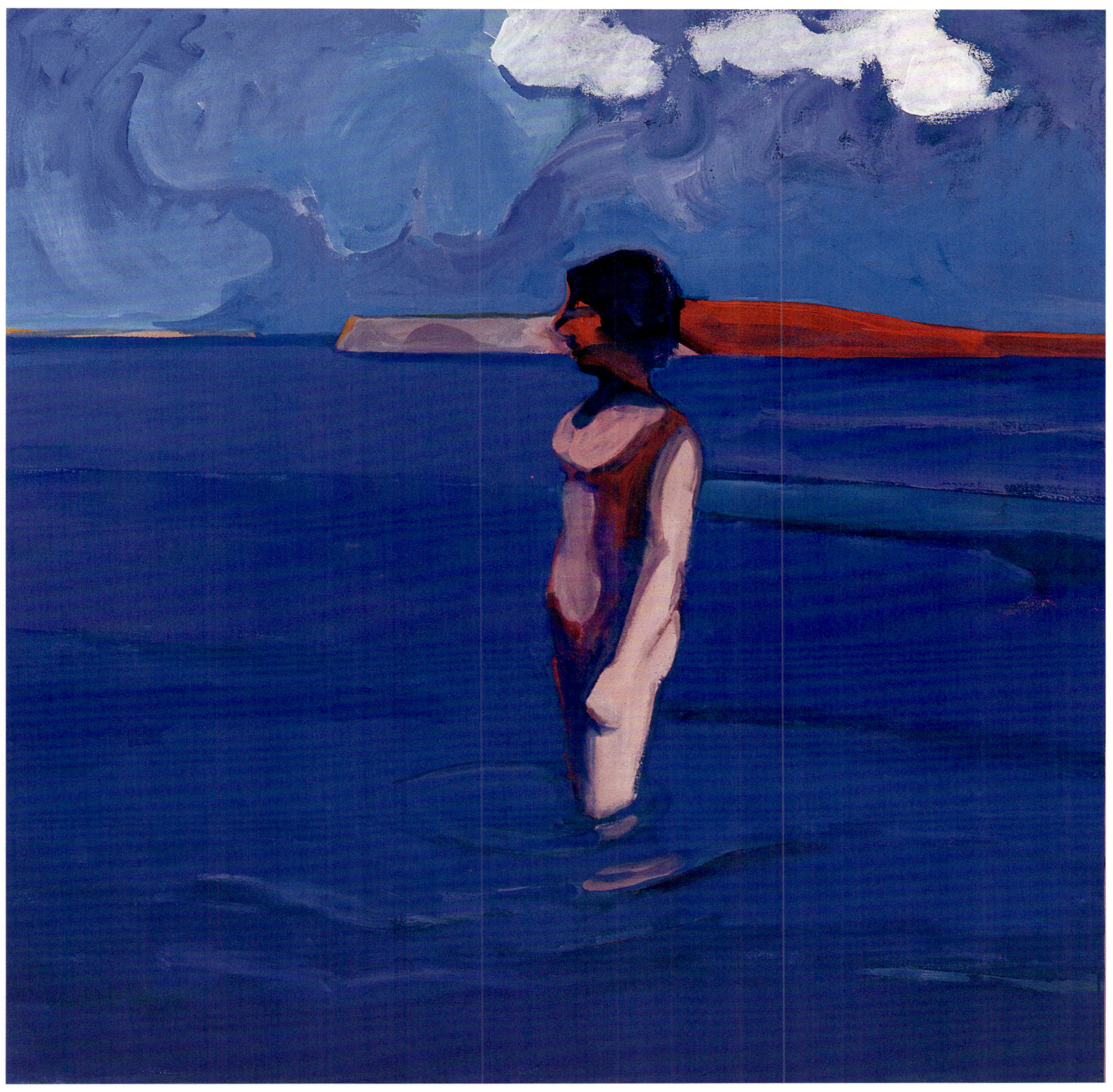

THE RED HILLS 1966, oil on canvas, 48 x 48 inches.

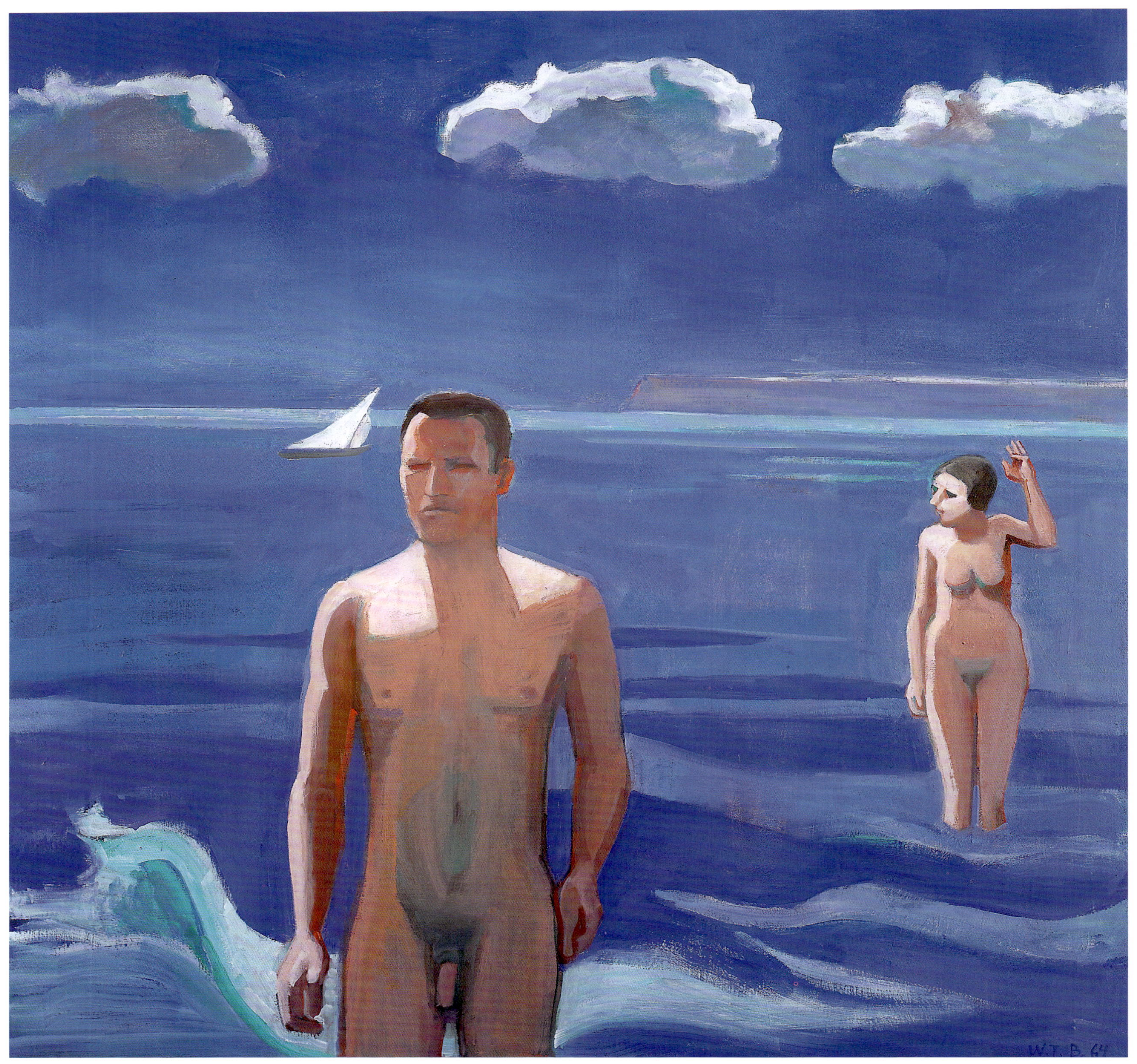

44   *UNTITLED* 1963, oil on canvas, 48 x 48 inches. Private Collection

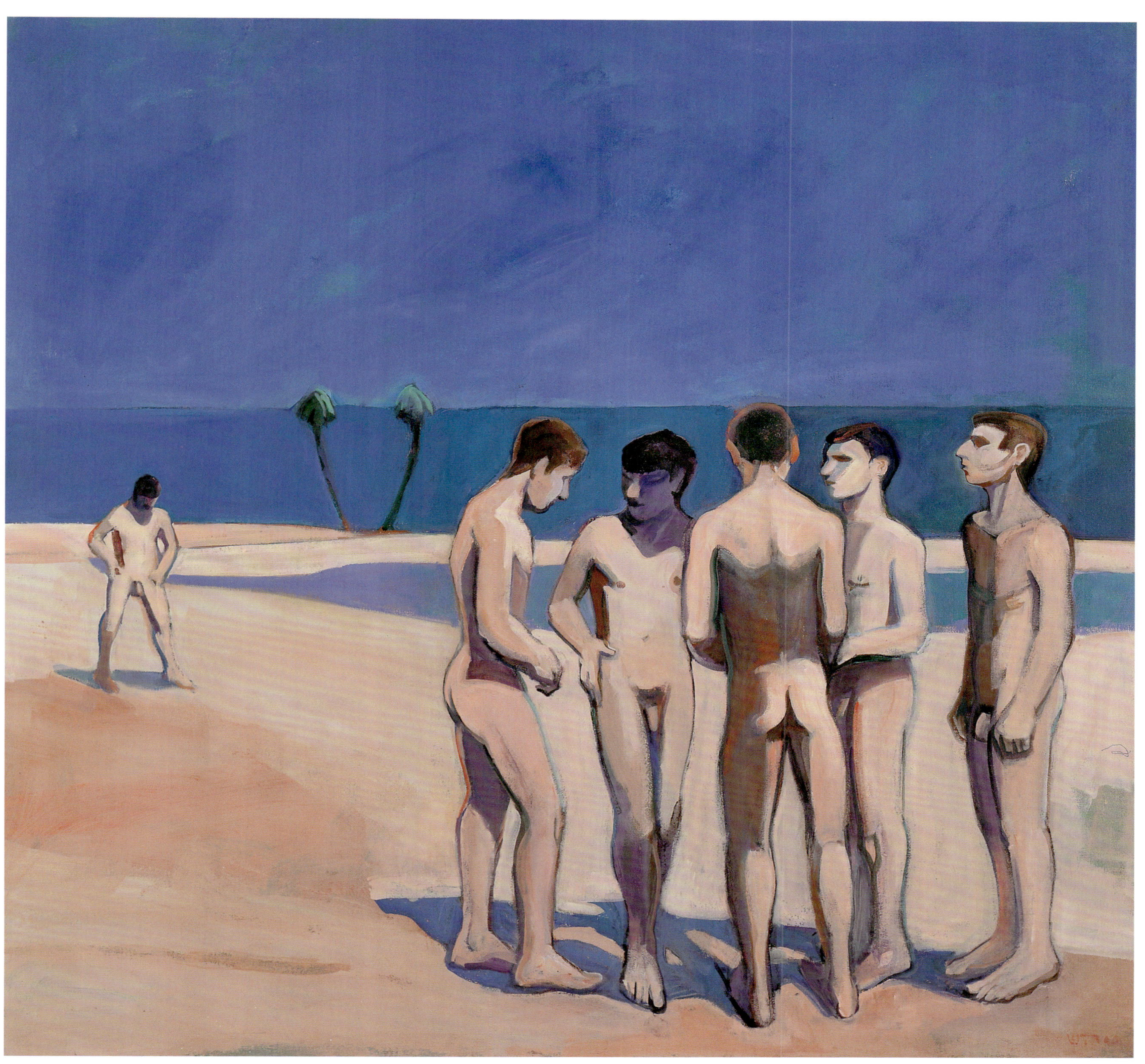

UNTITLED 1968, acrylic on canvas, 48 x 52 inches. Private Collection

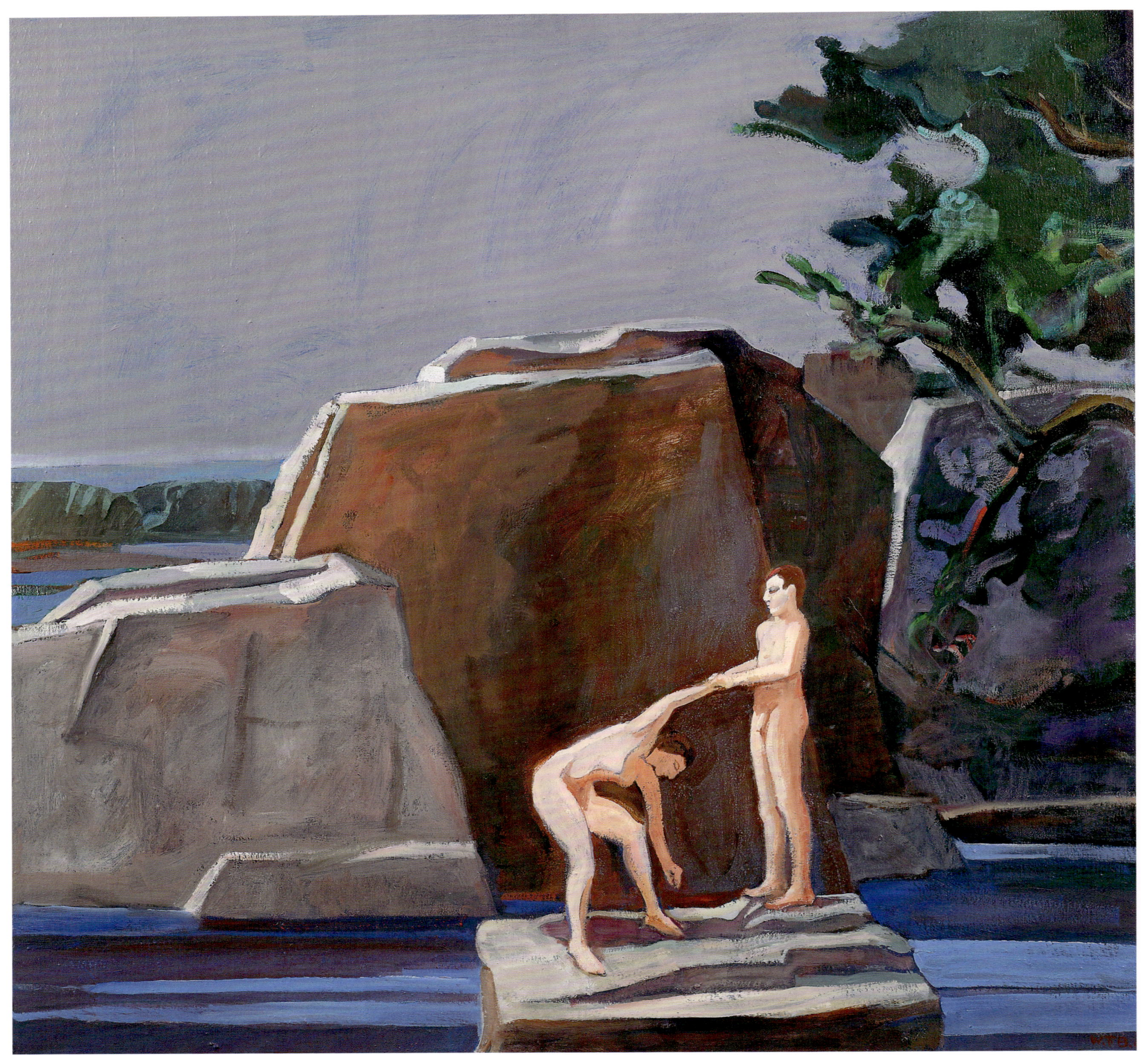

  TWO FIGURES ON A ROCK 1968, oil on canvas, 42 x 40 inches. Collection of Mr. & Mrs. Robert Chee, San Francisco

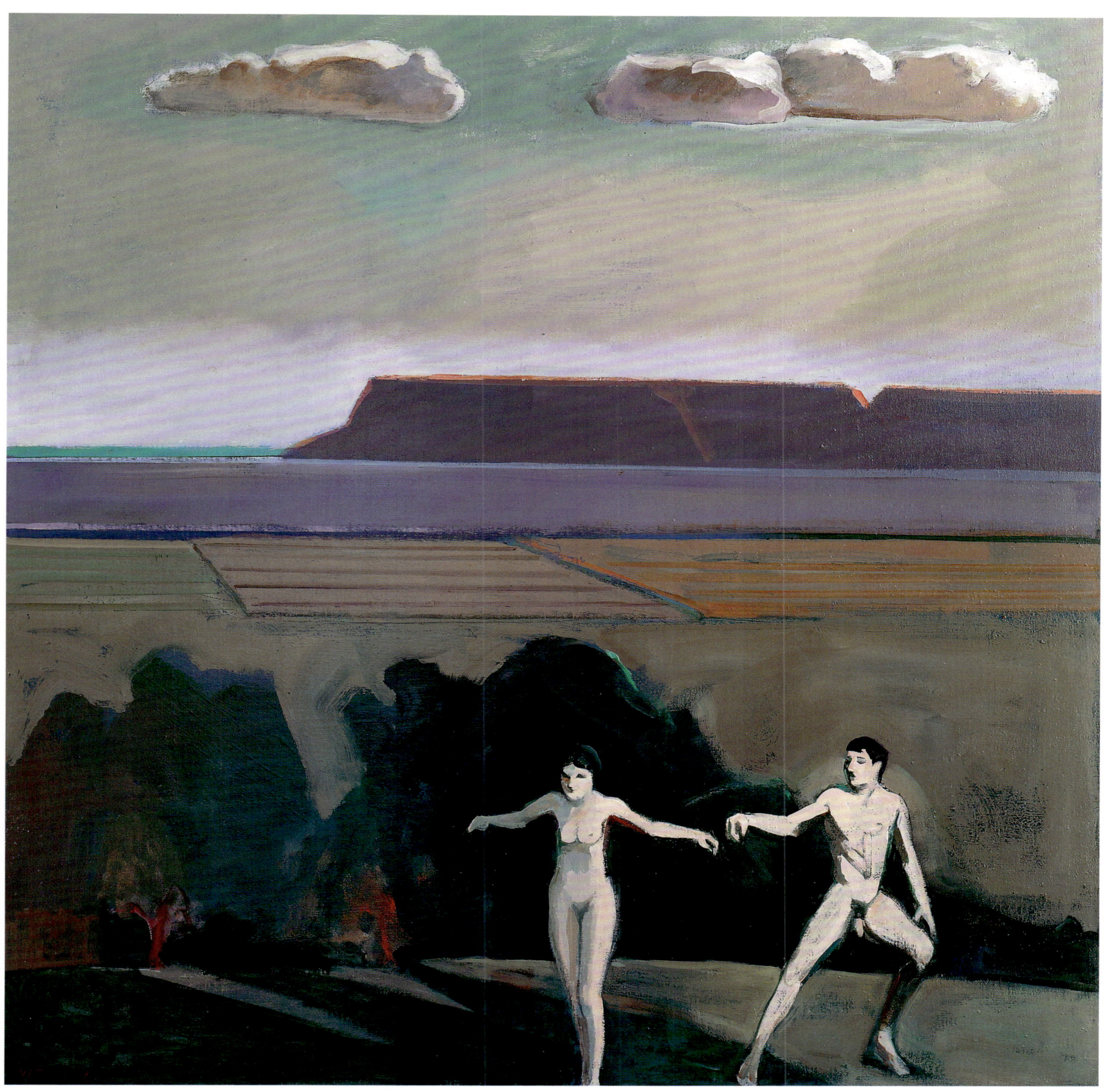

TWO FIGURES IN A FIELD 1968, oil on canvas, 48 x 40 inches. Collection of Ronald Casentini, Santa Rosa, California

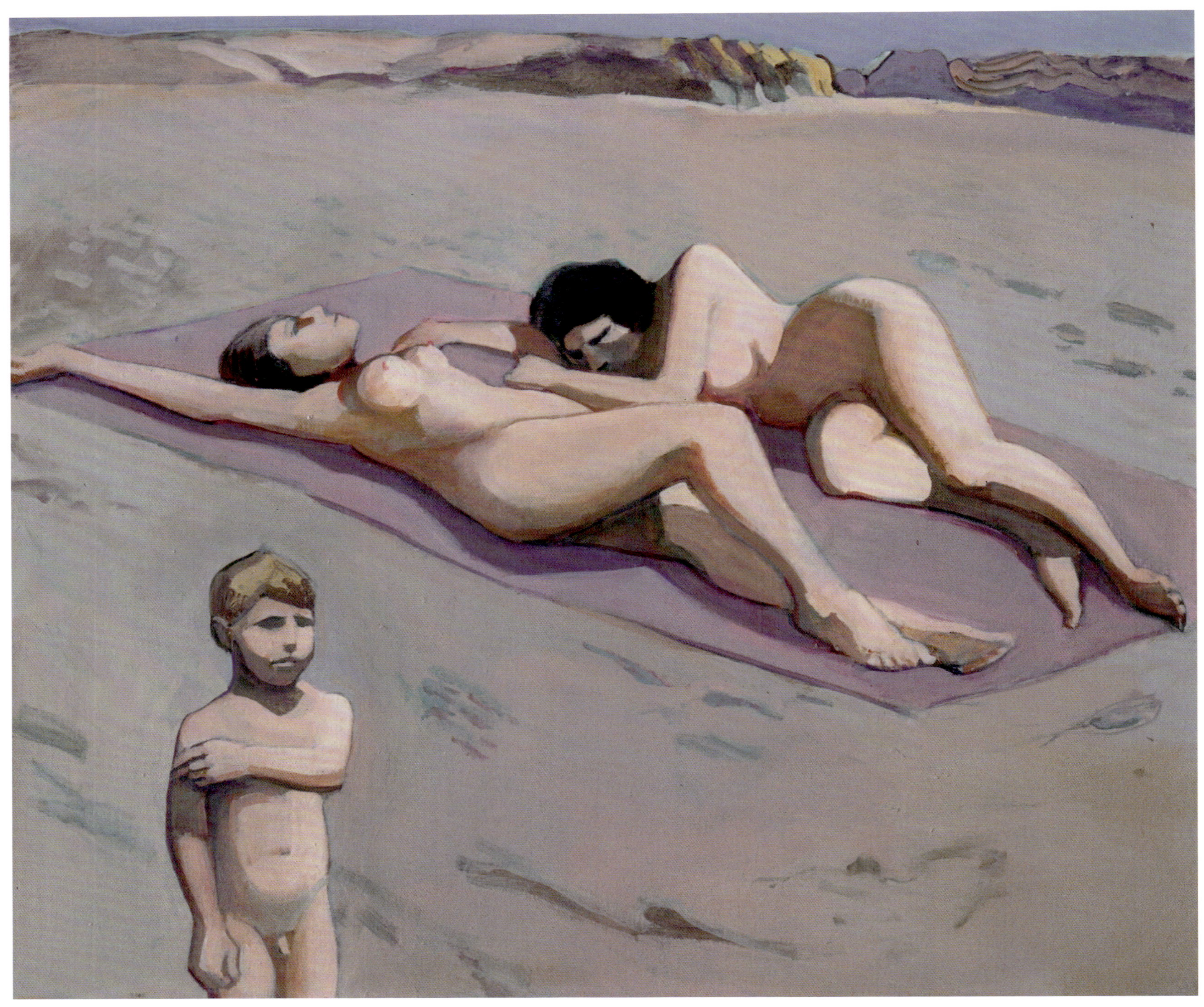

UNTITLED 1986–90, acrylic on canvas, 48 x 60 inches. Private Collection

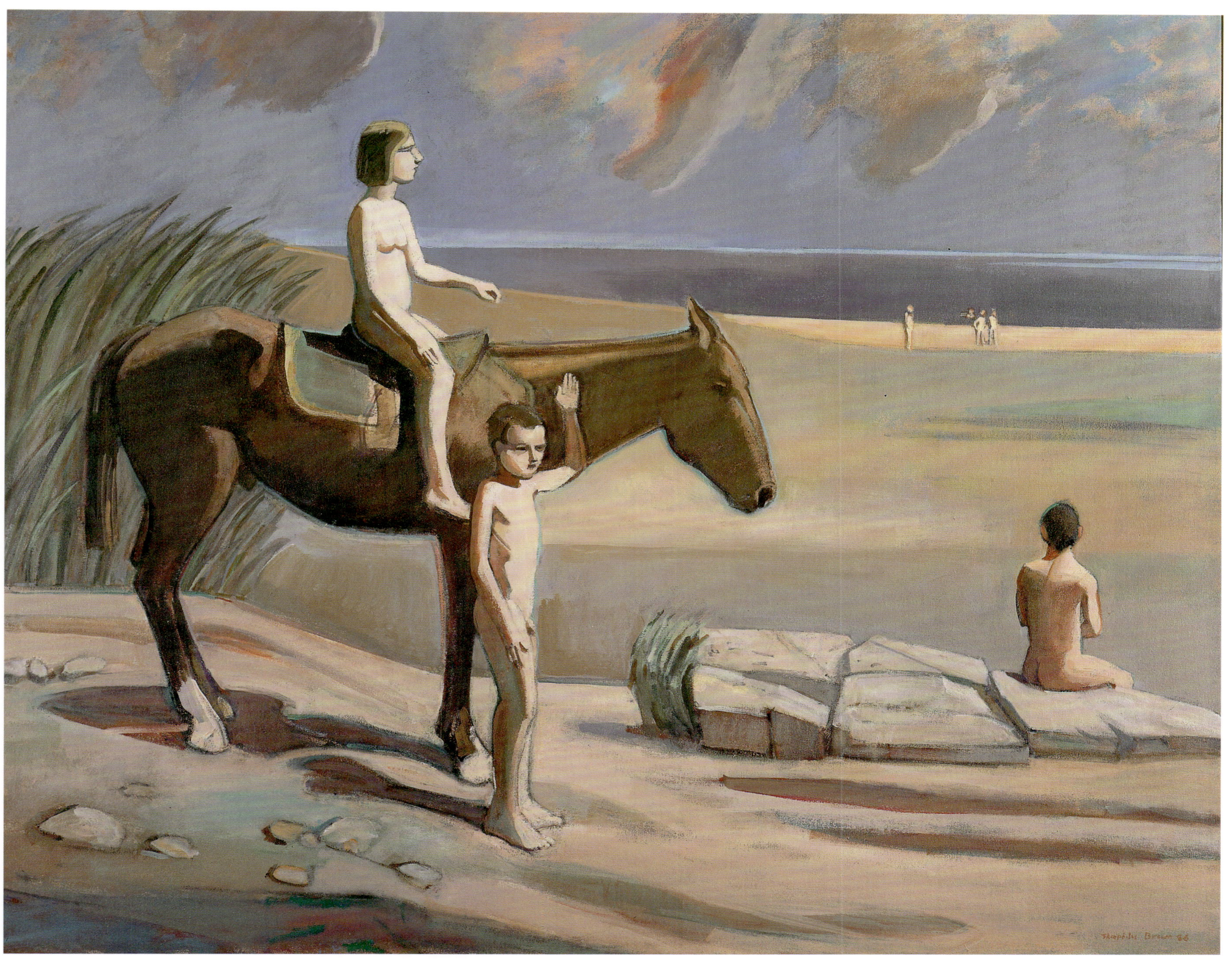

UNTITLED 1993, acrylic on canvas, 24 x 30 inches. Private Collection

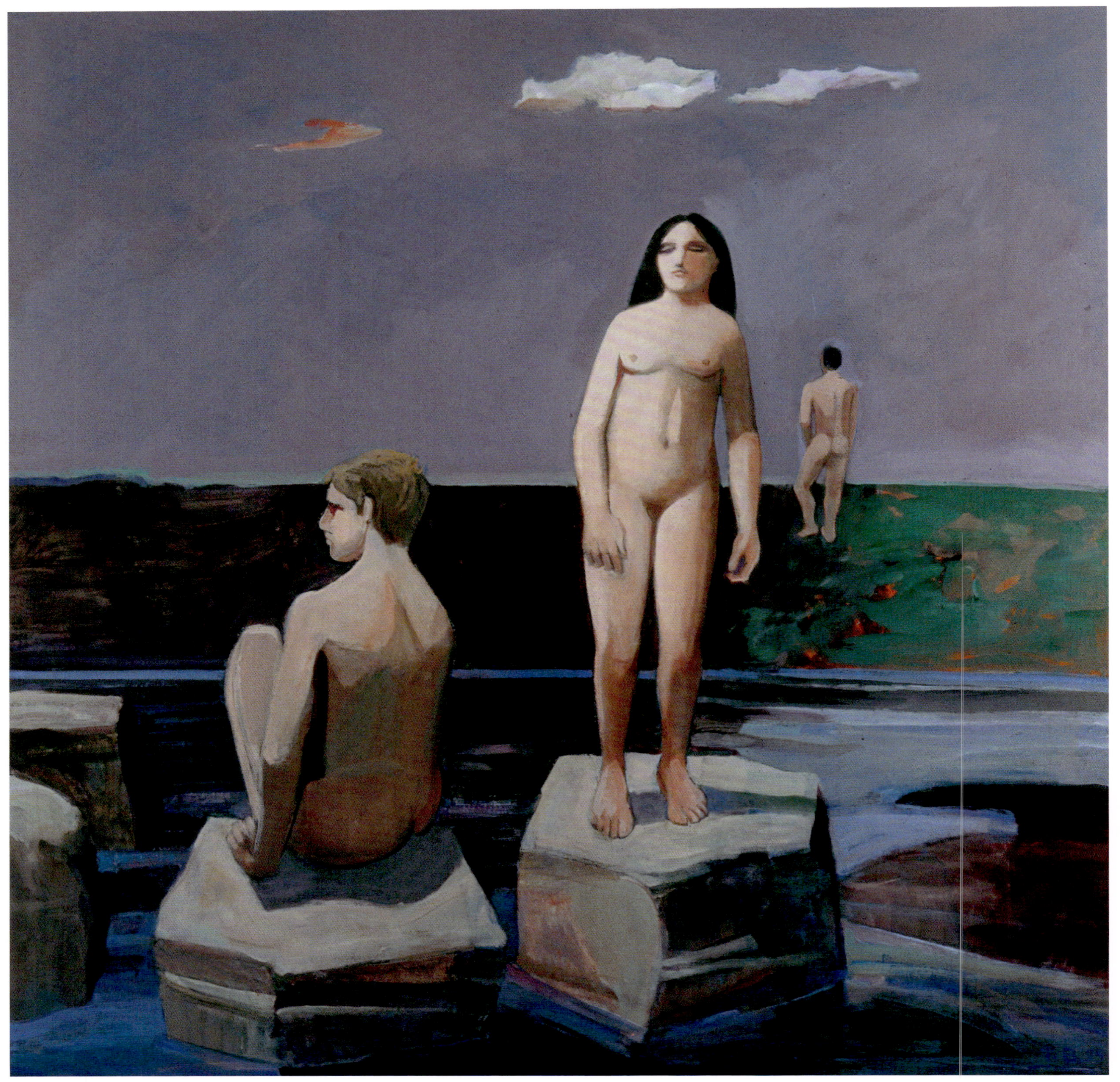

 UNTITLED 1990, acrylic on canvas, 48 x 48 inches. Collection of Loren Estrow & Brian Newkirk, Los Angeles

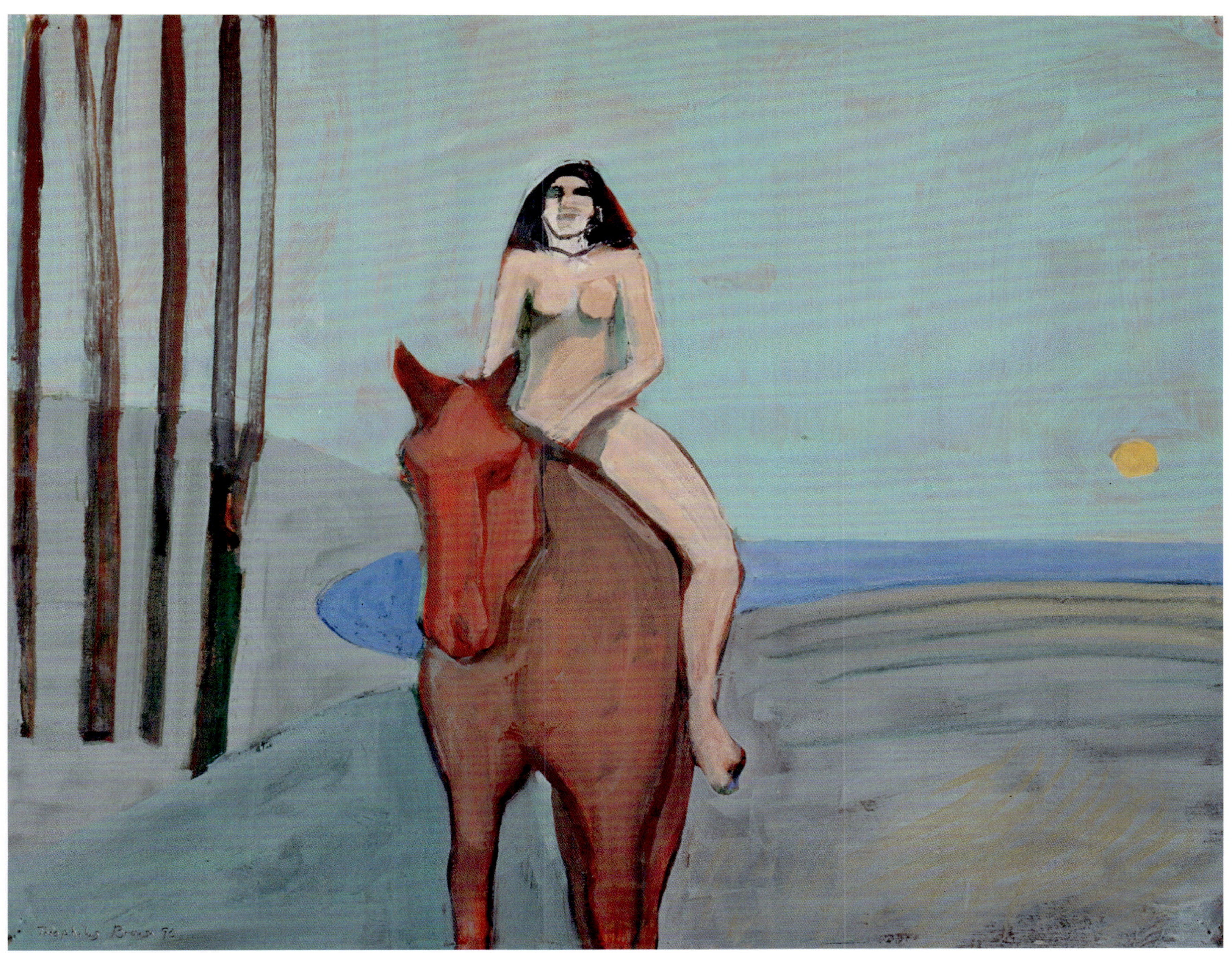

UNTITLED 1986–90, acrylic on canvas, 48 x 60 inches. Private Collection

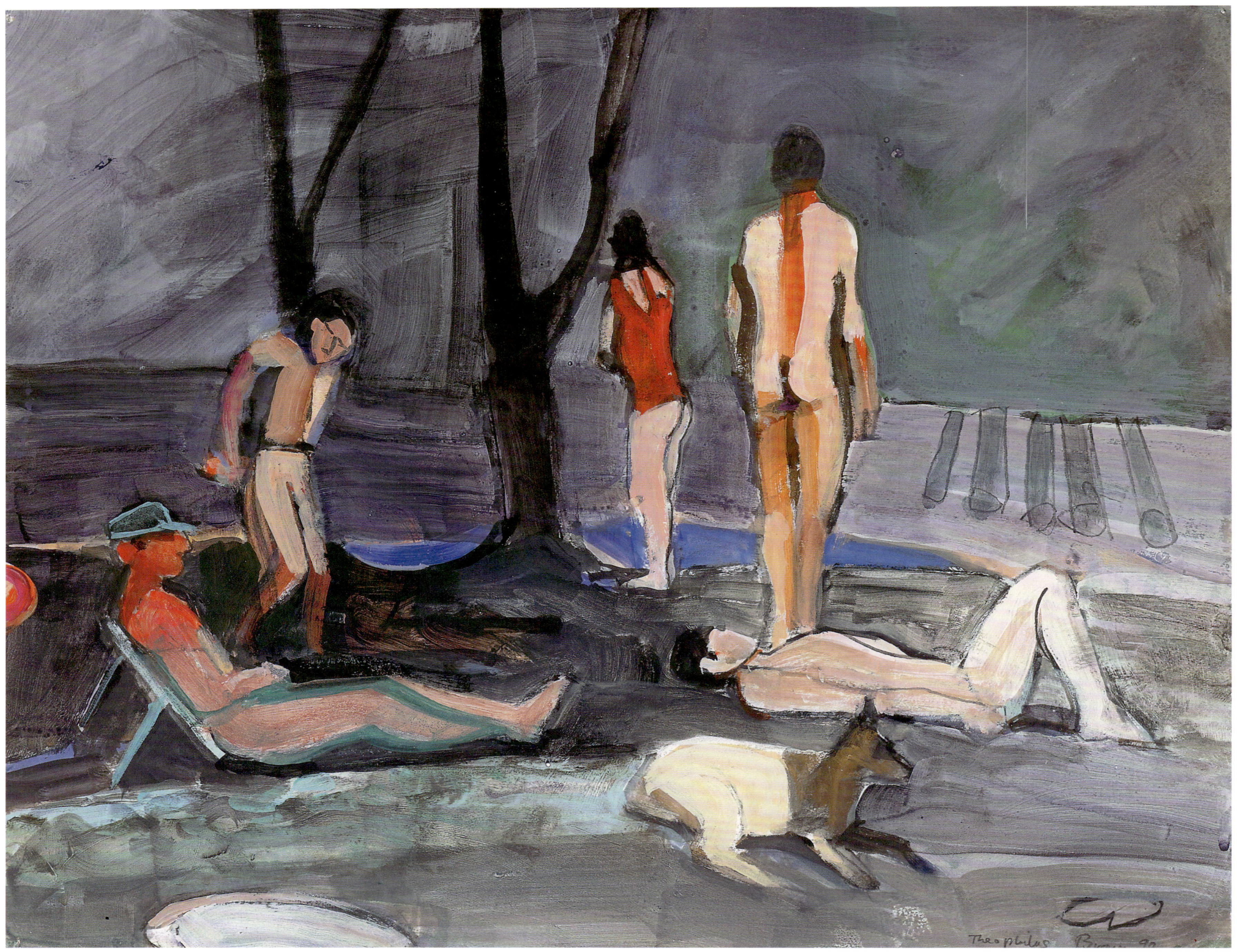

UNTITLED 1990, acrylic on paper, 11 1/2 x 14 1/2 inches (location unknown)

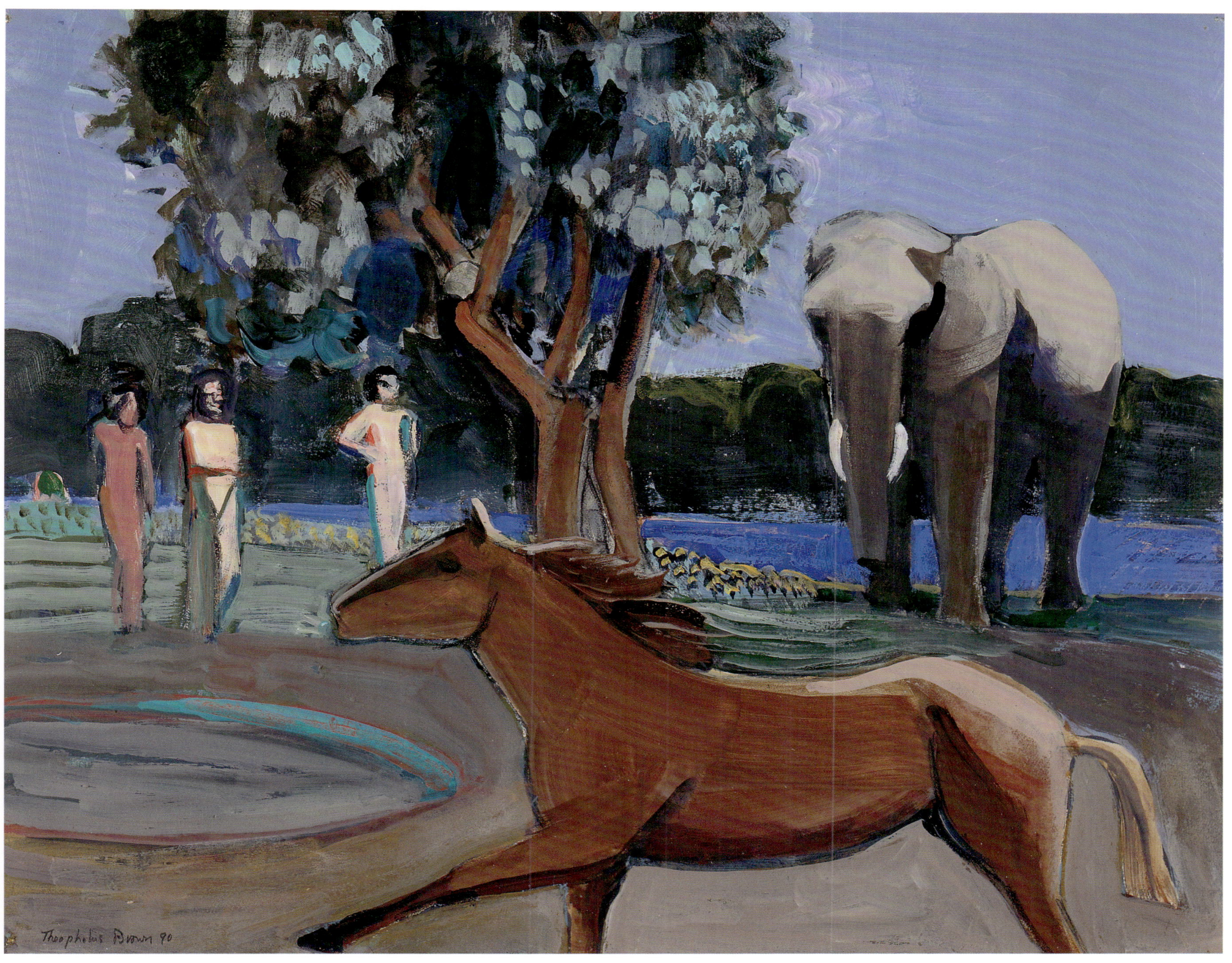

UNTITLED 1990, acrylic on paper, 11 x 14 inches. Collection of Peter Linenthal, San Francisco

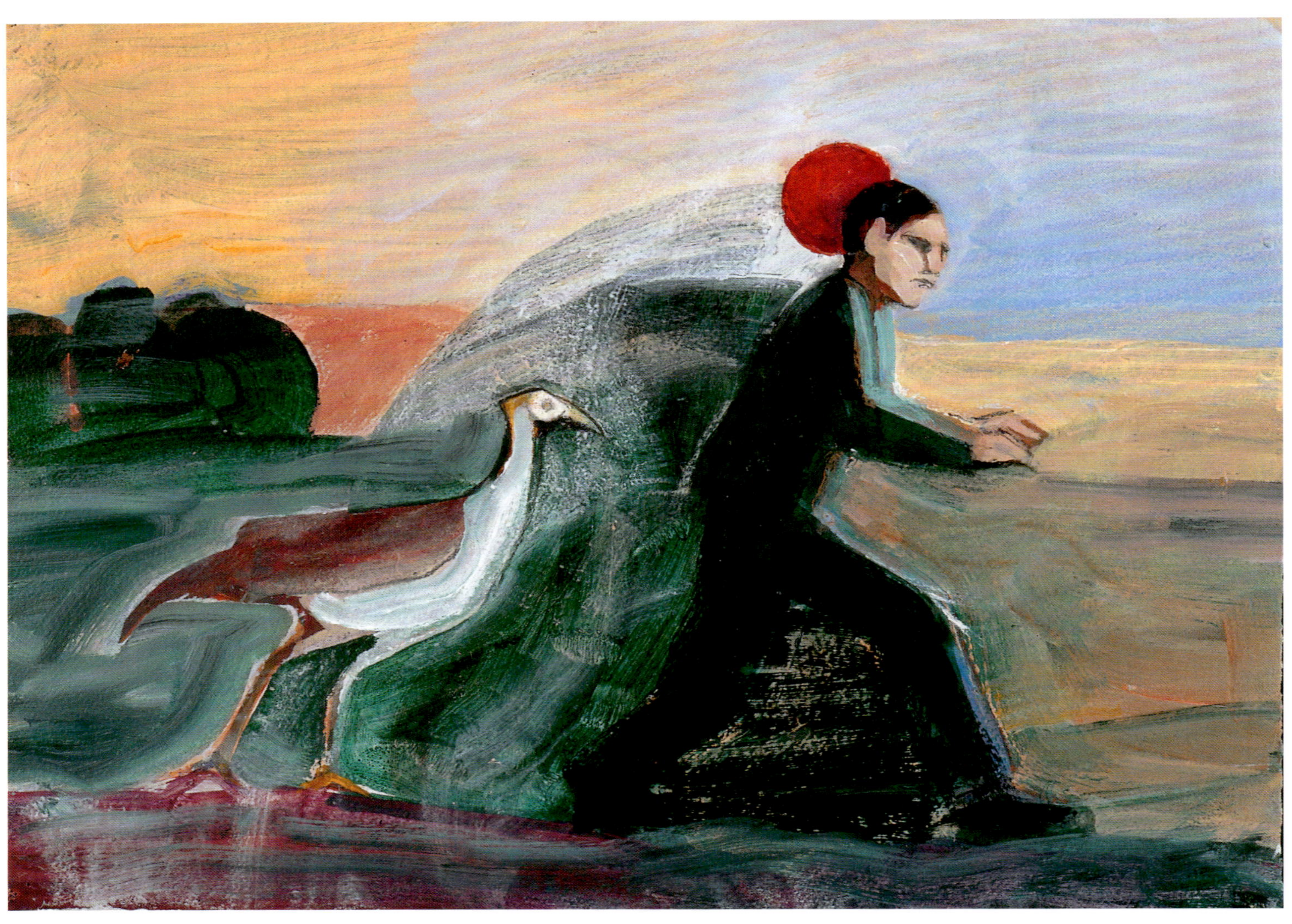

BIRD CHASING MAN 1980, acrylic on paper, 14 1/4 x 17 1/2 inches (location unknown)

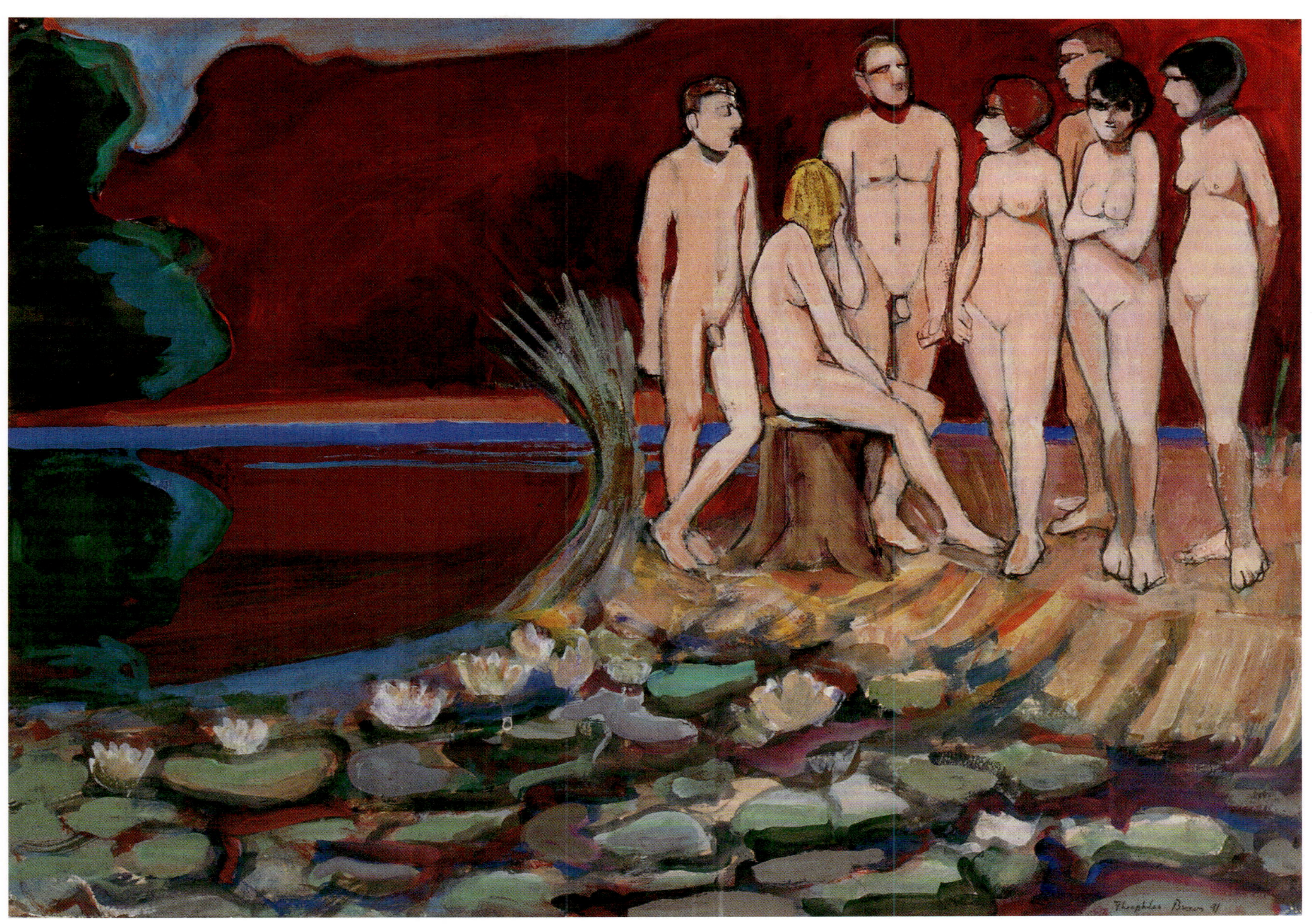

UNTITLED 1991, acrylic on paper, 14 3/4 x 21 inches. Private Collection

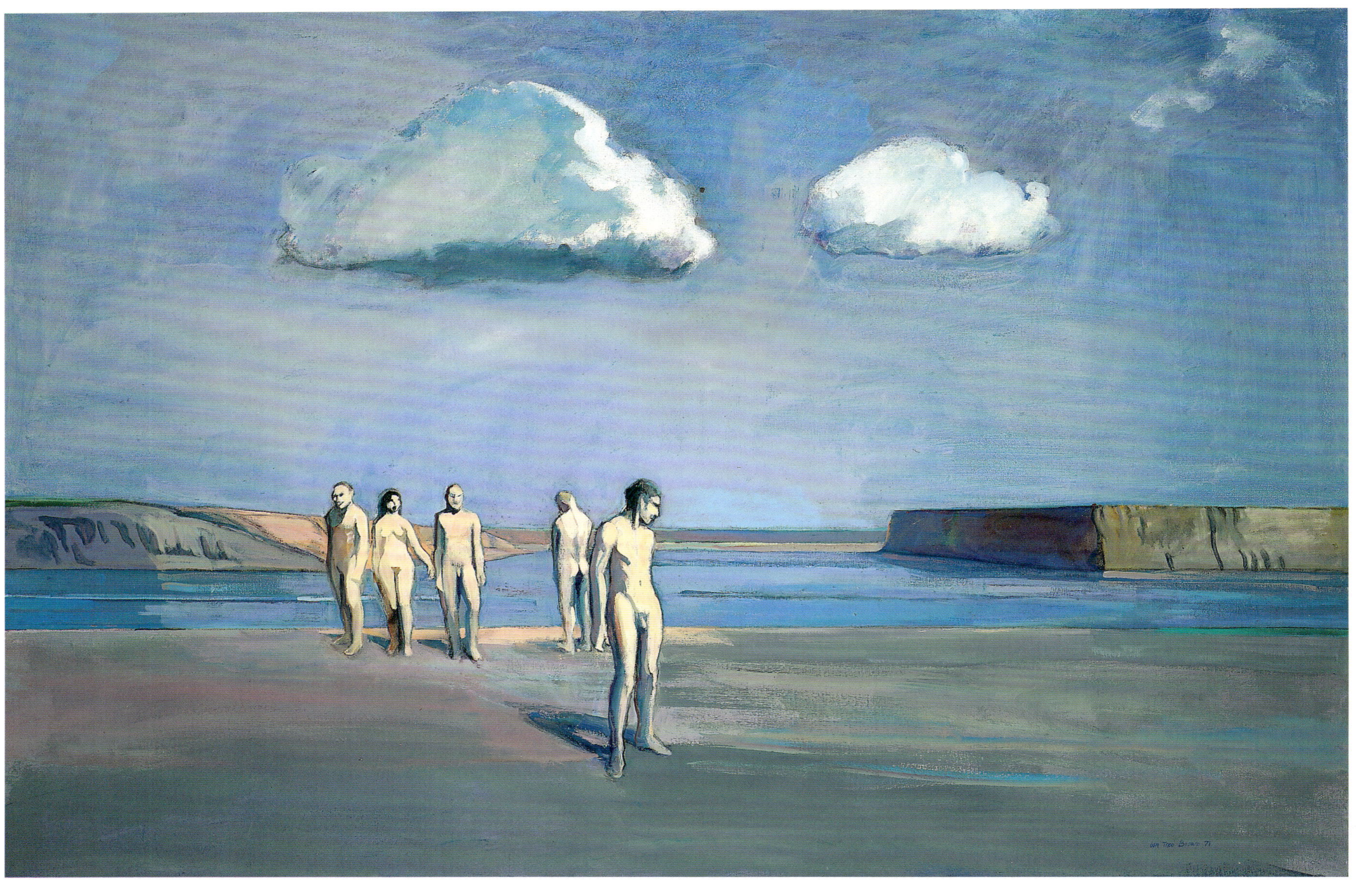

  NUDES ON A RIVERBANK 1968–72, acrylic on canvas, 48 x 72 inches. Collection of M. Koplin, Los Angeles

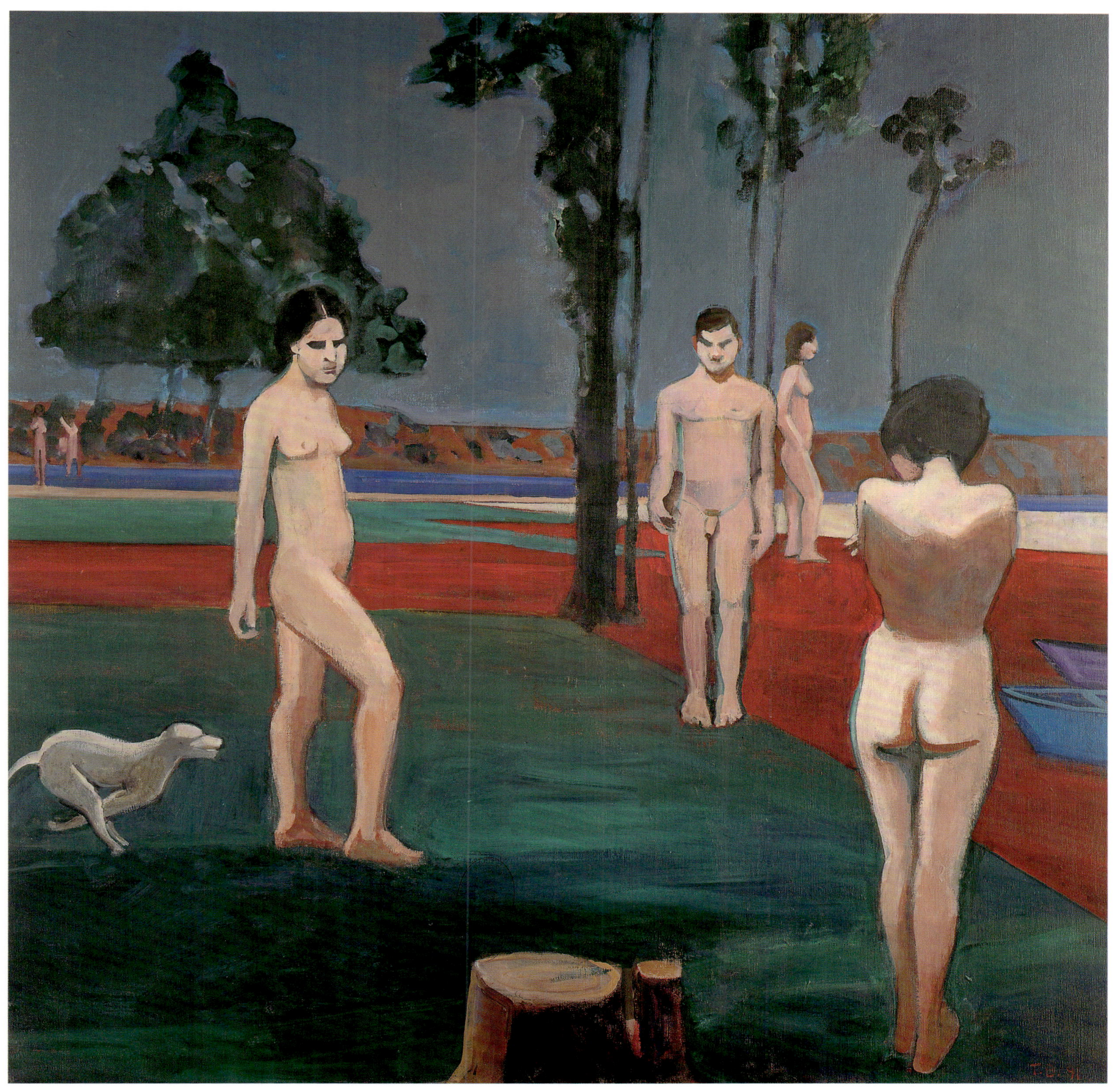

UNTITLED 1997, acrylic on canvas, 48 x 48 inches. Private Collection

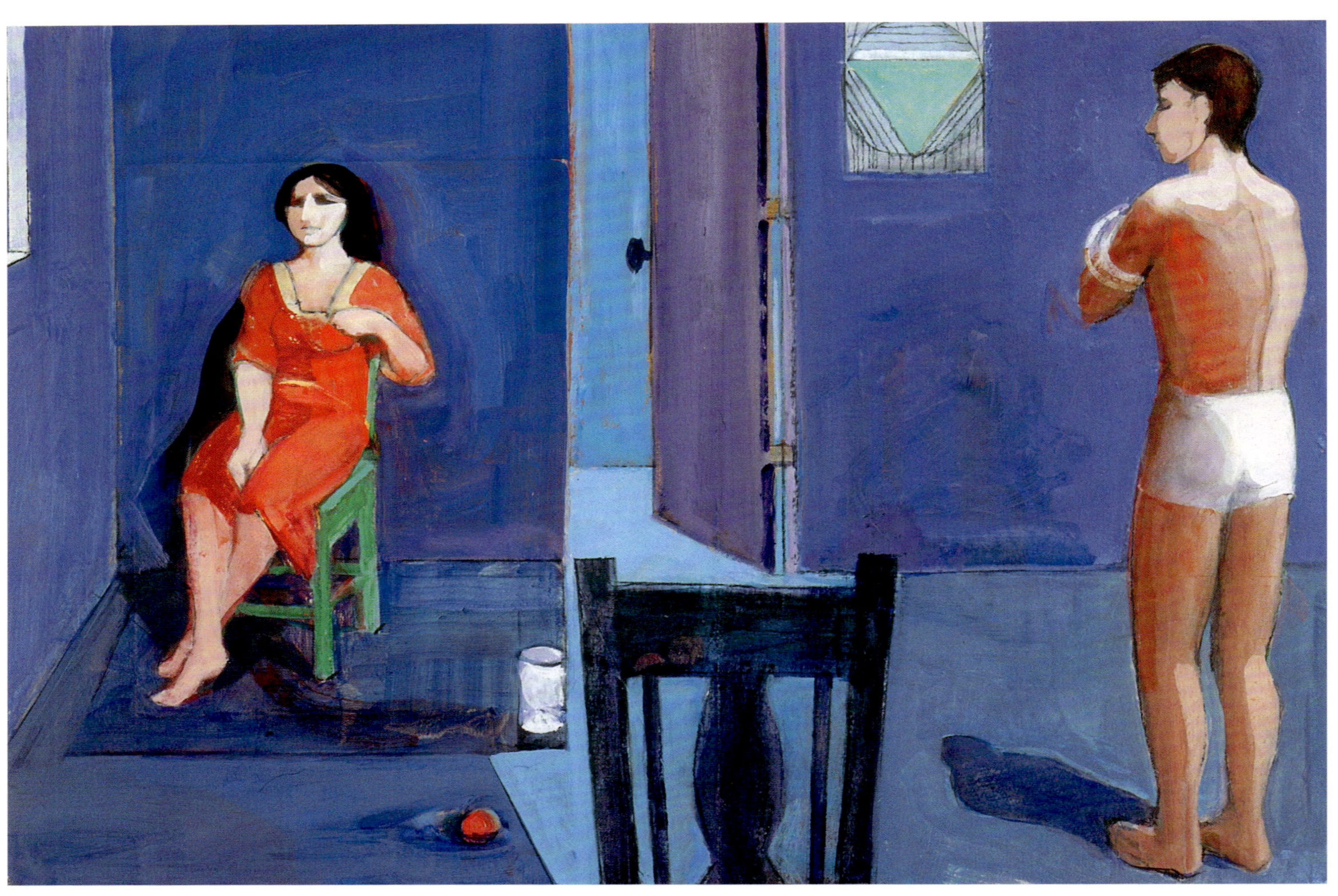

58   *OPEN DOOR* 1980, acrylic on paper, 141/4 x 171/2 inches (location unknown)

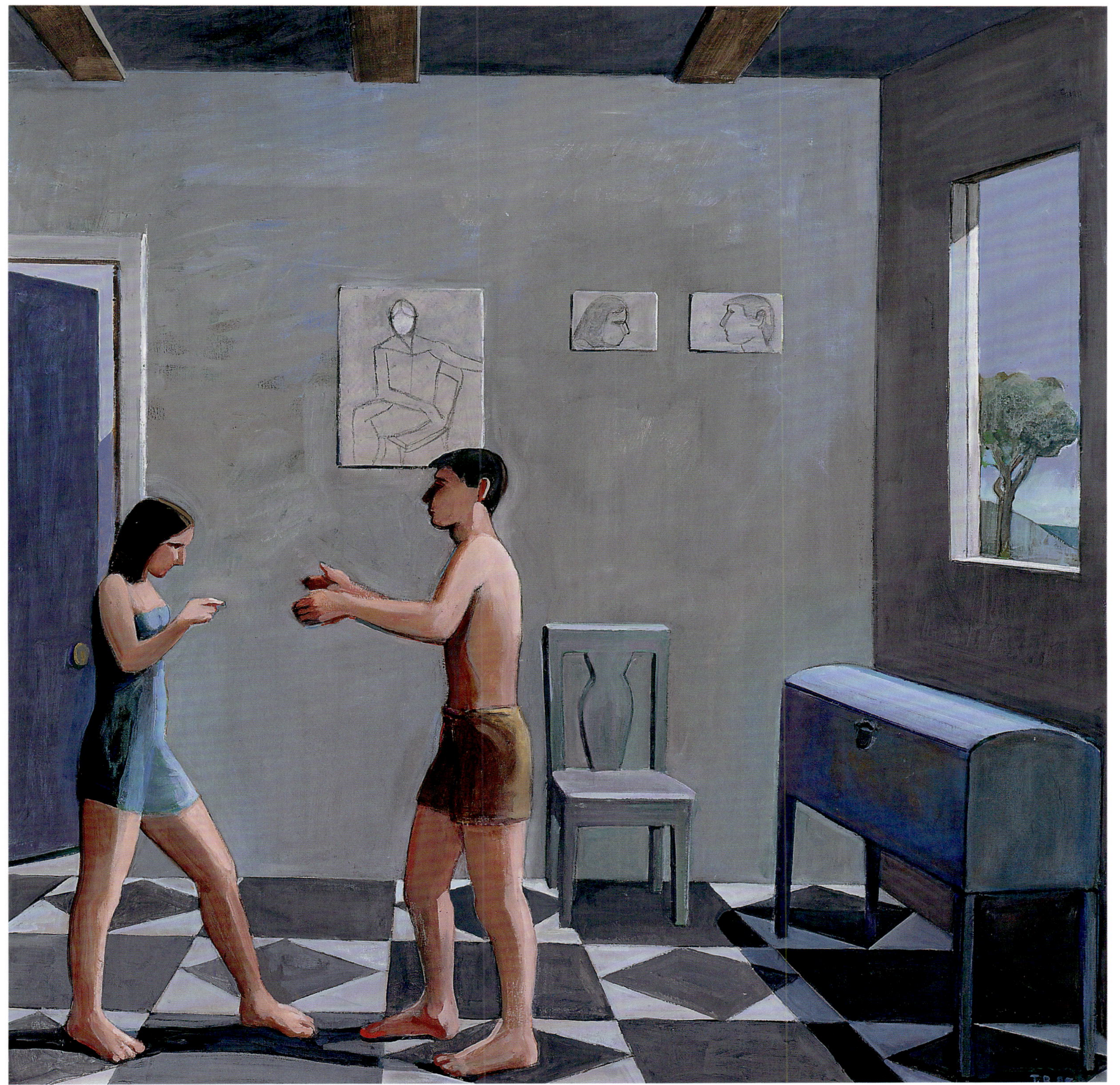

ENCOUNTER 1992–95, acrylic on canvas, 48 x 48 inches. Collection of Martha & Alan Armstrong, Hatfield, Massachusetts

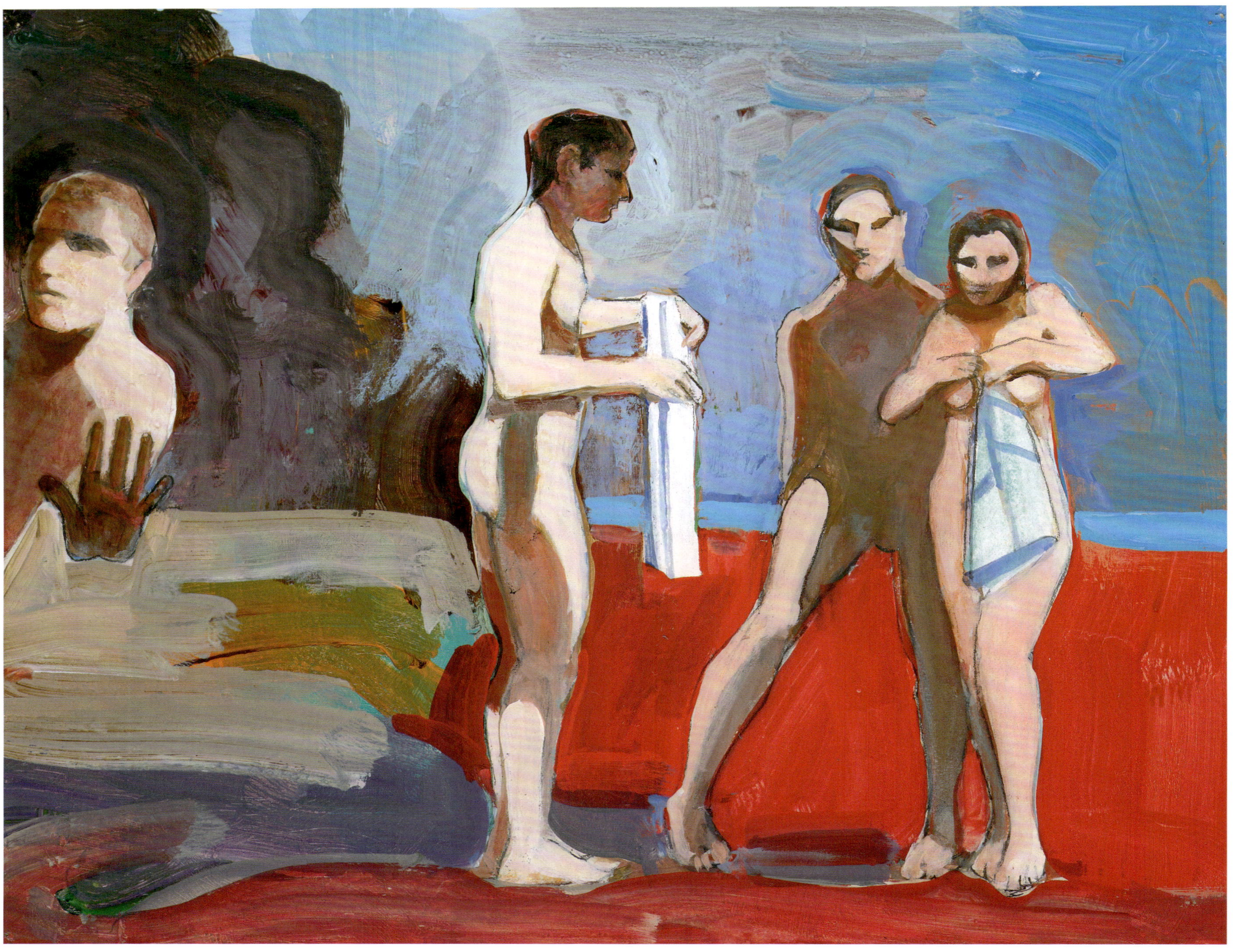

UNTITLED 1992, acrylic on paper, 14 1/2 x 17 inches. Collection of Jim Krozel, Portland, Oregon

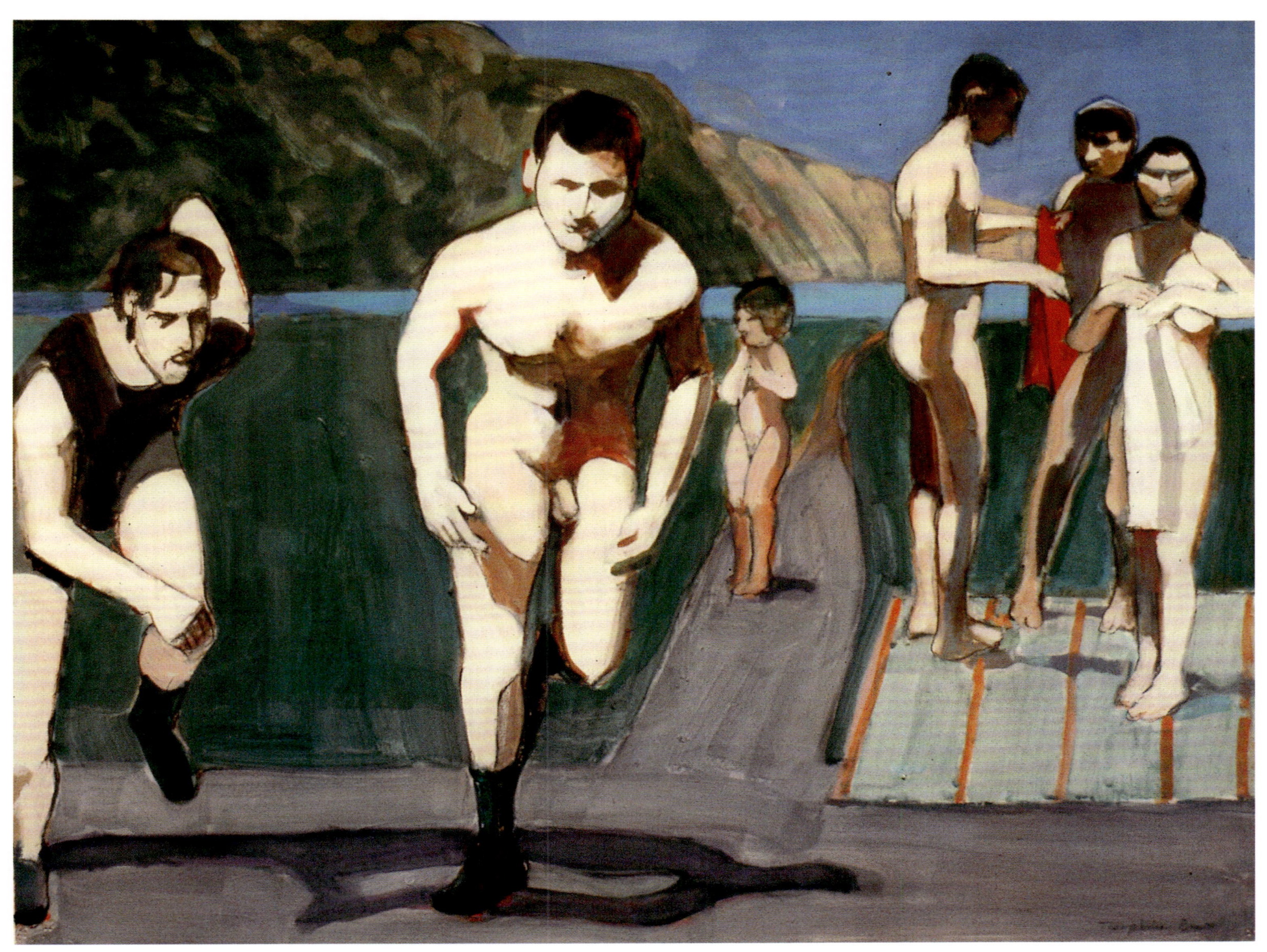

RACE 1991, acrylic on paper, 14 1/2 x 19 inches. Collection of Mr. & Mrs. Morgan Flagg

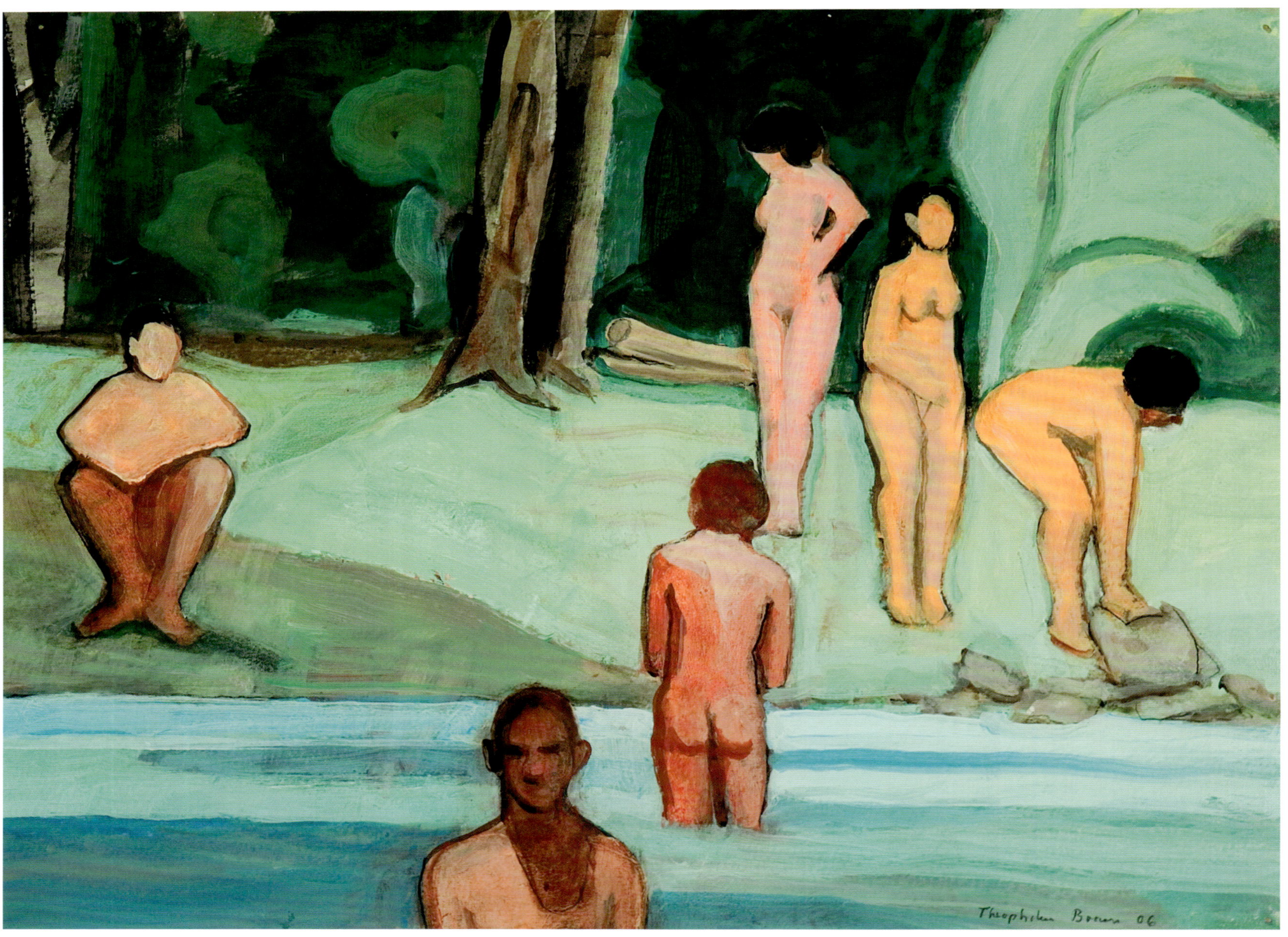

FIGURES BY A RIVER 2006, acrylic on paper, 10 x 131/2 inches. Collection of the Artist

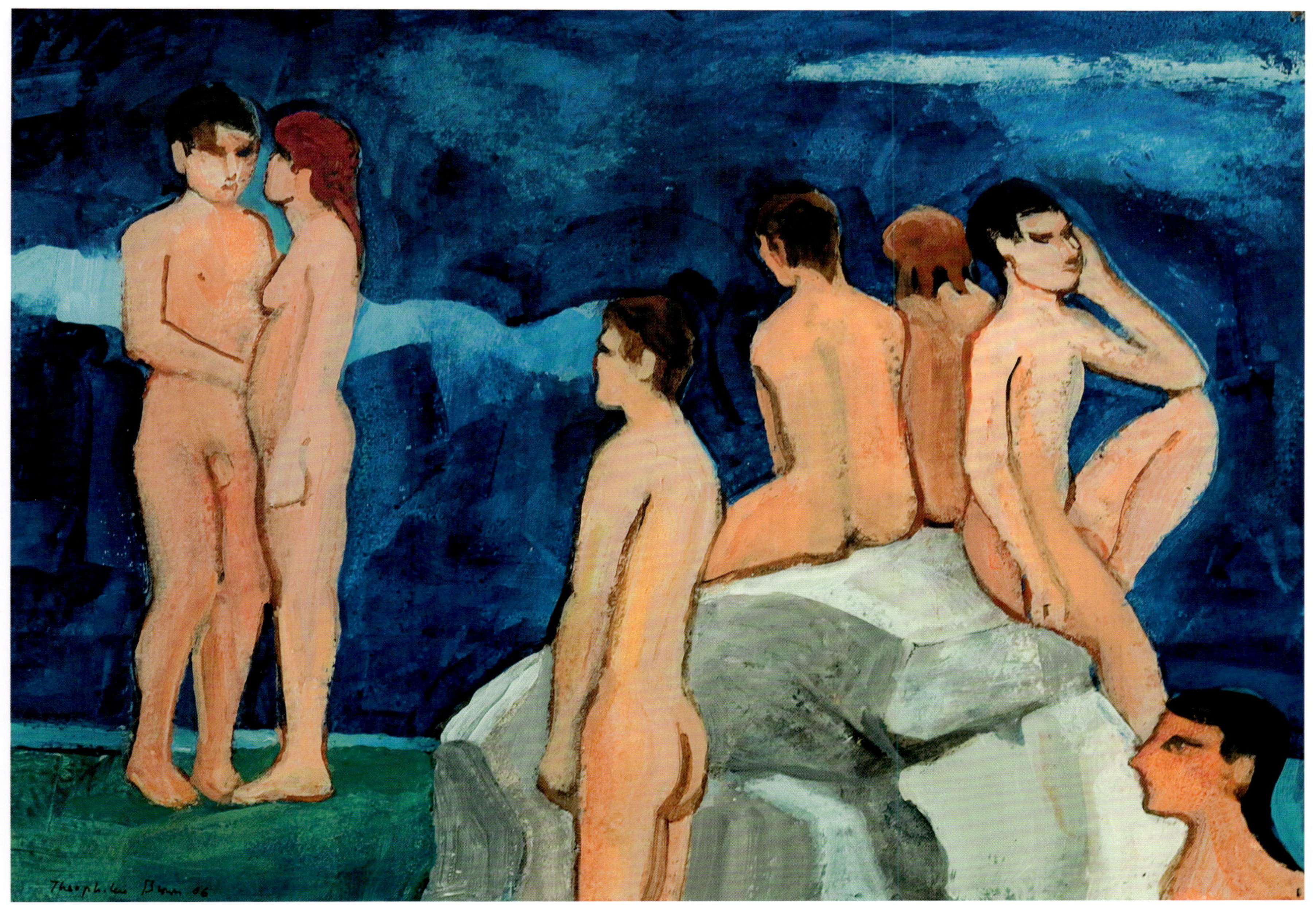

NUDES ON A ROCK 2006, acrylic on paper, 11 x 15 1/2 inches. Collection of the Artist

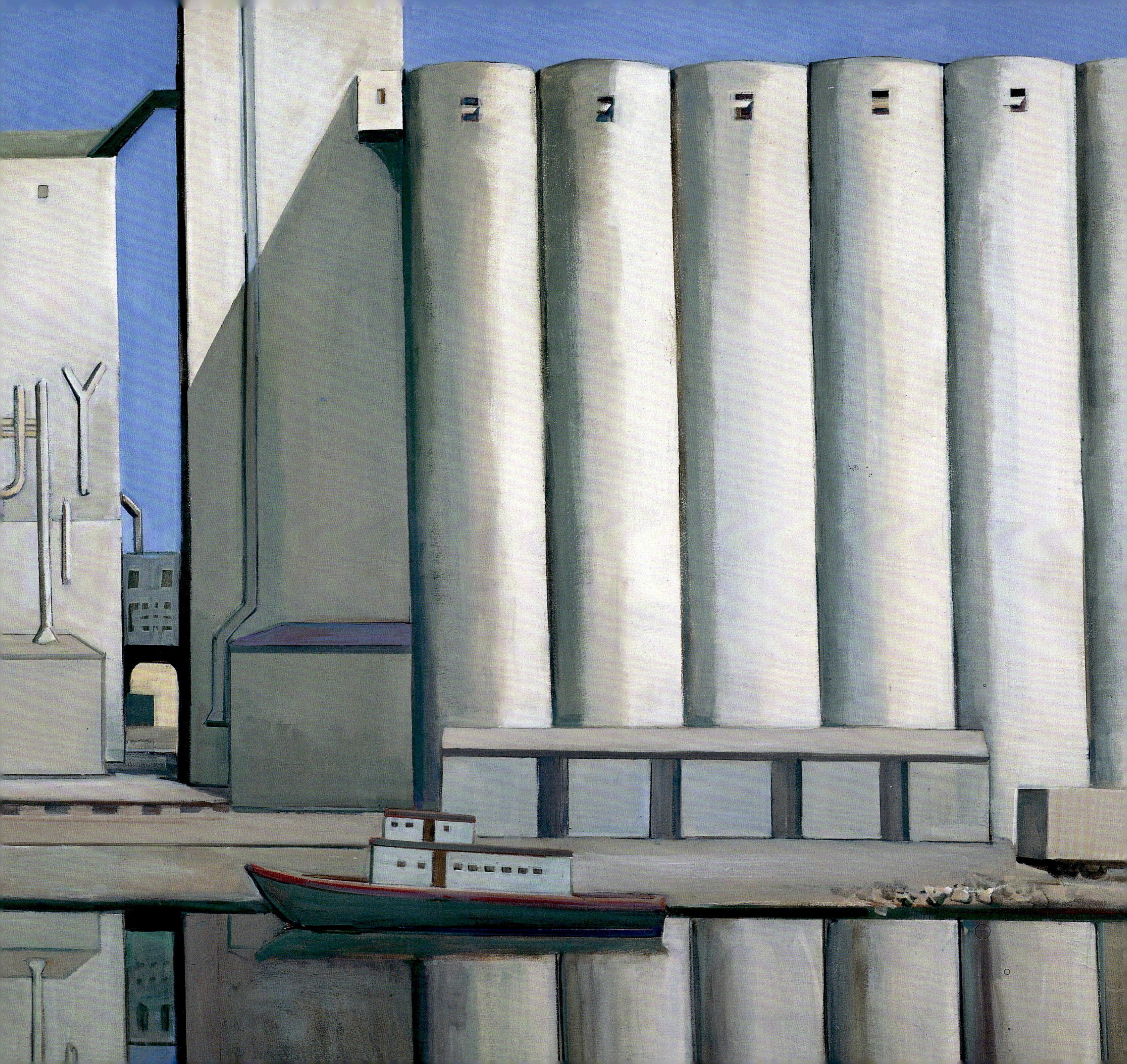

Urban and Industrial Landscapes

*To create beauty, he must simultaneously reject reality
and exalt certain of its aspects. Art disputes reality,
but does not hide from it.*

—Albert Camus

THEOPHILUS BROWN'S INDUSTRIAL landscapes evolved gradually from his landscapes, urban views, and interiors. Their roots lie in such earlier works as the enigmatic *Pedestrian Crossing* (p. 67), where the function of the architectural structure is obscured by the landscape; the simplified interior of *The Chase* (p. 40); *The Empty Room*; and *Studio Roof: Santa Barbara,* a tautly structured composition based on the view from the roof of Brown's and Wonner's studios. Most of the paintings of plants and factories were done between 1985 and 1990.

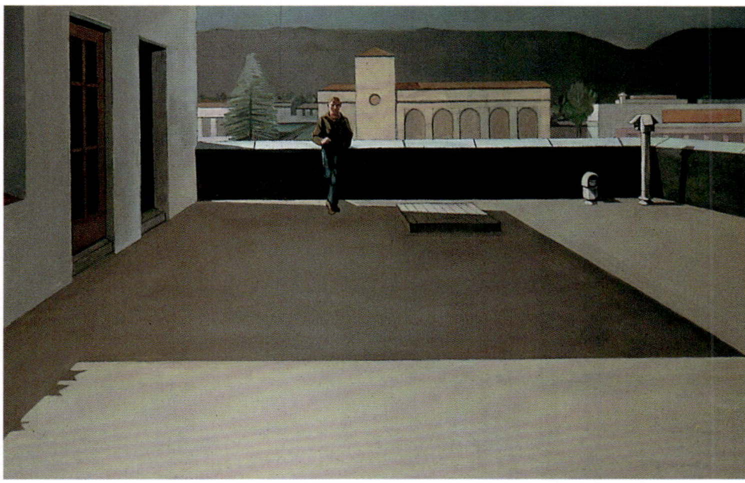

The industrial views are derived from small plein air sketches —a procedural means that insists on abbreviation and emphasis—and Brown's snapshots of factories in San Francisco, Oakland, and Alameda. He makes no attempt to convey their purpose, for they are not intended to be illustrations or narrative paintings. In fact, such specifics are of little interest to him, so their functions remain elusive.

Some are reminiscent of Giorgio de Chirico's sharp shadowed piazzas and dark arcades, but Brown's views are devoid of the melancholic airs and ominous allusions that permeate the Italian's metaphysical paintings. The traits they share lie in

the editing—the stripping of architectural details, forms, and figures to their pictorial essentials—and in the dreamlike quality of both painters' images. One is also reminded of the sense of serenity—so oddly out of place considering the monotonous and often backbreaking labors carried on within these factory walls—conveyed in Charles Sheeler's masterful images of plants and mills (qualities that are lost in his later double-exposed industrial structures and highly patterned agrarian abstractions), but Brown has little interest in Sheeler's lack of painterly sensuality or his dryly rendered precisionism. One could argue, given the sensuality of Brown's paintings, that they are more similar to the timbre and poetics of the early architectural works of Charles Demuth.

Brown's factories, usually untitled, are distinctly marked by a sense of stillness—even more heightened than in most of his beach paintings. This quality—unlike the depicted or implied activity in his figurative paintings—is intensified and brought to the forefront. One of the most lucid examples is the serenely classical, primary forms of cylindrical, sun-bleached silos flanked on the left by an arrangement of rectangles and cubes. These sculptural shapes are redoubled, and the hull of a docked tug is mirrored in the waterway, but the boat's cabin casts no reflection, illustrating the freedom Brown takes with his subjects (p. 76). Considered as a group, the industrial views serve as marvelous reminders that "exactitude is not truth."

These images are consistently keyed to a palette of faded pinks, dusty greens, silvery tones, and umberish shadows. While devoid of airiness, all emphatically convey a sense of openness

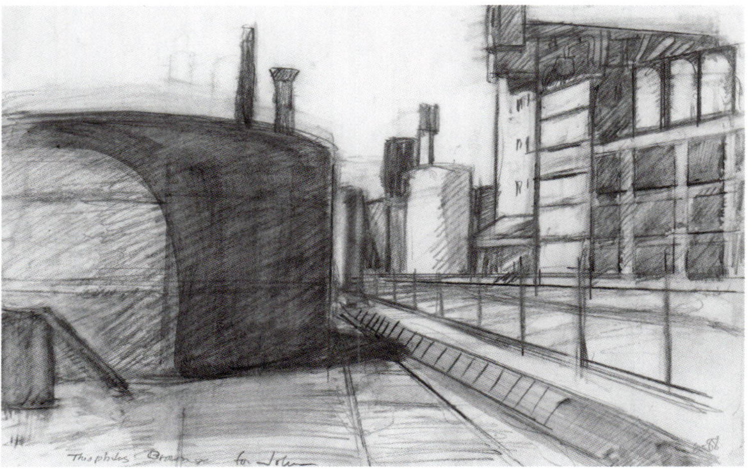

STUDIO ROOF, SANTA BARBARA 1971, oil on canvas, 40 x 60 inches
Collection of the University of California at Irvine

STUDY FOR AN INDUSTRIAL LANDSCAPE 1988
pencil and wash on paper, 51/2 x 81/2 inches (p. 74)

and spatiality. The forms of these silos, tanks, and industrial buildings as well as the spaces they occupy are defined almost entirely by the use of shadows and linear perspective. Roads and tracks lead from the foreground toward those stark, artless structures, and the fences, poles, and smokestacks rhythmically mark off these spatial recessions.

The hum and din of activity is tacit, but it is never shown. Occasionally Muybridge's mongrel, Dread, makes an appearance. He has strayed far from the beach, and here, with hot feet, tail down, and wary, Dread moves cautiously through the graceless and inhospitable environment.

In turn, the formal strategies acquired in painting these stark industrial views spill over and rejuvenate the urban scenes and figurative compositions that follow them—aspects that are quite clear in some of Brown's later small gouaches and acrylics on paper of cityscapes, parks, and village scenes. Like the wandering Dread, the figures in these works are delegated to peripheral roles.

Brown is incapable of obsequiousness and far too intelligent to deal in ironies, and these gritty industrial views—without doubt his least ingratiating subjects—are among his most noteworthy and inscrutable paintings.

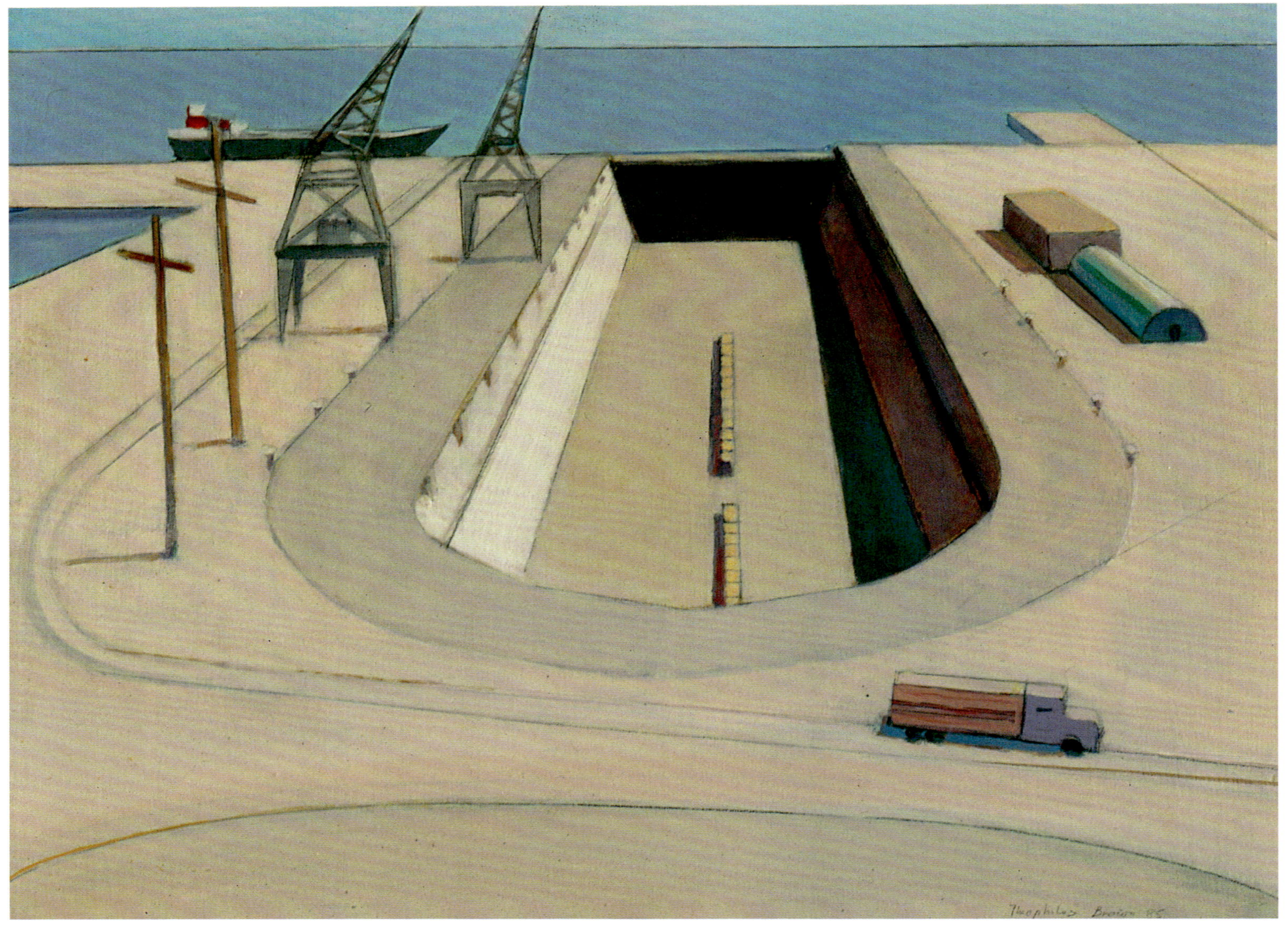

UNTITLED (DRY DOCK) 1985, acrylic on plywood, 9 x 12 inches. Collection of Mr. & Mrs. John Murray, Paris, France

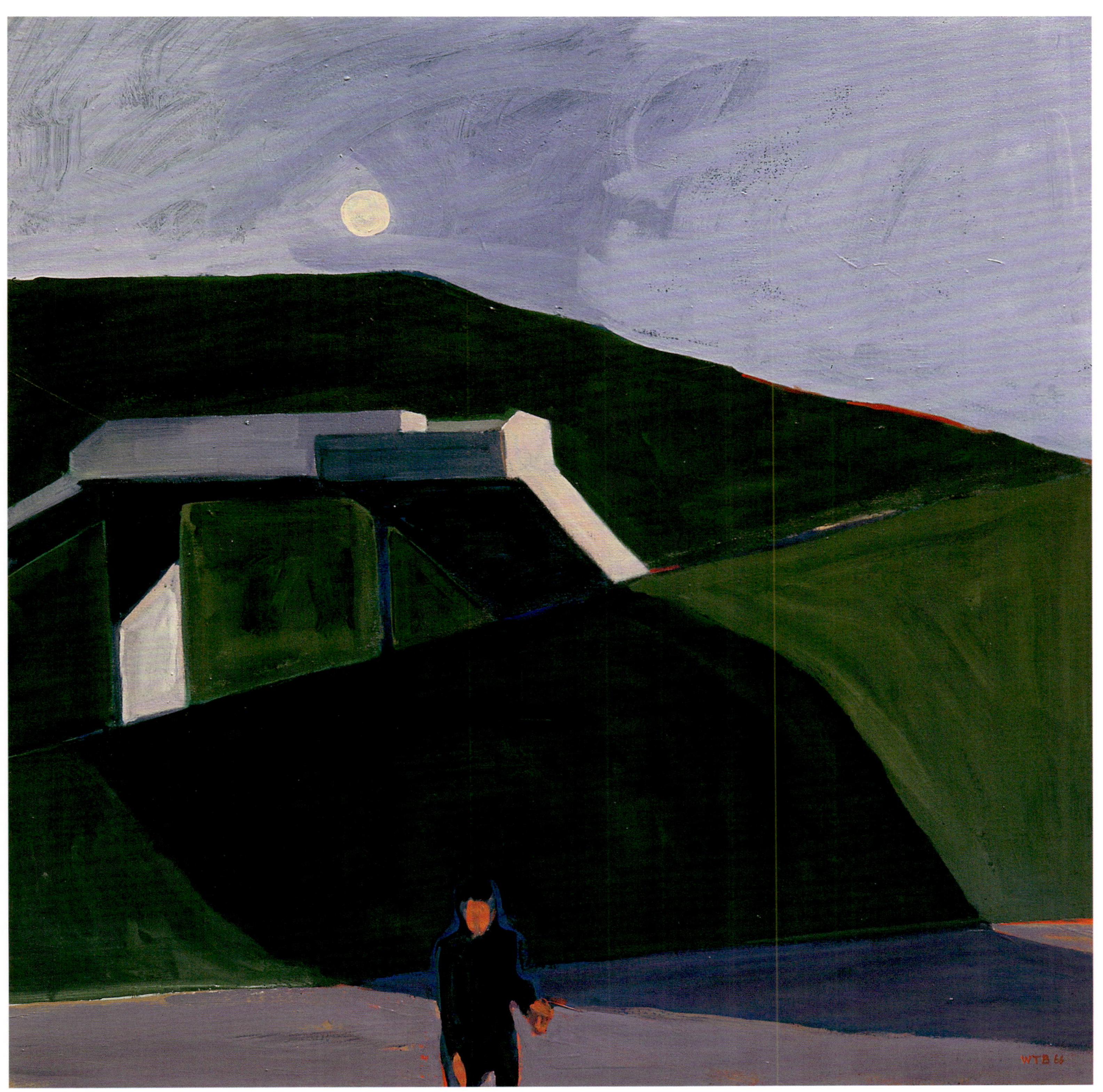

PEDESTRIAN CROSSING 1966, acrylic on canvas, 48 x 471/2 inches. Hirshhorn Museum and Sculpture Garden, Washington, D.C.

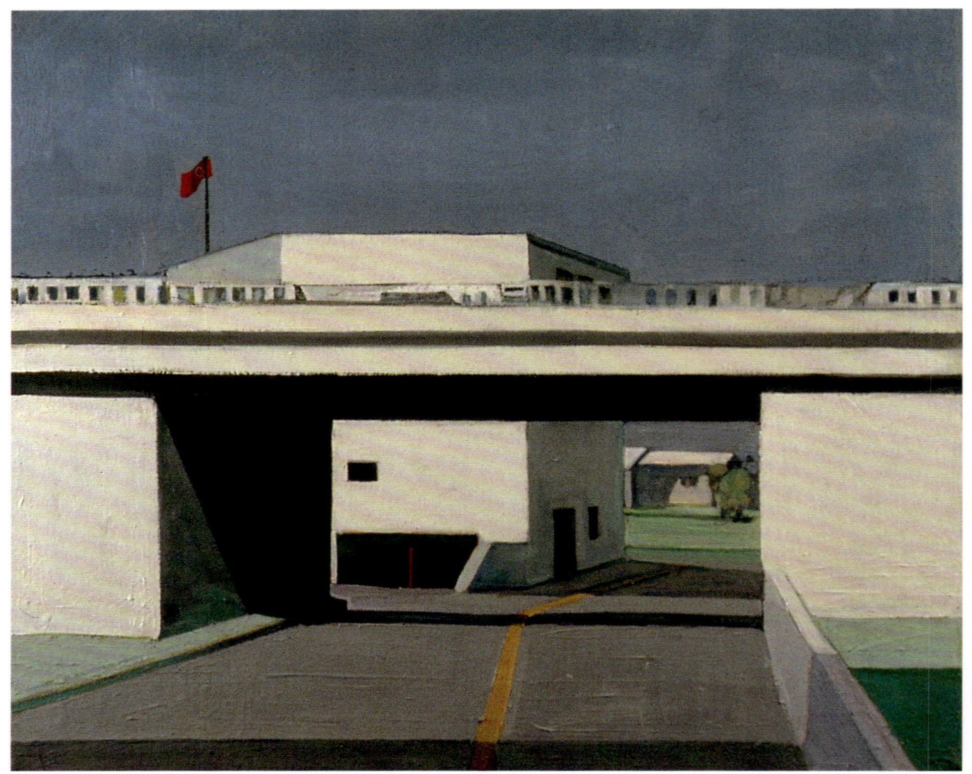

UNDERPASS, OAKLAND 1985, acrylic on canvas, 18 x 24 inches. Private Collection

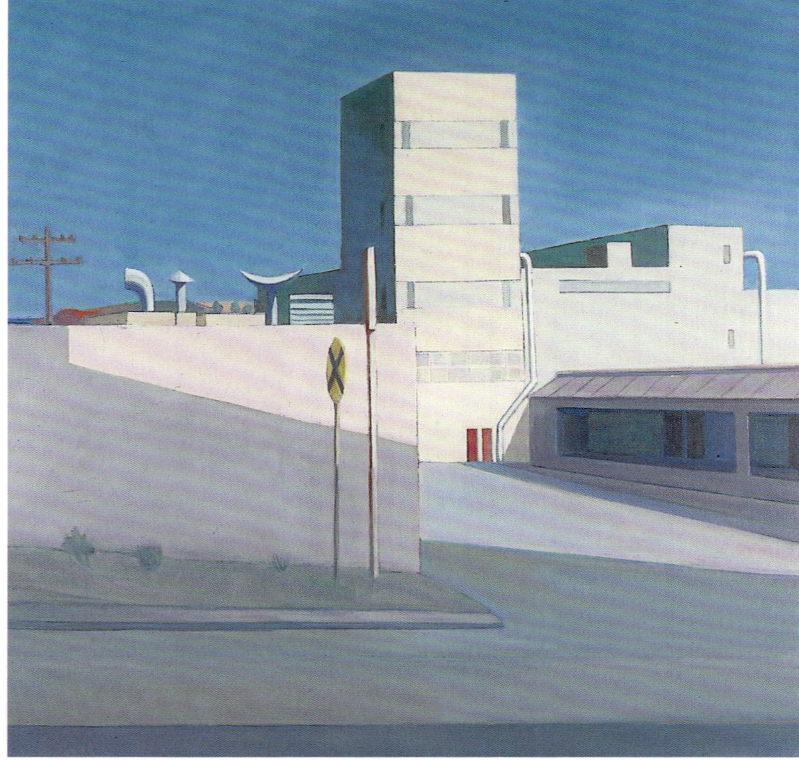

UNTITLED 1983, acrylic on canvas, 37 x 37 inches
Collection of Mr. & Mrs. John Berggruen, San Francisco

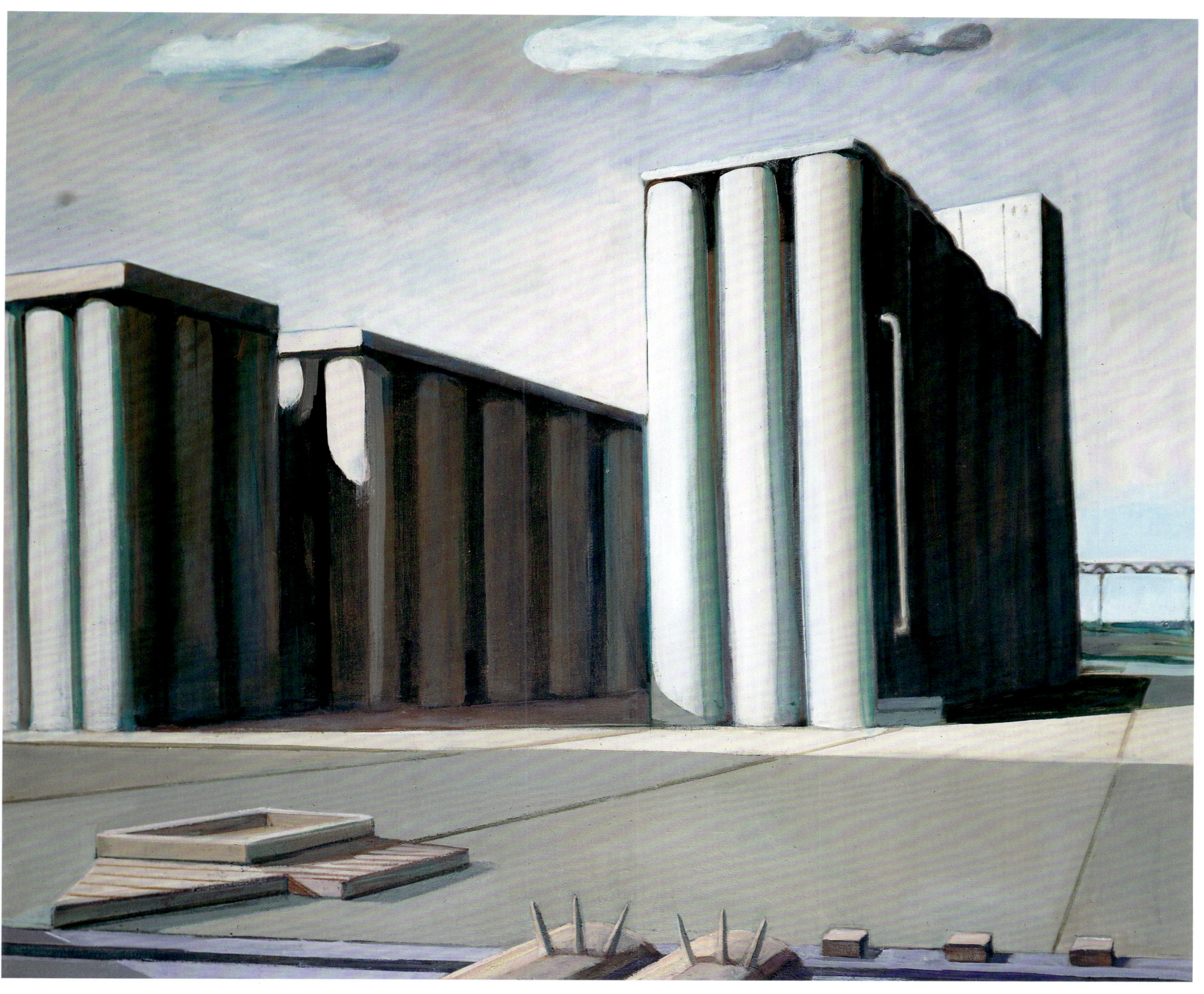

UNTITLED 1987–88, acrylic on canvas, 30 x 36 inches. Private Collection

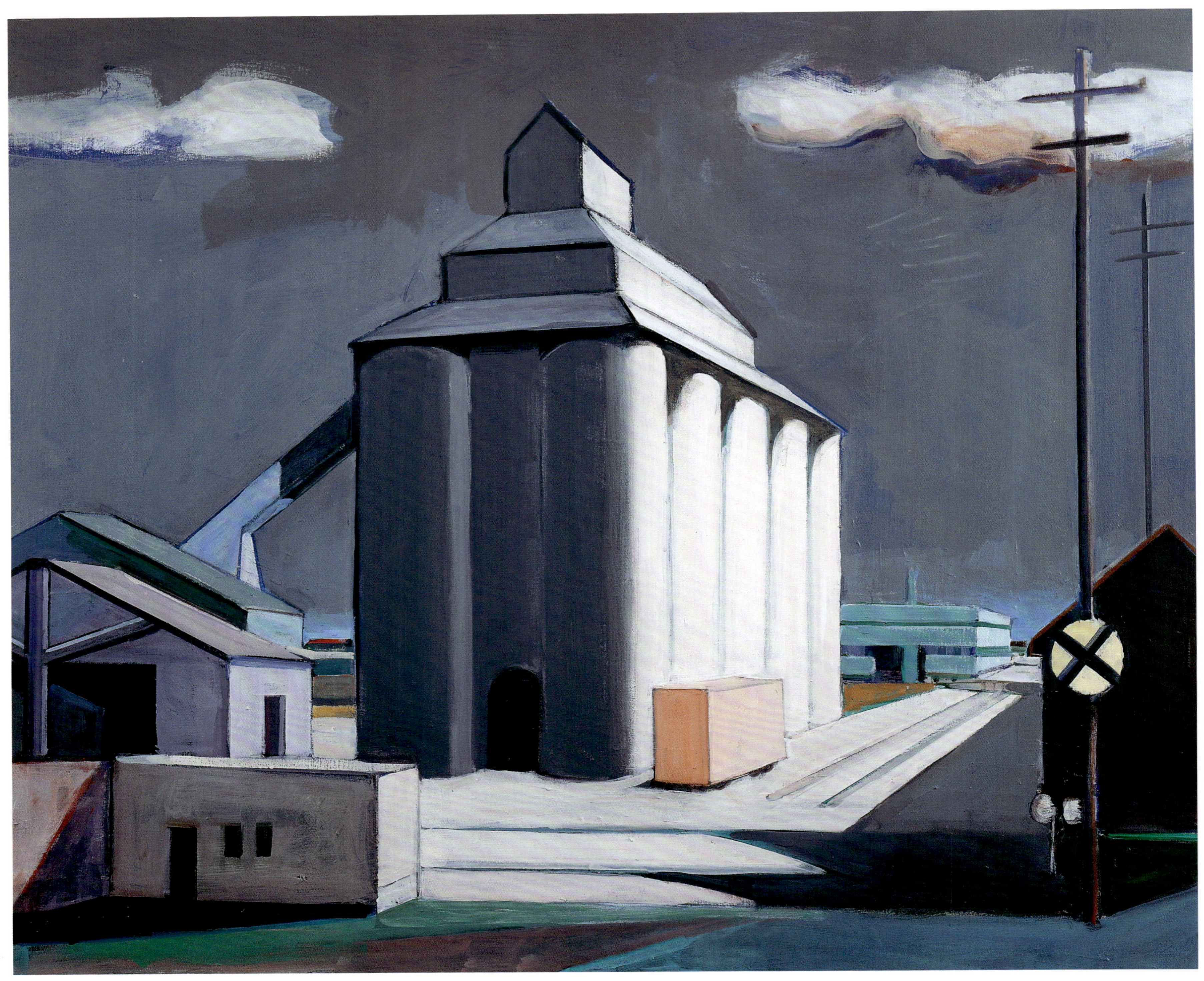

 UNTITLED 1989, acrylic on canvas, 30 x 36 inches. Collection of Robert Schneider & Jamie Summers, San Francisco

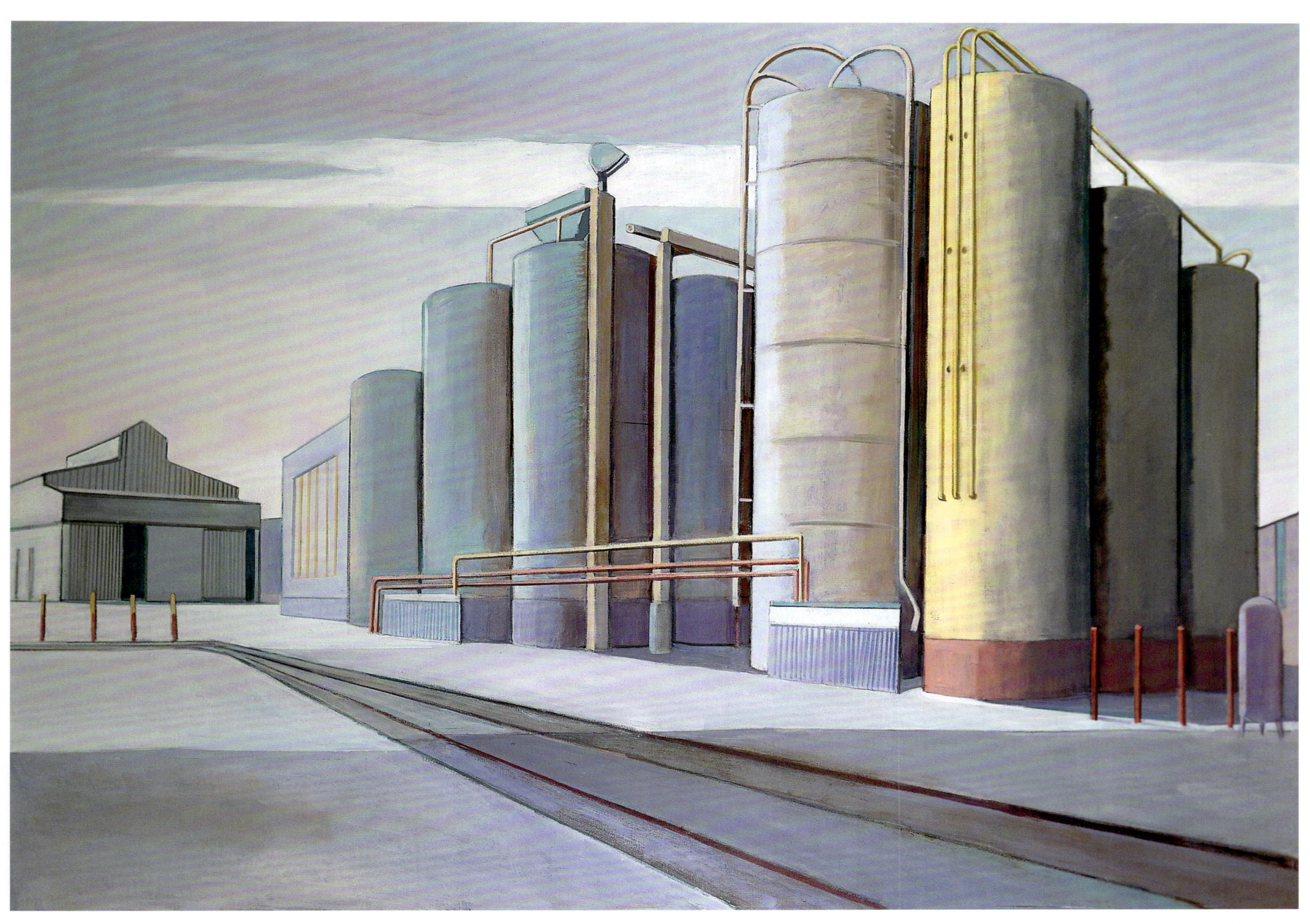

UNTITLED 1989, acrylic on canvas, 54 x 76 inches. Collection of the Artist

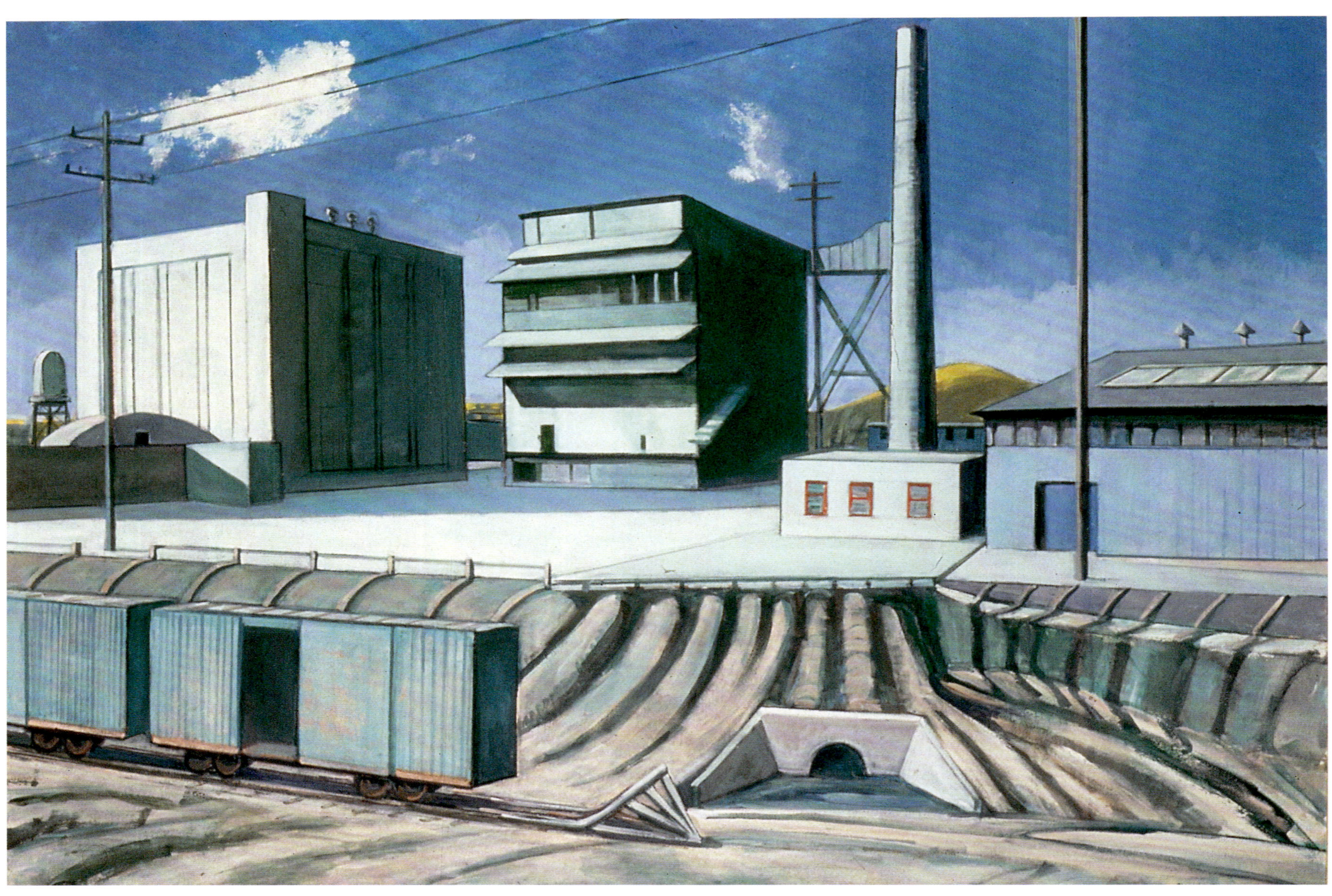

UNTITLED 1988, acrylic on canvas, 54 x 78 inches. Collection of Mr. & Mrs. Kevin Kearney, Sabastopol, California

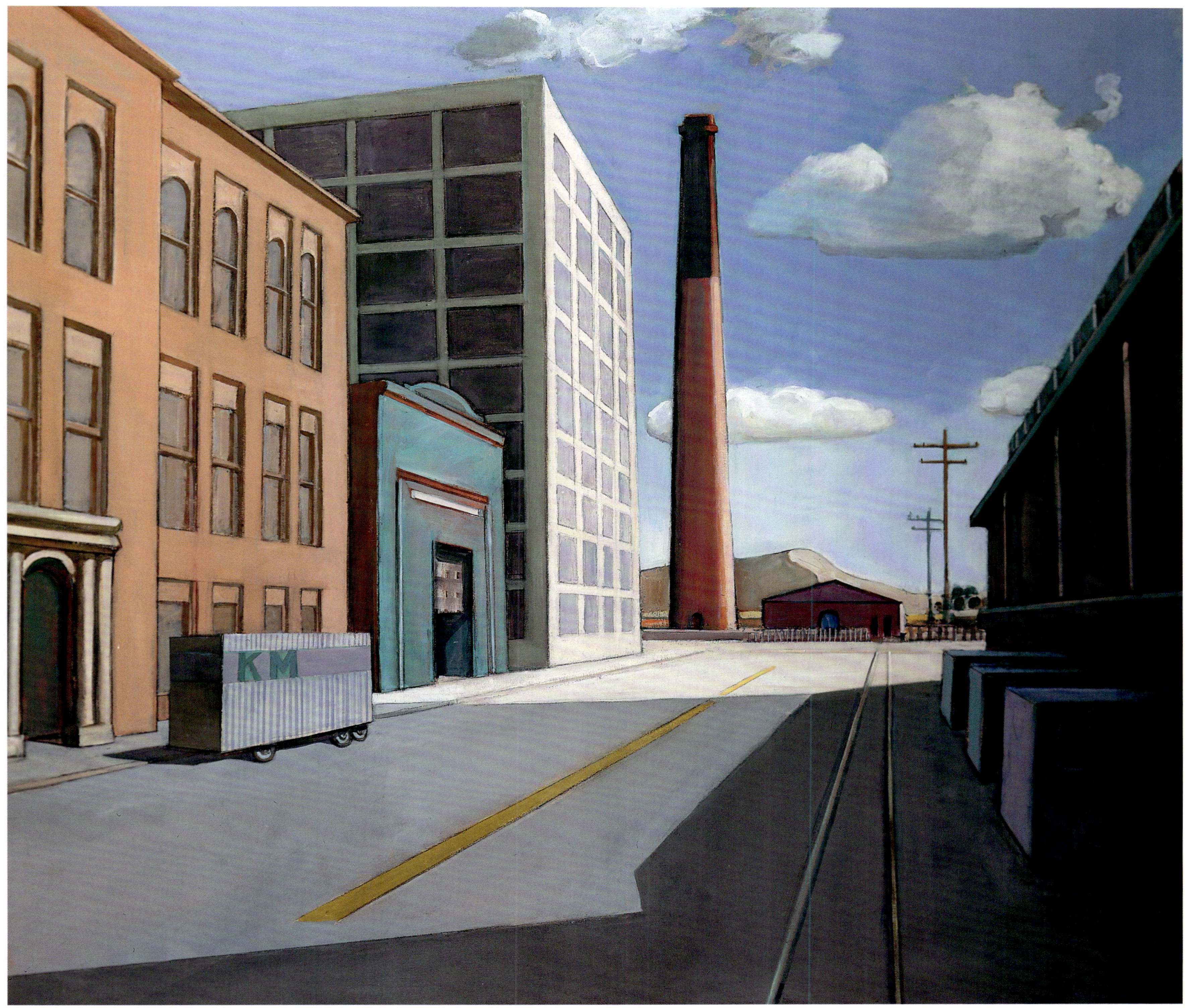

UNTITLED 1988, acrylic on canvas, 54 x 60 inches. Private Collection

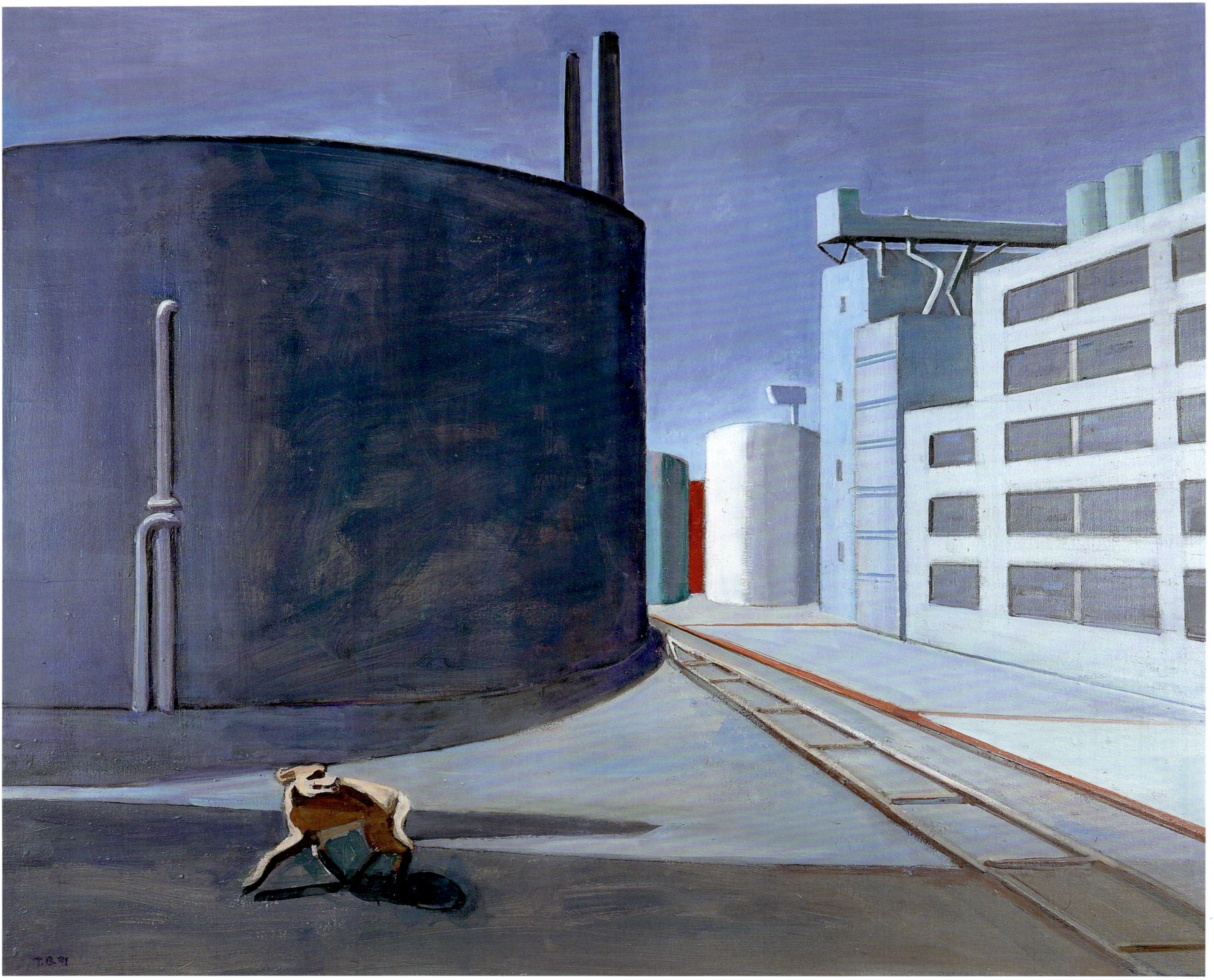

UNTITLED 1988, acrylic on canvas, 30 x 36 inches. Private Collection

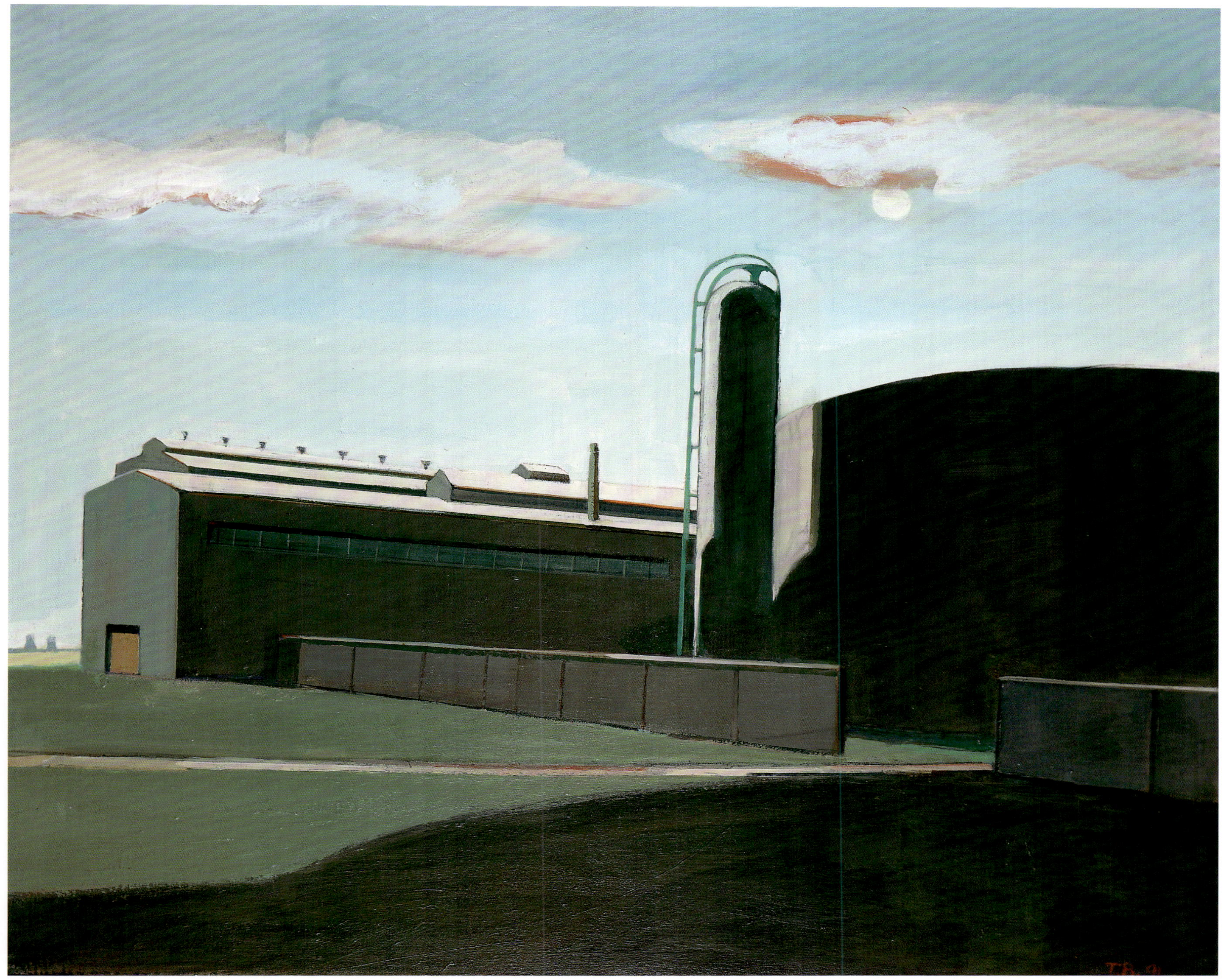

UNTITLED 1989–91, acrylic on canvas, 31 x 36 1/2 inches. Collection of the Artist

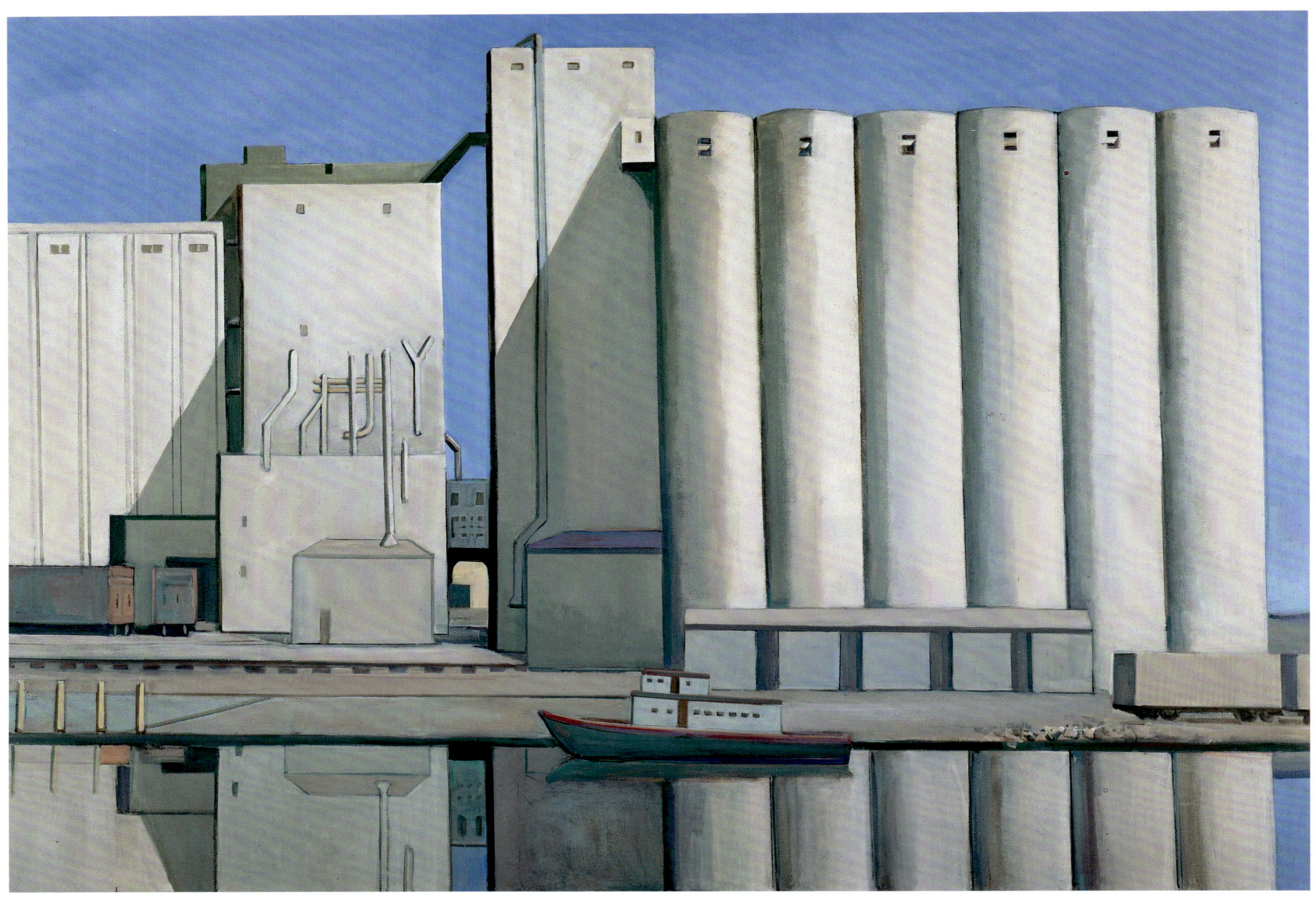

UNTITLED 1989, acrylic on canvas, 54 x 64 inches. Private Collection

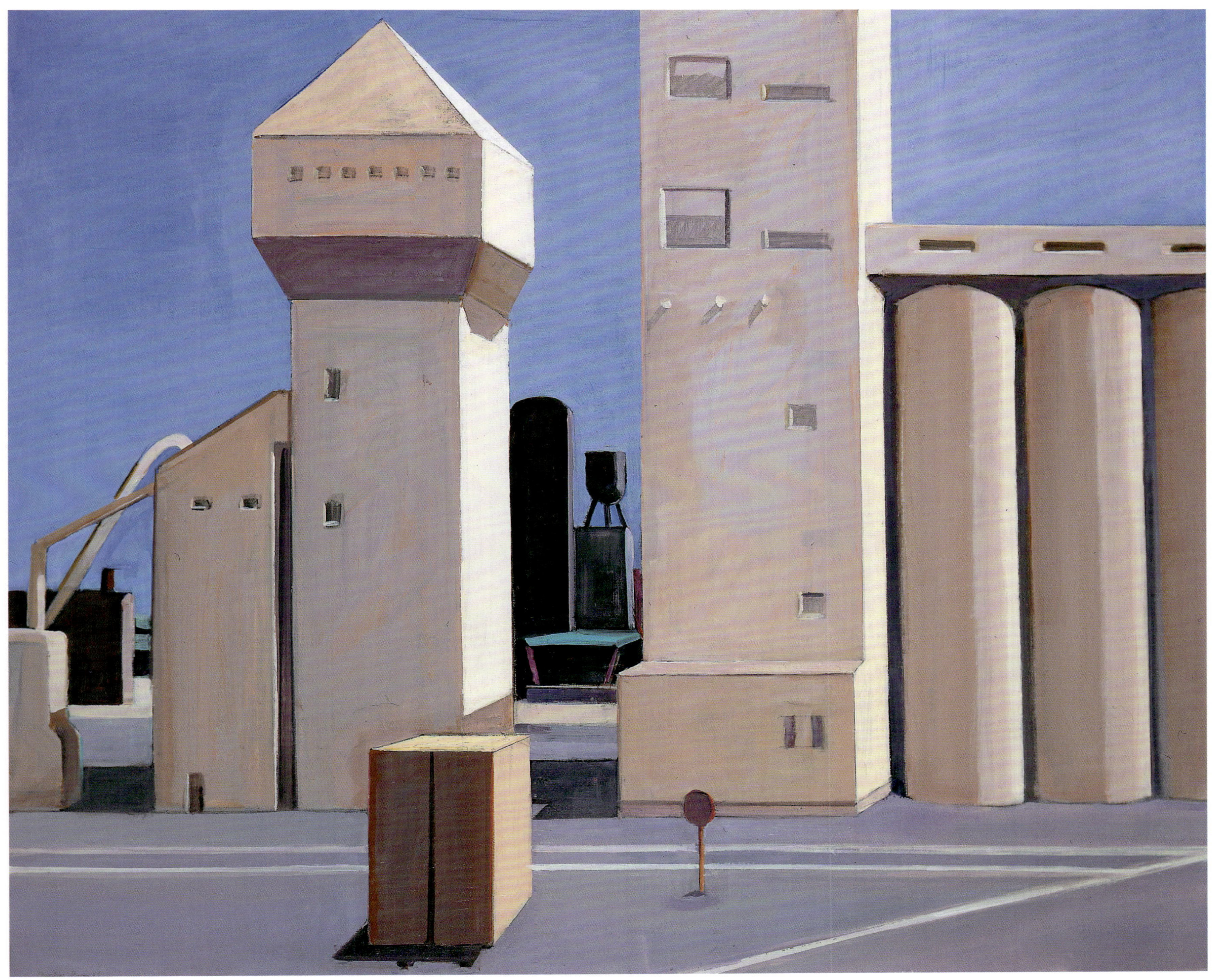

UNTITLED 1989, acrylic on canvas, 30 x 36 inches. Collection of the Artist

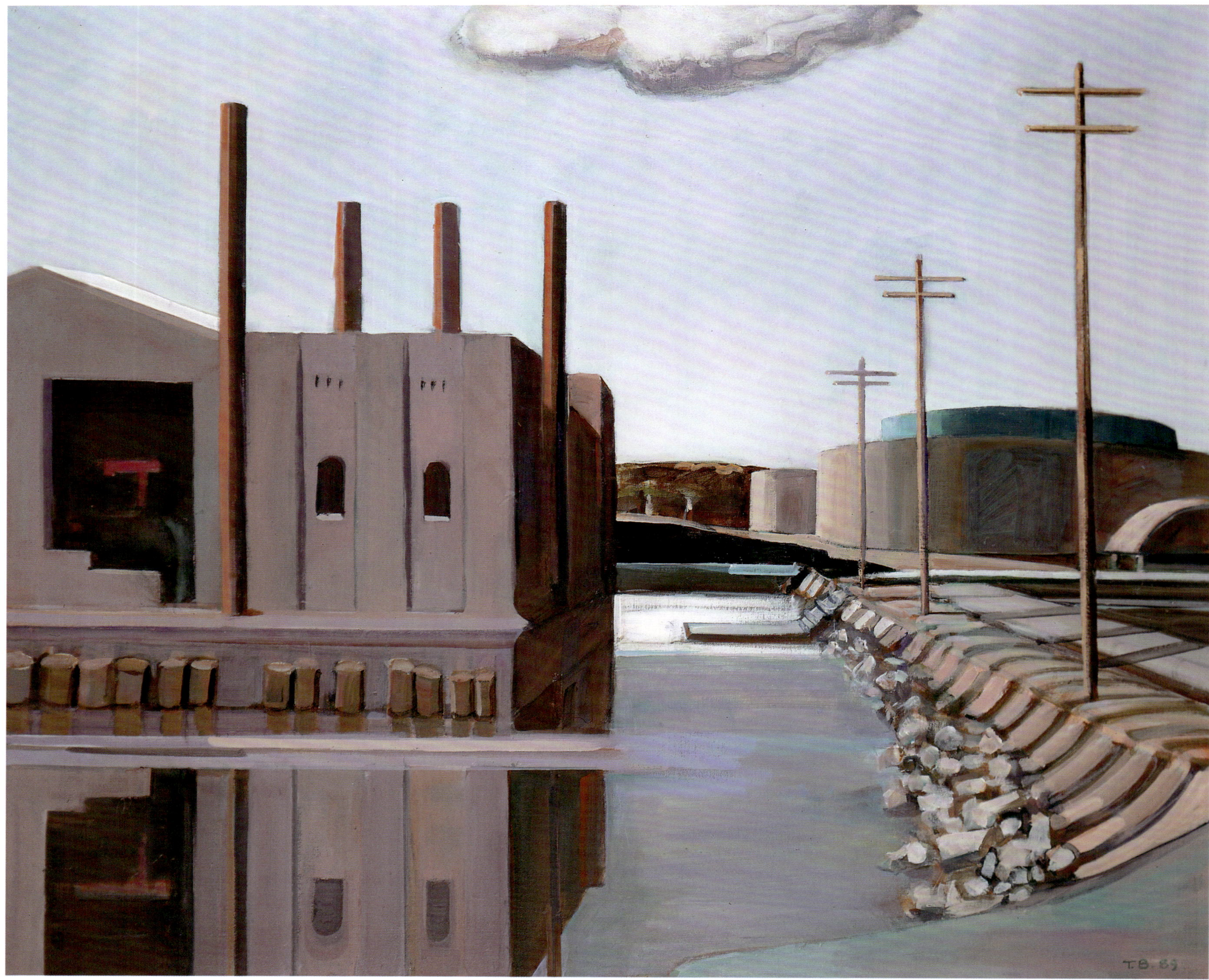

UNTITLED 1989, acrylic on canvas, 30 x 36 inches. Private Collection

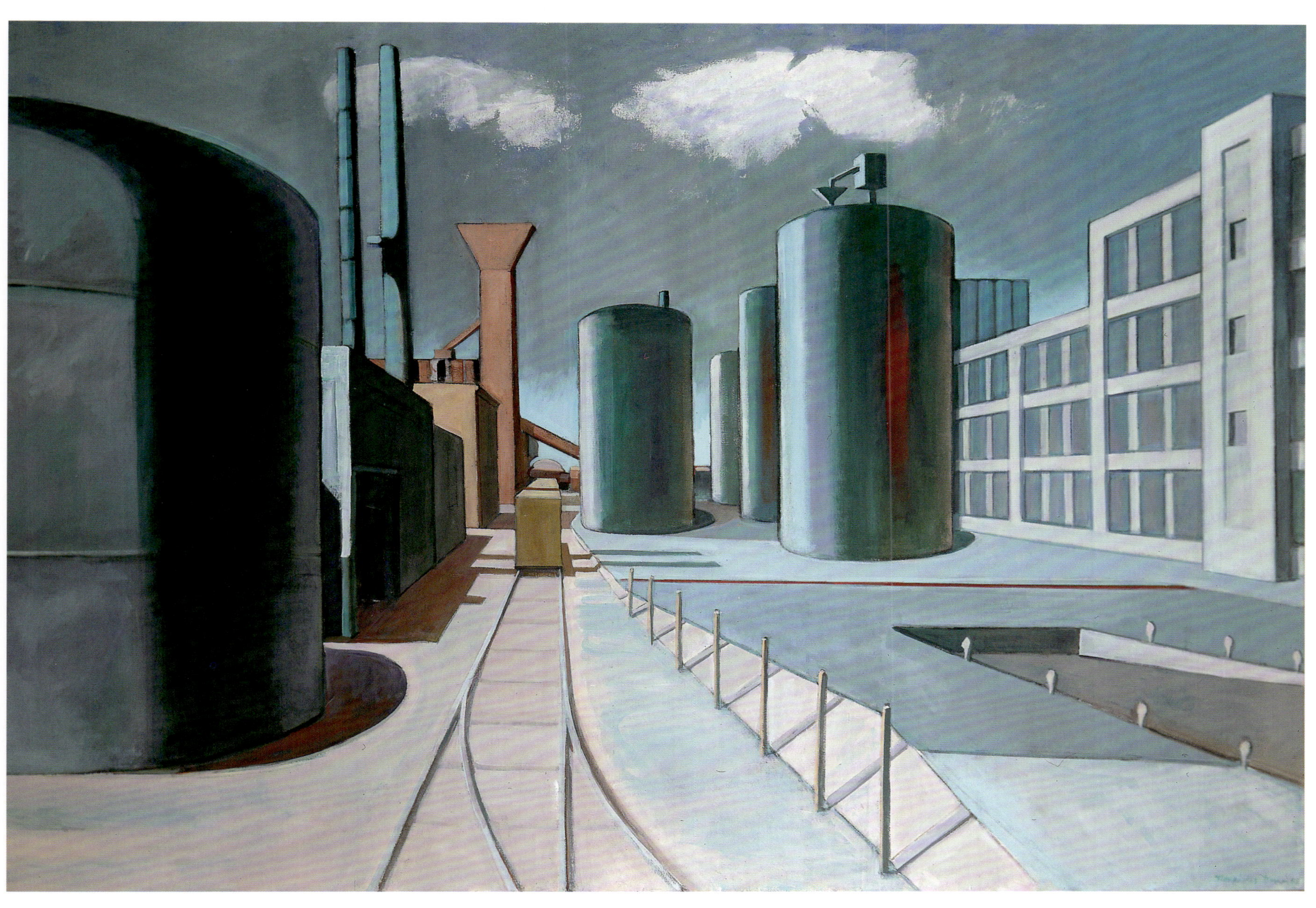

UNTITLED 1988, acrylic on canvas, 54 x 78 inches. Collection of Dr. & Mrs. John Murray, San Francisco

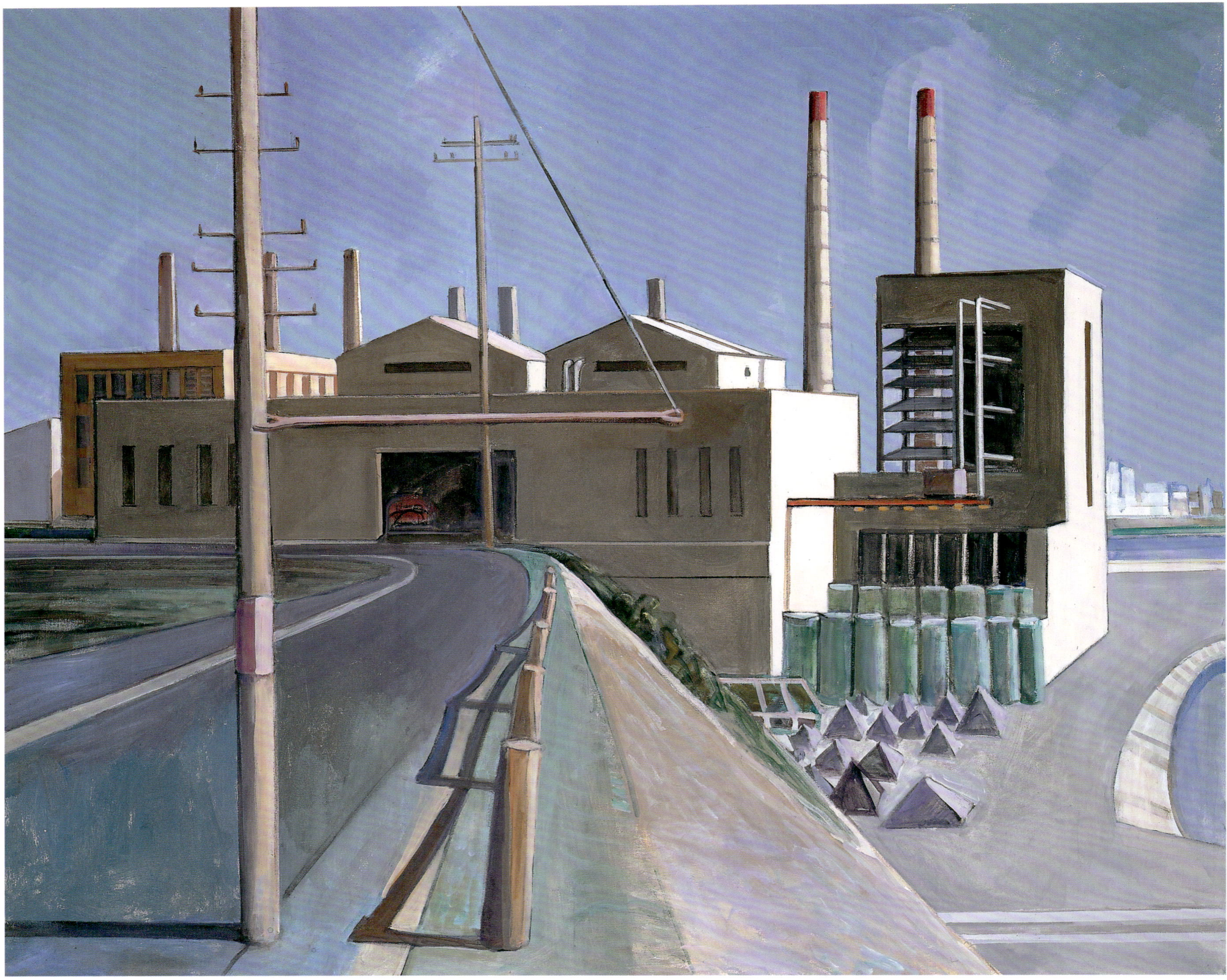

   UNTITLED 1988, acrylic on canvas, 56 1/2 x 68 inches. Collection of the Artist

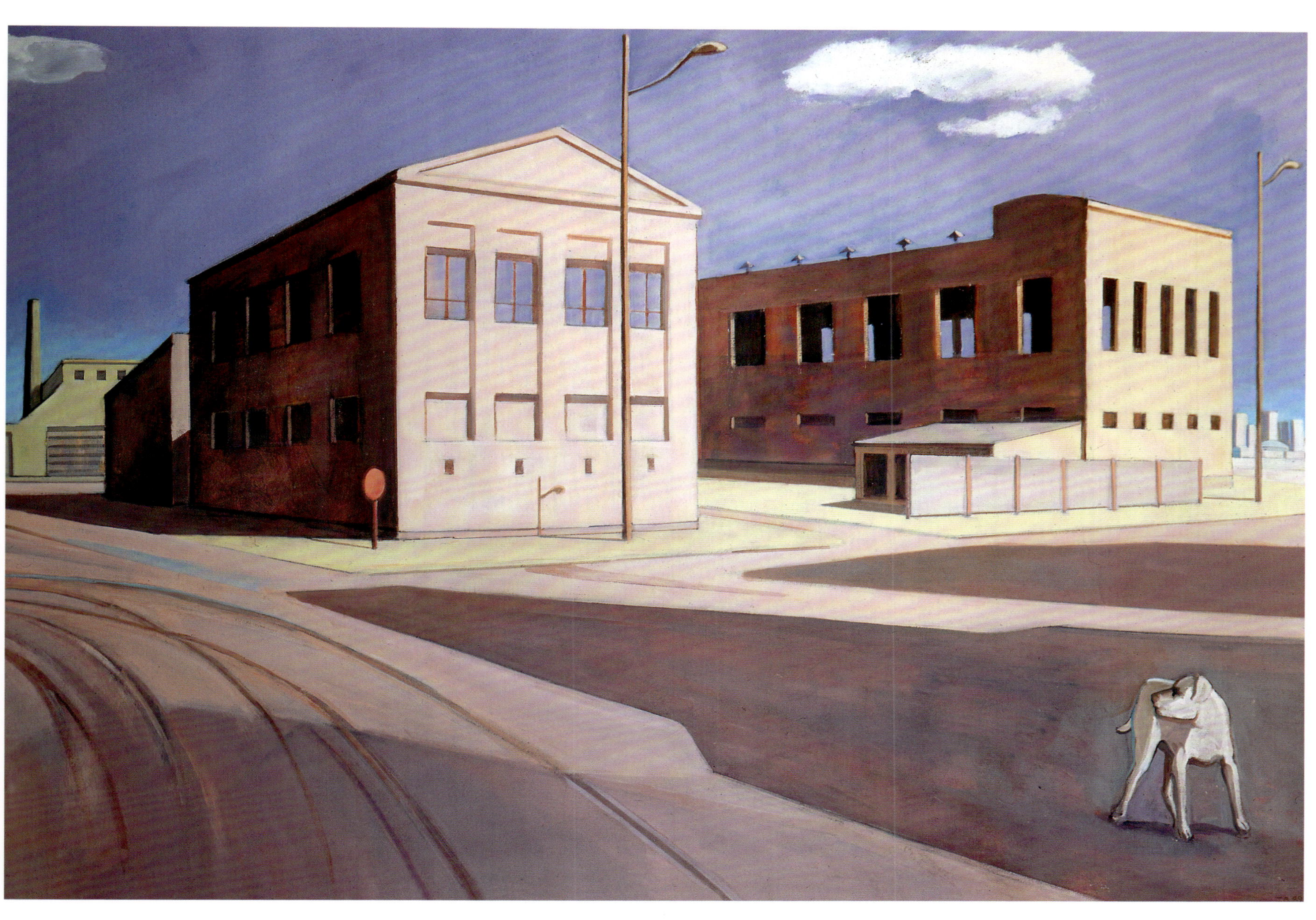

A BACKWARD GLANCE 1989, acrylic on canvas, 54 x 76½ inches. Collection of Mr. & Mrs. Kevin Kearney, Sebastopol, California   81

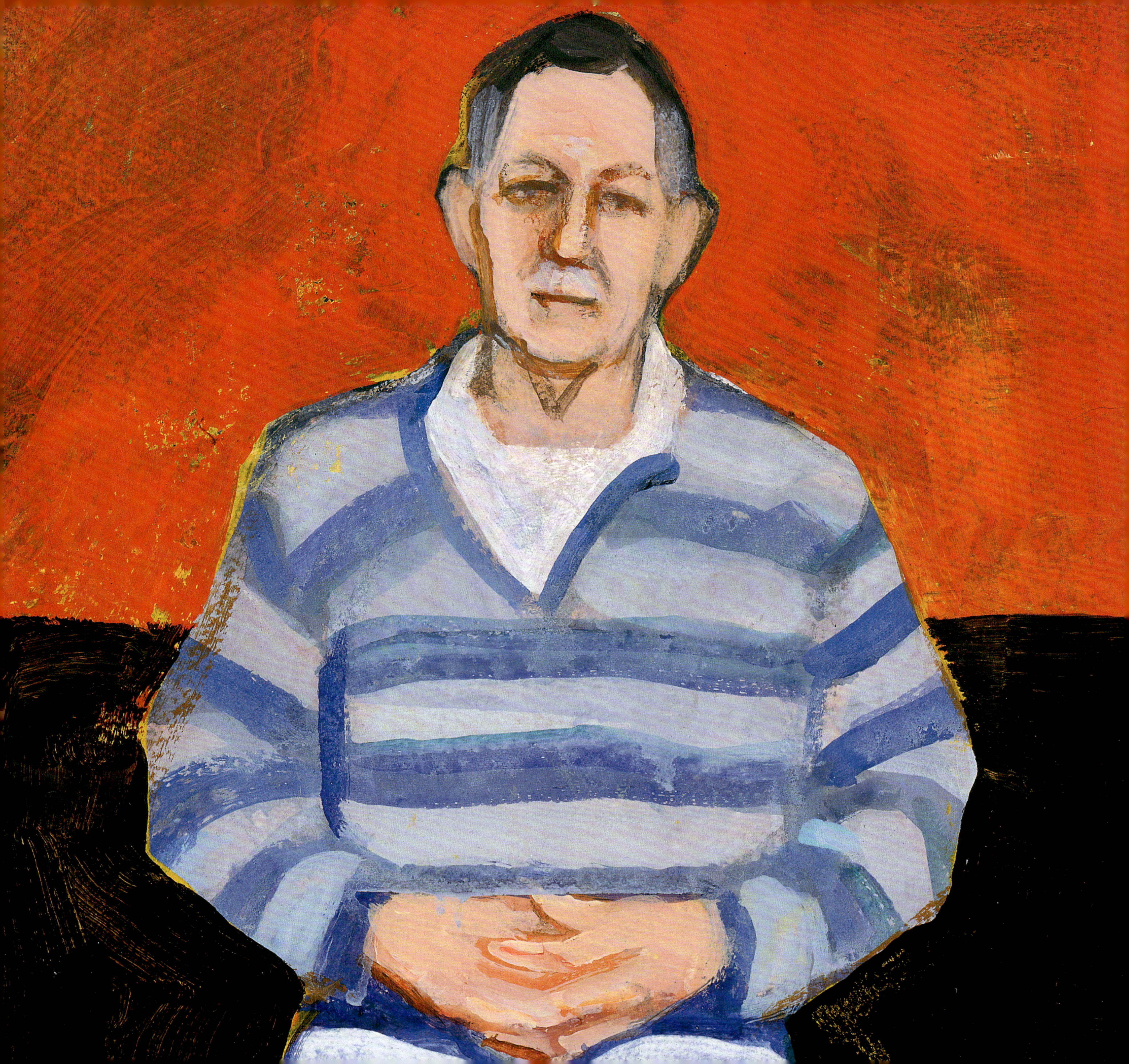

Portraits and Self-Portraits

*What is a face, really? Its own photo? Its make-up?
Or is it a face as painted by such and such a painter?
That which is in front? Inside? Behind?*

   —PICASSO

*I believe, however, that the essential expression of a
work depends almost entirely on the projection of
the feeling of the artist in relation to his model
rather than the organic accuracy of the model.*

*The art of portraiture is one of the most remarkable.
It demands special gifts of the artist, and the possibility
of an almost total identification of the painter with
his model. The painter should come to his model with
no preconceived ideas.*

   —HENRI MATISSE

THE PORTRAIT has long played a major role in Theophilus Brown's oeuvre. With regard to the large number of paintings, drawings, and acrylics on paper depicting sitters in his studio, it is second only to his numerous explorations of the theme of the bathers.

While some of the subjects are not named, such as *Man in a Red Chair* (p. 89), or are drastically simplified, like *Portrait of D.K.* (Don Knudson) (p. 88), they clearly depict individuals. As mentioned earlier, Brown is an accomplished draftsman and has always drawn from the figure. Over the decades he has participated regularly in drawing sessions with Wonner, David Park, Richard Diebenkorn, Elmer Bischoff, James Weeks, Nathan Oliveira, and other illustrious Bay Area painters. During the years Brown and Wonner lived in Los Angeles, he and Don Bachardy drew together. When they moved back to San Francisco in

1976, Brown worked from a model weekly with Gordon Cook, Mark Adams, Beth Van Hoesen, and Wayne Thiebaud.

This experience is abundantly clear in the concisely rendered portraits *Kevin Kearney* (p. 97), *Buck McCreary* (p. 92), and *Michael MacDowell* (p. 93). In the first, a young man is seated in the studio, which is filled with various accoutrements of the painter's trade—a saw, an unfinished study on the drafting table, drawings pinned to the wall, a pencil sharpener—all described with a studied reductivism. Most of the colors are applied flat, with the various planes and recessions defined by the course of the shadows of the figure and chair and through linear perspective. A smaller canvas depicts Buck McCreary sitting with his legs crossed and a hand to his face. He appears to be lost in contemplation. All three portraits are rendered in volumetric slabs of tone and color, and in each the interior is parallel to the picture plane. As in the *Kevin Kearney* painting, each of the interior spaces is articulated by overlapping forms and the course of the shadows.

The marvelous totemic figure of *Hilde Heidt* (p. 91)—her physical attractiveness and sensuality in sharp contrast with the geometrical patterns of her dress—is set against the hard-edged, minimal rigidity of the diamond ornamentation of the background. The entire figure is executed in a palette of pinks, sepias, and worn grays, like the tones in a fading photograph, except for the two small accent points of color provided by Hilde's blue beads and an emerald ring. As the invented background indicates, Brown seldom adheres to the constraints of empirical representation in his paintings and drawings.

Another full-length figure, *Peter Liashkov* (p. 90), is emotionally and formally the polar opposite of *Hilde Heidt*. First, it is less frontal and totemic due to Liashkov's Praxitelean stance. The handsome youth stands with one hand hooked in his belt and the other on his chest. He glances to the side with a troubled

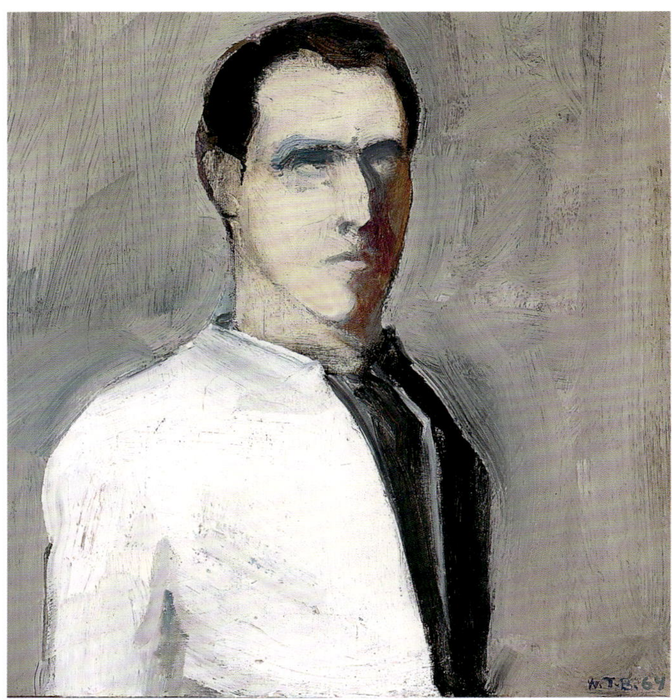

SELF-PORTRAIT 1964, oil on canvas, 14 x 13 inches
Collection of John Modell, San Francisco

expression, like a young Hamlet. Liashkov appears to be a narcissistic poseur in a practiced attitude and gesture. Adding to his theatrical mannerism, the exaggerated perspective of the plank-like background conveys the artifice of a stage set.

Over the decades, Brown's numerous portraits and self-portraits have consistently followed an expressive vein. Of the contemporary artists, his painterly accounts are closest to those of Alice Neel, but Brown has never indulged in Neel's emphatic focus on the sitter's physical and emotional frailties and her frequent use of flaying wit. Conversely, he instills his subjects with dignity and focuses on their sensuality. Brown's way of rendering with paint—green daubs for eyes and brows, for example—and his incisive distillation of each subject to his or her most pertinent and revealing essentials recall the late figurative works of Edvard Munch.

Many of the figure studies, portraits, and self-portraits are on paper. Often they are sketches of various sitters from the drawing sessions that Brown paints over later in his studio. While some of the small acrylics, such as *Woman in Red and Blue* (p. 101) and *Woman in a Red Chair* (p. 102), are not as sharply delineated, all maintain distinct traces of the individual. The palimpsest of overpainted shapes indicates that even in these small works, Brown's open-ended procedure is similar to that of Matisse; it is one of continual modification and condensation. Like the minute and elusively eerie expressive shifts of a Noh mask infused by the slight tilt or turn of an actor's head in the flickering light of a torch, Brown places the weight

on an emphatic pose or characteristic gesture rather than relying on a glut of physiognomic details.

The small monochromatic heads of Allen Ginsberg and Jack Kerouac were painted in oil and casein from magazine photographs in 1961. They crowd their perimeters like old film noir close-ups, and their reductive likenesses are vigorously rendered in sharply contrasting patterns of chiaroscuro. *On the Road,* Kerouac's semi-autobiographical chronicle of sex, drugs, and jazz, had been published four years earlier and *Howl*, Ginsberg's epic poem, was first printed in 1956. Kerouac and Ginsberg were vivid icons of the counterculture at the time Brown painted the portraits, and the two literary works have served as leitmotifs of the Beat Generation from that time on. In Brown's small paintings, an attentive Kerouac presses his forefinger to his chin. A contemplative Ginsberg, spectacled, already balding, and with short hair, covers his mouth, perhaps to stifle a yawn. These and other portraits illuminate Brown's literate, discerning, and unending inquisitiveness. Formally, they illustrate that for the past half century, he has had the self-assurance to frequently leave awkward passages alone.

None of Brown's portraits are commissioned, which explains why they bear no evidence of catering or appeasement. Instead, the paintings carry innuendos of closeness and at times possess insinuations of intimacy. In the art of portraiture, there is always a tacit understanding between the sitter and the painter. It is a consensual, participatory act on both sides of the easel, and at least two egos are involved. The subject is cast in the role of his own persona, and, in the most revealing portraits, is coaxed into divulging a private and carefully hidden facet of his interior life. For example, we best know the stout, mannish Gertrude Stein through Picasso's portrait, just as he predicted we would. And portraiture can take a fictive turn. Whether the implications are psychologically misleading or not, our perception of André Derain is through the Balthus depiction of him, clad in pajamas and bathrobe with his alluring nubile niece.

The portrait is a pact entered into with a certain amount of vanity and good hope, and apparently, without dwelling too long on Goethe's augury, "One is never satisfied with a portrait of a person that one knows." But it is important to bear in mind that in Brown's paintings physical exactitude is rarely the goal. While he does not indulge in flattery, his intimate, diminutive portraits are never cruel, nor are they indifferent. It

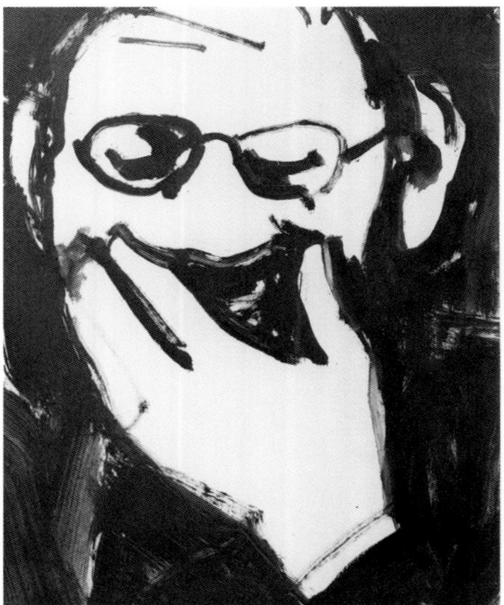

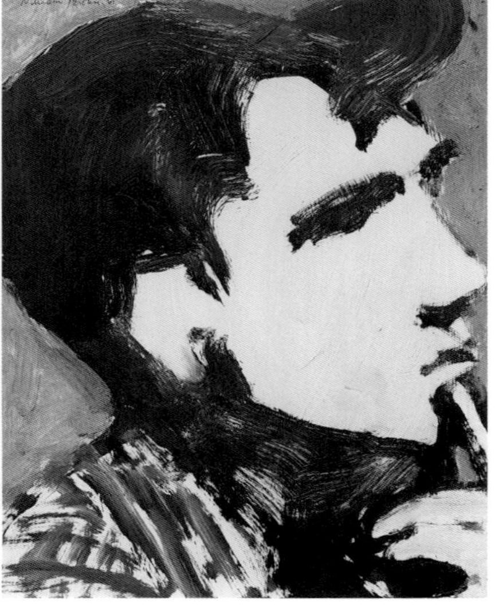

ALLAN GINSBERG 1961, oil and casein on paper, 107/8 x 81/2 inches
Hirshhorn Museum and Sculpture Garden, Washington, D.C.

JACK KEROUAC 1961, oil and casein on paper, 107/8 x 81/2 inches
Hirshhorn Museum and Sculpture Garden, Washington, D.C.

is readily apparent that he is attracted to his sitters and feels a great deal of affection for them—and, it bears repeating, most are among his close circle of friends.

Many of the portraits are small drawings or acrylics on paper. But large or small, all are rendered with verve and wit. The painterly vigor of the works on paper recalls his canvases of the late fifties and sixties. Some of his subjects, including his self-portraits, appear clothed and nude, and there is never a hint of self-consciousness or awkwardness in Brown's voyeurism.

Seth and Jamie are depicted both individually and together. Jamie variously appears with a goatee, with a beard, and beardless, clearly indicating that he, Seth, David, and others are frequent visitors to the painter's studio. The painting *David and Jamie* (p. 86) is one of Brown's finest double portraits. Like salt and pepper shakers, they sit on identical stools and in similar poses, with the exception of David's arm around Jamie's shoulder. The rich handling of their clothing and the viscous swash of gray-blue outlining their feet recall the early days of Bay Area figuration.

There are various portraits of Evie Lincoln, an art historian. In Brown's study, *Evie with Cat* (p. 98), the painter indicates both his warmth for her and his fondness for cats. Her face is rendered with economy and subtle opposing colors, like those incorporated in Munch's Fauve-like *Self-Portrait in Front of the House Wall* (1926) and in his later canvases, such as *Self-Portrait with Bottles* (1940–44). One portrait (p. 101)—reminiscent of a Mughal miniature—shows a woman in a green chair outlined against a bright red background. The rendering of her breasts and the charged brushwork refer de Kooning's *Women,* but without their implications of misogyny.

Over the years, Paul Wonner has also made repeated appearances in Brown's paintings. He is depicted several times in a familiar blue-striped shirt and faded jeans in small acrylics on paper. In the first (p. 94) he sits patiently and pensively, hands clasped in his lap, and framed against a rich red background. More than half a century of Brown and Wonner's shared experiences seems to float to the surface. In another painting, the shirt's stripes are blue-green. Wonner sits in an old office chair, its back melding into an abstract shadow that follows around the sitter's shoulder and head (p. 95). With only the most diminutive variations—the tilt of his head and an almost imperceptible downturn of the mouth—Wonner's emo-

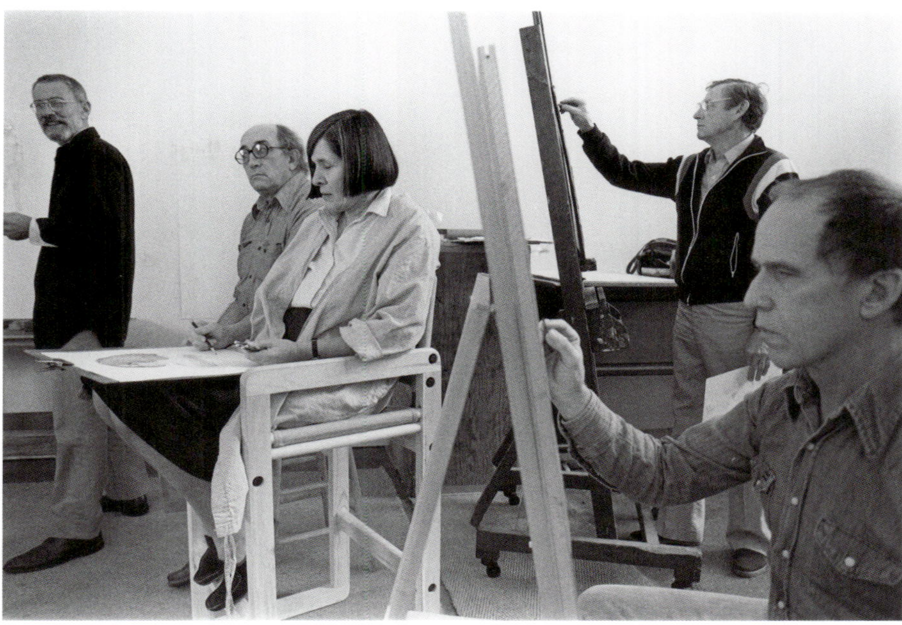

Mark Adams, Gordon Cook, Beth Van Hoesen, Wayne Thiebaud, and Theophilus Brown. Photograph by Diana Crane Citret

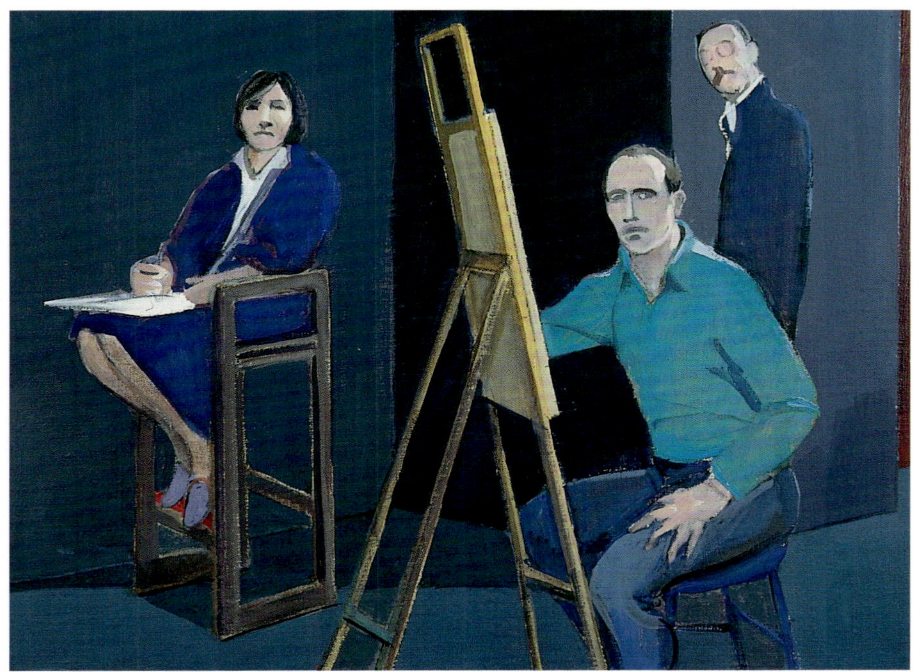

BETH VAN HOESEN, THEOPHILUS BROWN, AND MARK ADAMS 1982
acrylic on board, 20 x 24 inches. Beth Van Hoesen and Estate of Mark Adams

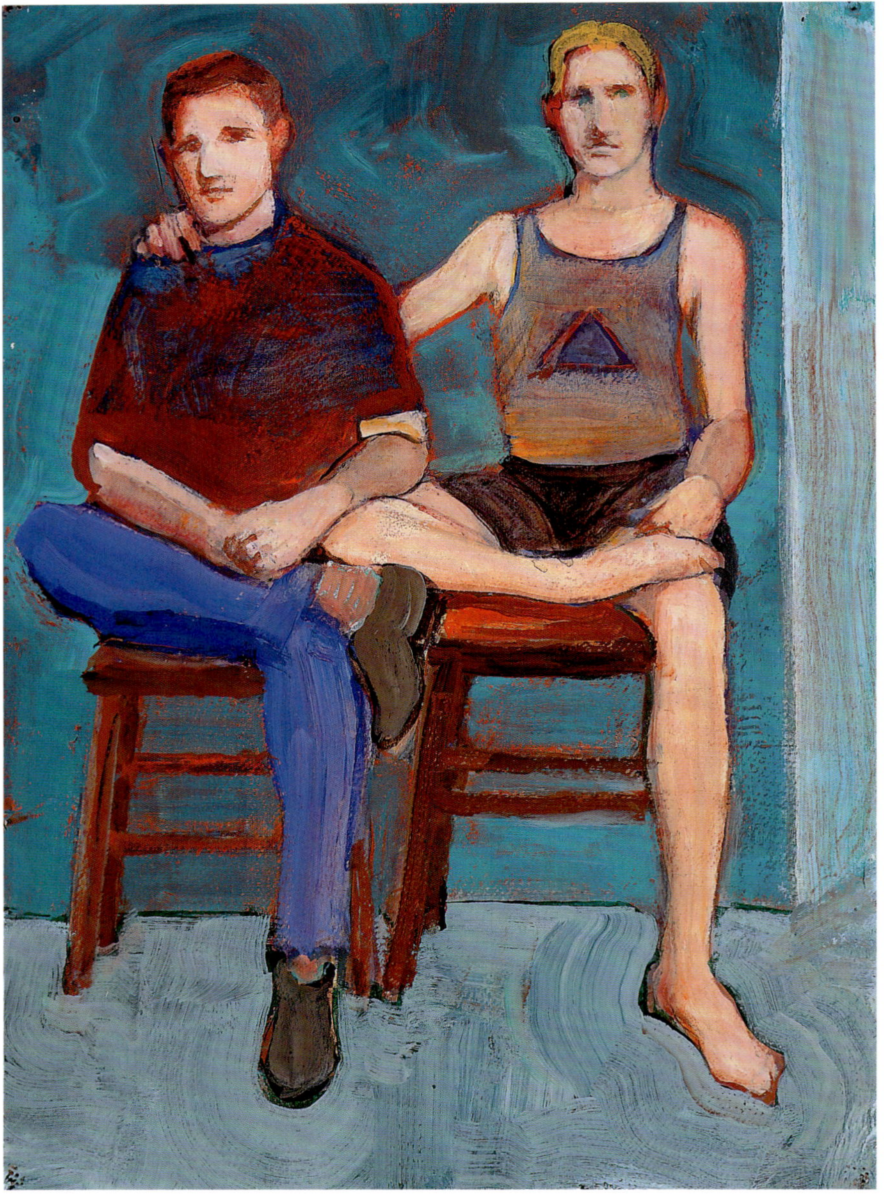

JAMIE AND DAVID 1999, acrylic on paper, 14 x 10 inches. Private collection

tional state is completely altered.

Within the probity of Brown's unvarnished self-observations there is a kaleidoscopic range of physical, formal, and expressive facets. More than in the various portrait and figure studies, Brown's self-portraits reveal the fluent coupling of his skills of observation and carefully honed formal instincts with his seasoned facility for distilling his image to the most relevant details. Perhaps nowhere in his oeuvre is the evidence of his deftness as a draftsman and the mark of his brush more succinct.

For example, the icon-like symmetry of a very frontal composition of the painter (p. 105) is broken by his crossed leg, the thin legs of his folding chair turned very slightly off center, and the addition of another chair jutting in from the right. Much of the drawing remains visible, as does the evolutionary path from the near blacks of the more specifically rendered interior to the painterly background of rose, pink, and pale lavender. There is a similar painting—the least flattering of all the self-portraits—of Brown in a dark T-shirt, arms folded and legs crossed (p. 109). Again, the folding chair floats in a pale palimpsest sea of paint.

In another, Brown sits on a red stool, knees spread and hands together (p. 104). It is a severely symmetrical arrangement with the exception of the profile view of the head, which has signs of being repositioned from an earlier rendering. A blue stroke covers the drawing of his neck. The rendering of his jumpsuit has been washed with a thin brown stain. A dark ovoid shape defines the back of the head and frames the painter's profile like an old cameo. Silhouetted against a pale green background, the round head, spread legs, and emphatically pointed ends of Brown's sleeves, knees, and cuffs are reminiscent of an insect pinned to a specimen board.

Frontal, legs crossed, mouth open, and clad in white (p. 106), the painter stares at his reflection. Behind him is the familiar worktable and a scattered assortment of objects. Sheets of paper on the wall have been altered, others on the floor have been painted over, but they have not been completely obliterated. The geometry of the various gridded shapes recalls the more elaborate compositions of Piet Mondrian, but without his severity, or, perhaps, Mondrian as recalled through the gestural brush of an Abstract Expressionist.

There are also a few small works of the artist nude. In one he is seated on the floor with an abstract drawing to his right (p. 107). Following the Flemish practice, the figure has been underpainted with green. Parts of the drawing have been rein-

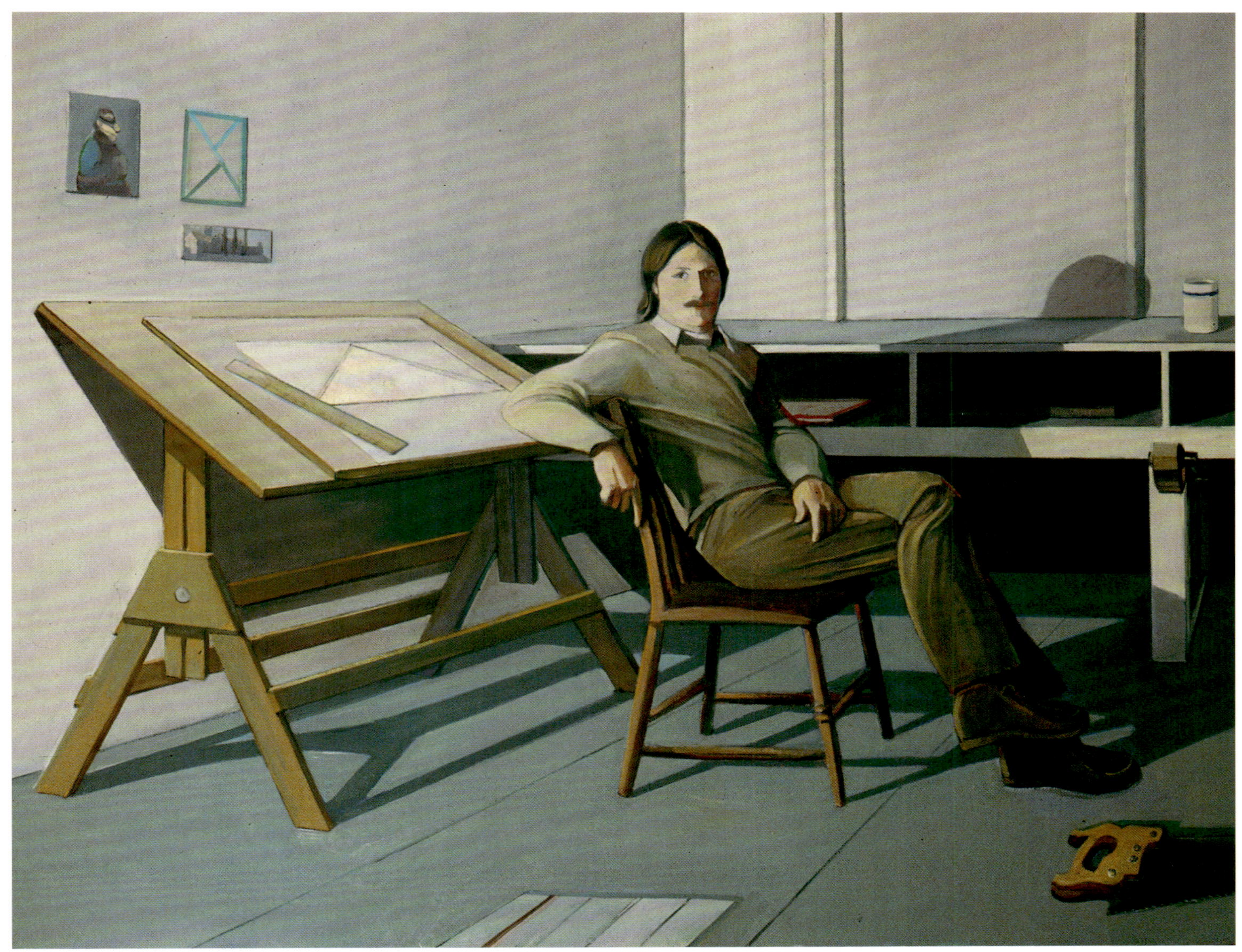

KEVIN KEARNEY 1976, oil on canvas, 60 x 72 inches. Collection of the Metropolitan Museum of Art, New York

forced with red. These studies, and several of those of Jamie, are among Brown's finest figure paintings.

While these small works on paper connect with Theophilus Brown's earlier beach figures and studies gleaned from old nudist magazine illustrations, they are very much accounts of the present. Their freshness is quite youthful in spirit, and while this seems to have been easily achieved, it is in fact quite deceptive. Everything, as always, has been carefully considered. There are no peripheral details, for Brown has never been prone to elaborate or embellish. Instead, he puts down, adjusts, paints out, and in the end leaves only what is needed. A coffee cup, a book, or stretched canvases leaning against a wall serve as a compositional counterbalance, spatial marker, or defining narrative element.

His inclinations have not changed over the years, but the deftness and succinctness Brown displays in these works has evolved over the past half century in the studio. It is a shrewd, delicately nuanced, and seasoned performance.

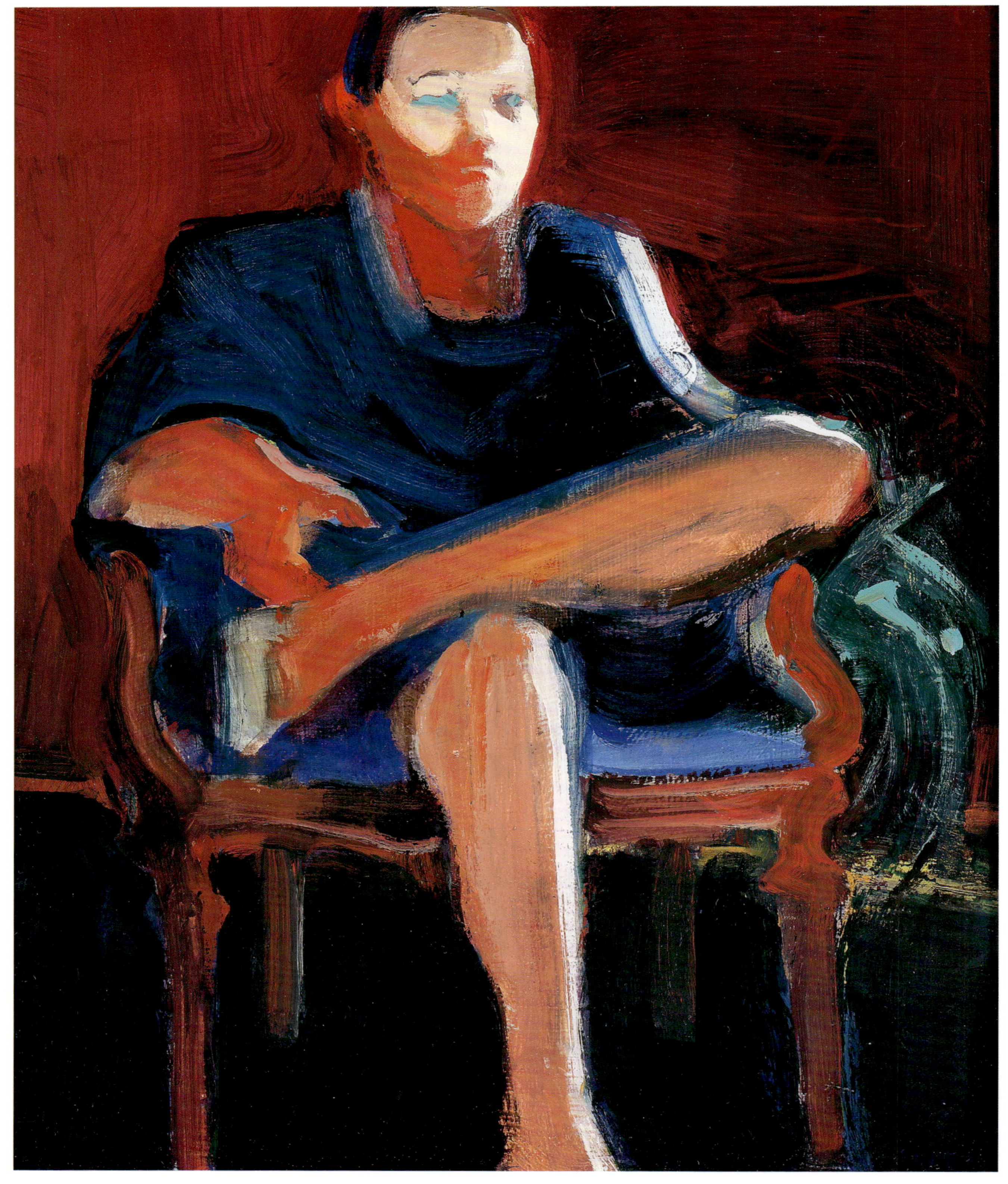

PORTRAIT OF D.K. 1964, oil on canvas board, 11 1/2 x 9 3/4 inches. Private Collection

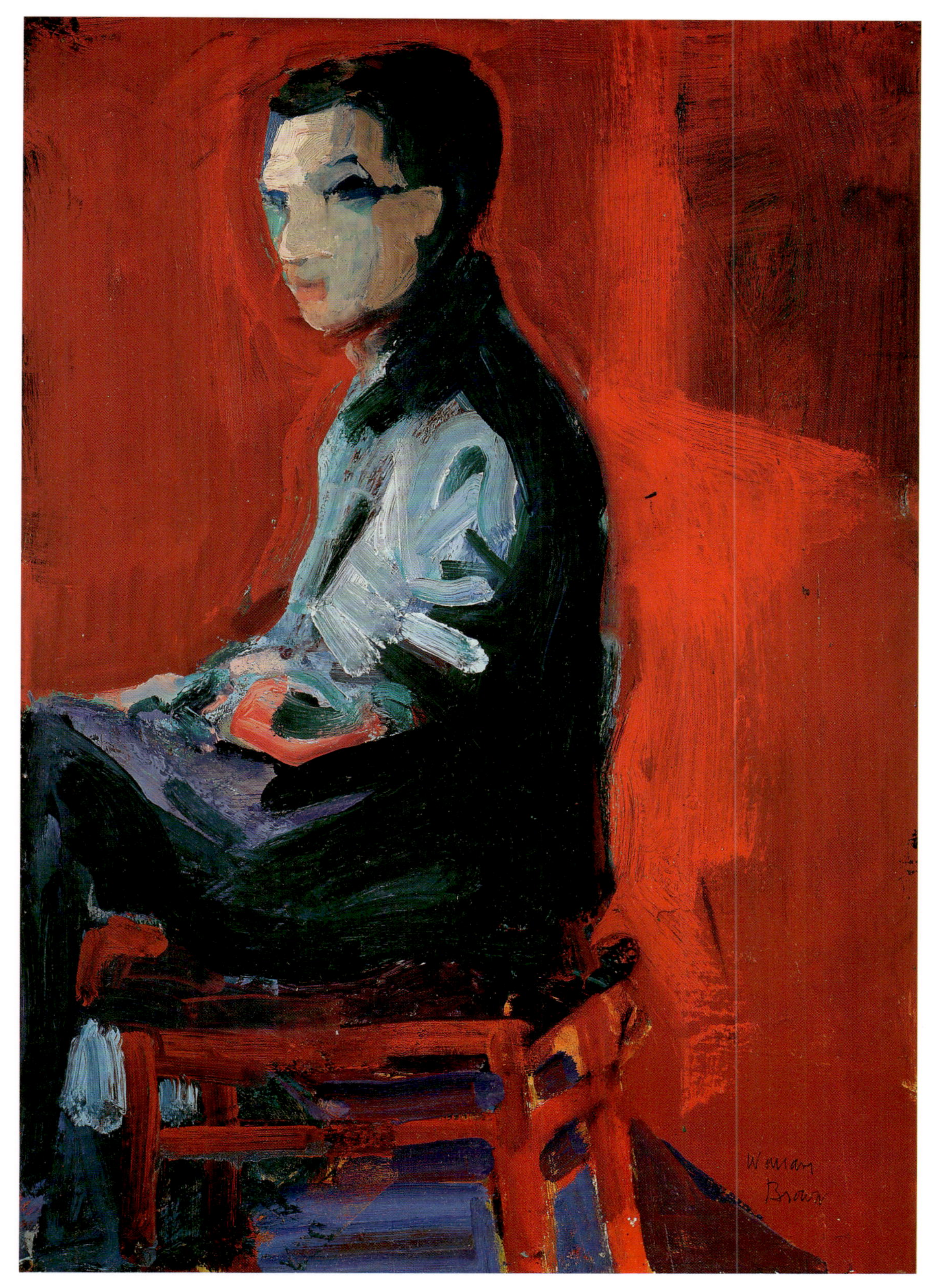

MAN IN RED CHAIR 1962, oil on canvas, 17½ x 12¼ inches. Collection of John Modell, San Francisco

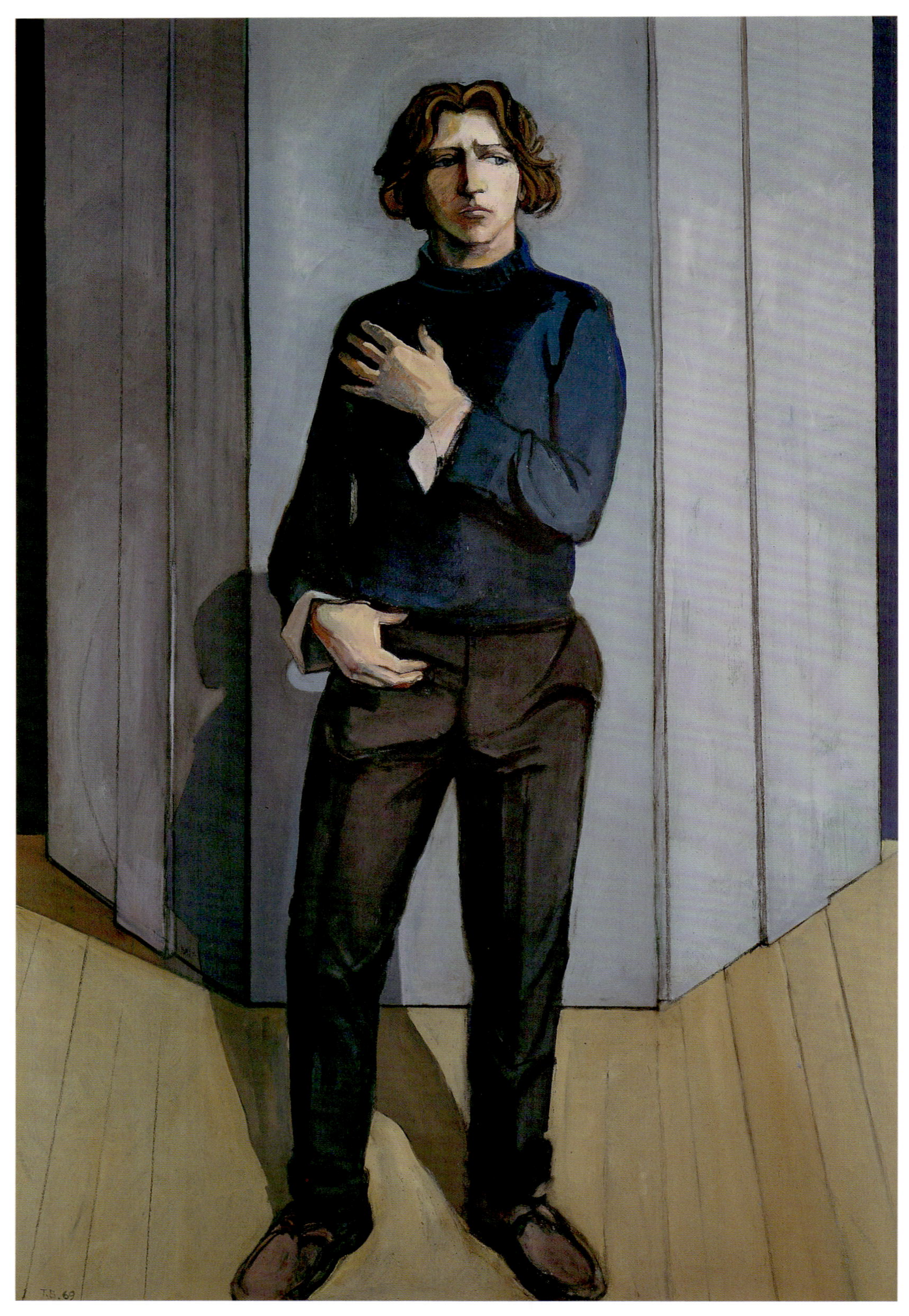

PETER LIASHKOV 1969, acrylic on canvas, 72 x 48 inches. Collection of the Artist

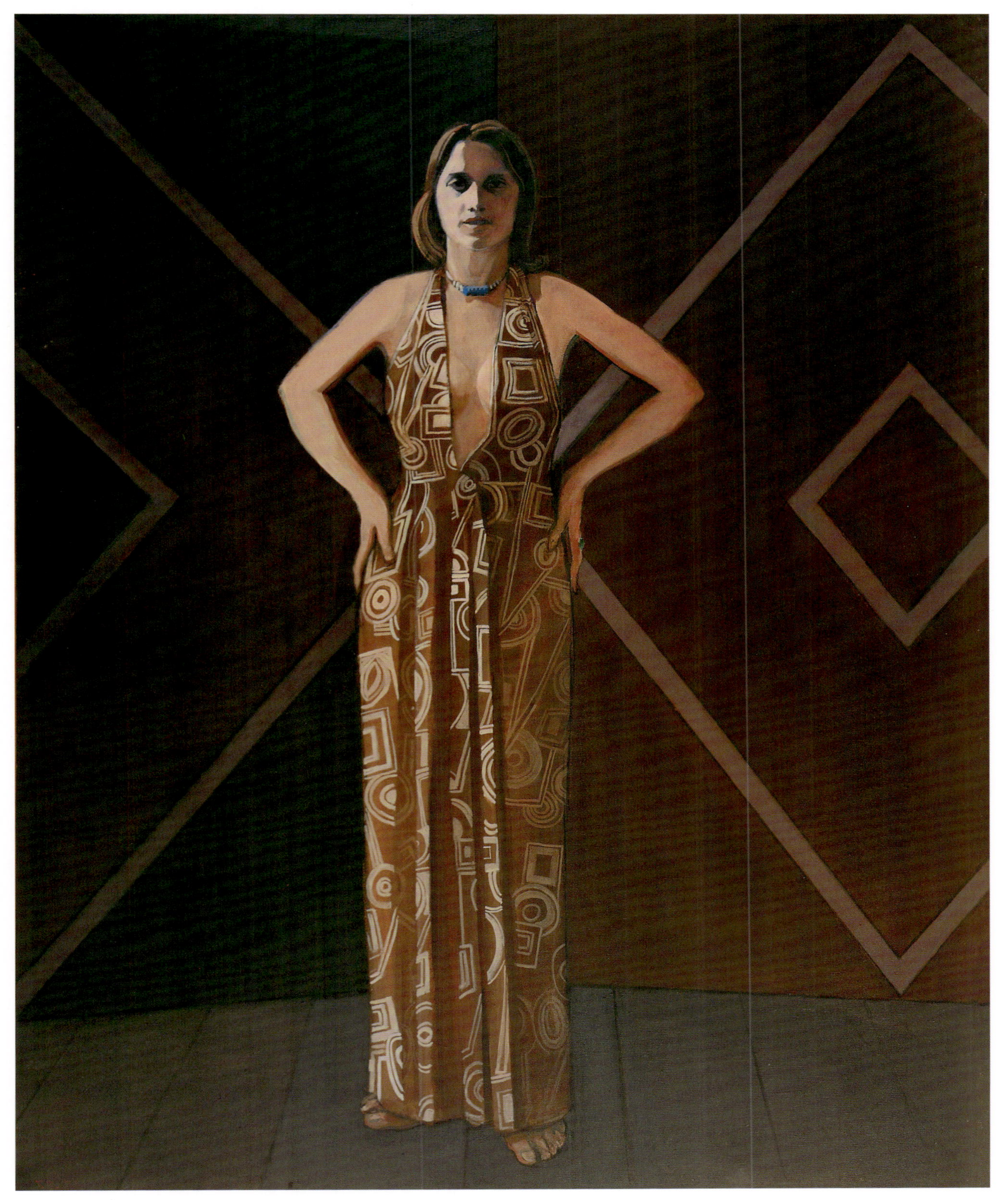

HILDE HEIDT 1970, acrylic in canvas, 60 x 48 inches. Collection of Bill Imhoff & Hilde Heidt, Santa Monica

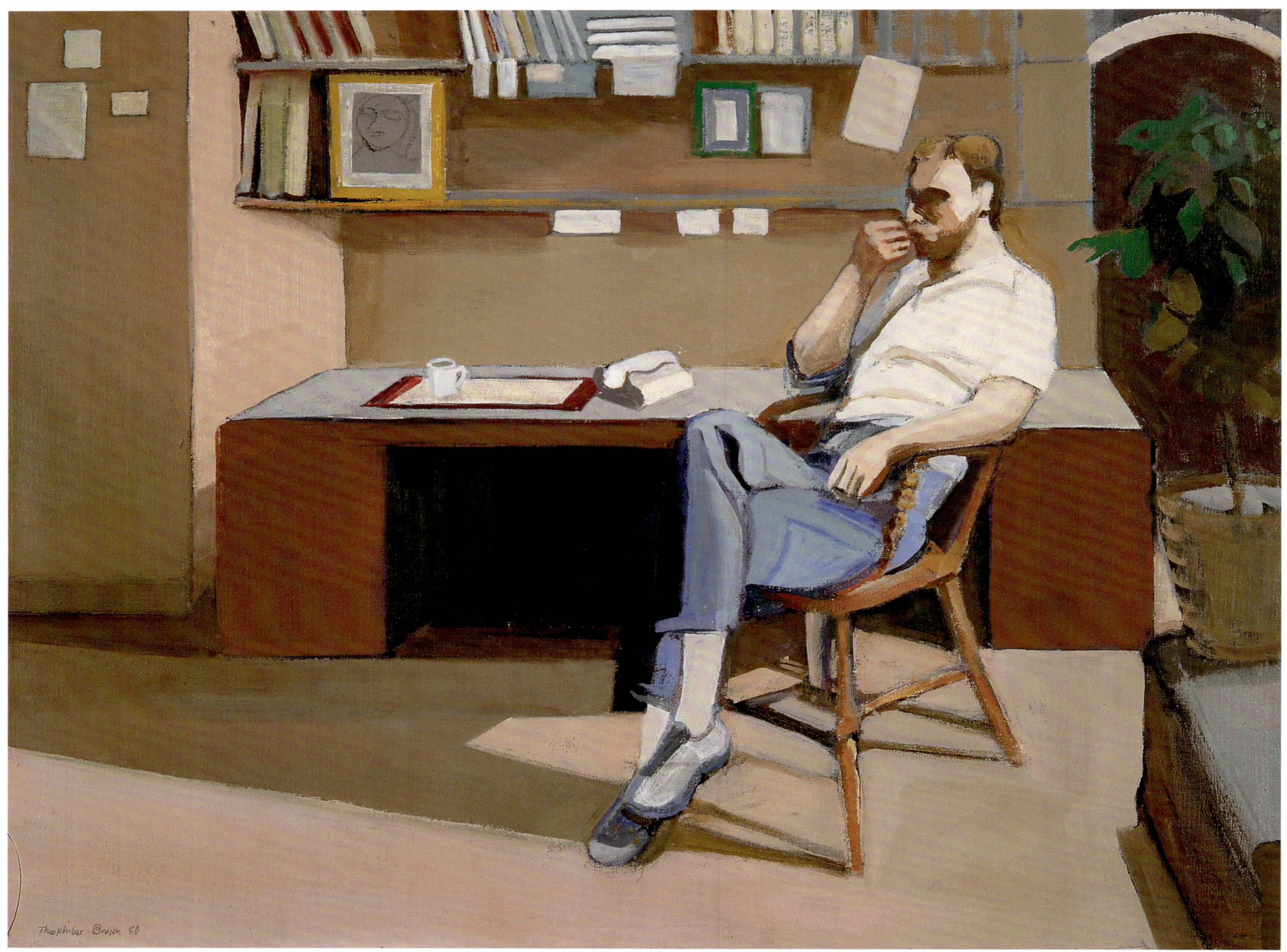

BUCK McCREARY 1978, oil on canvas, 18 x 24 inches. Private Collection

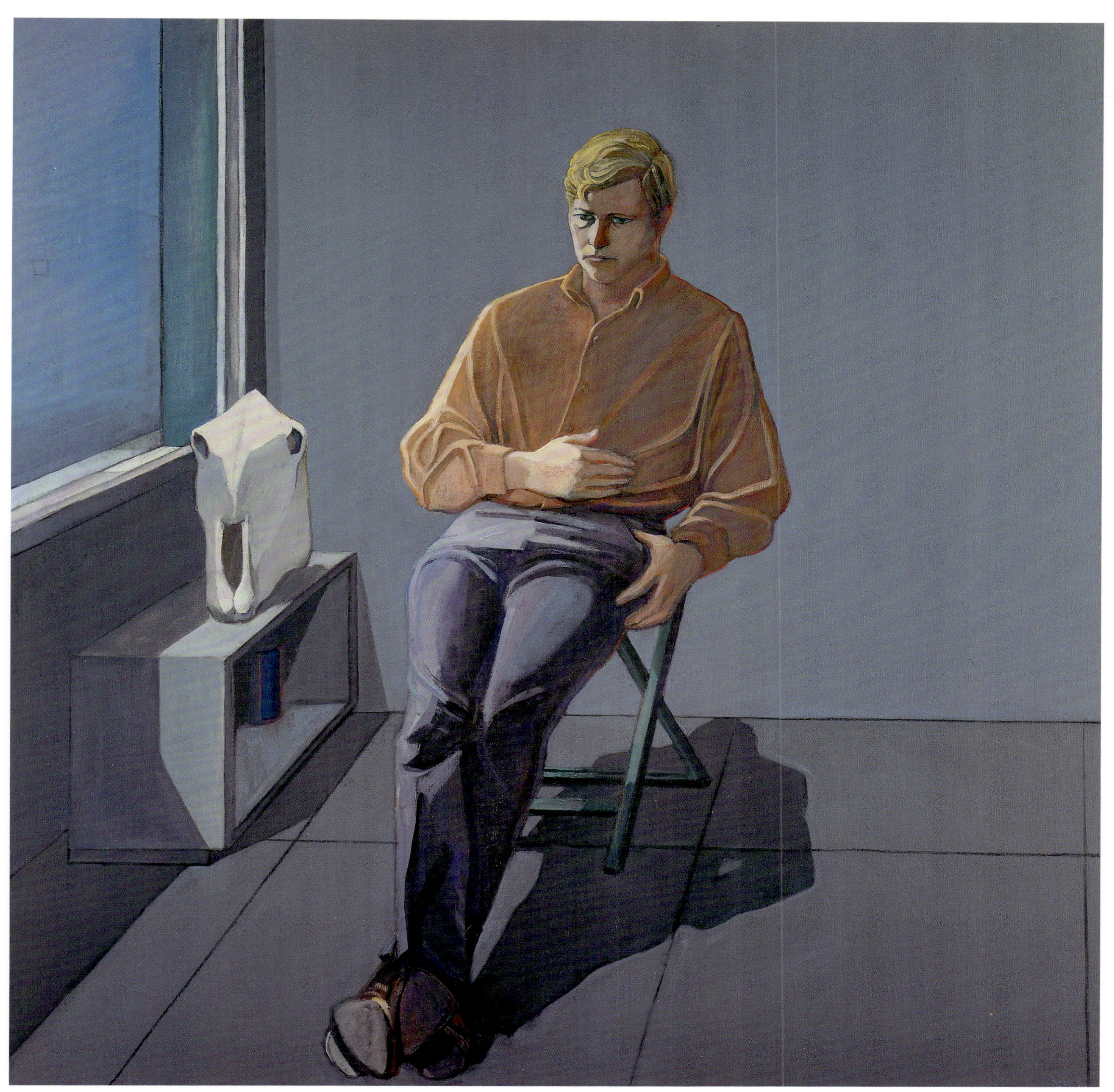

MICHAEL MACDOWELL 1970, acrylic on canvas, 48 x 48 inches. Collection of the Artist

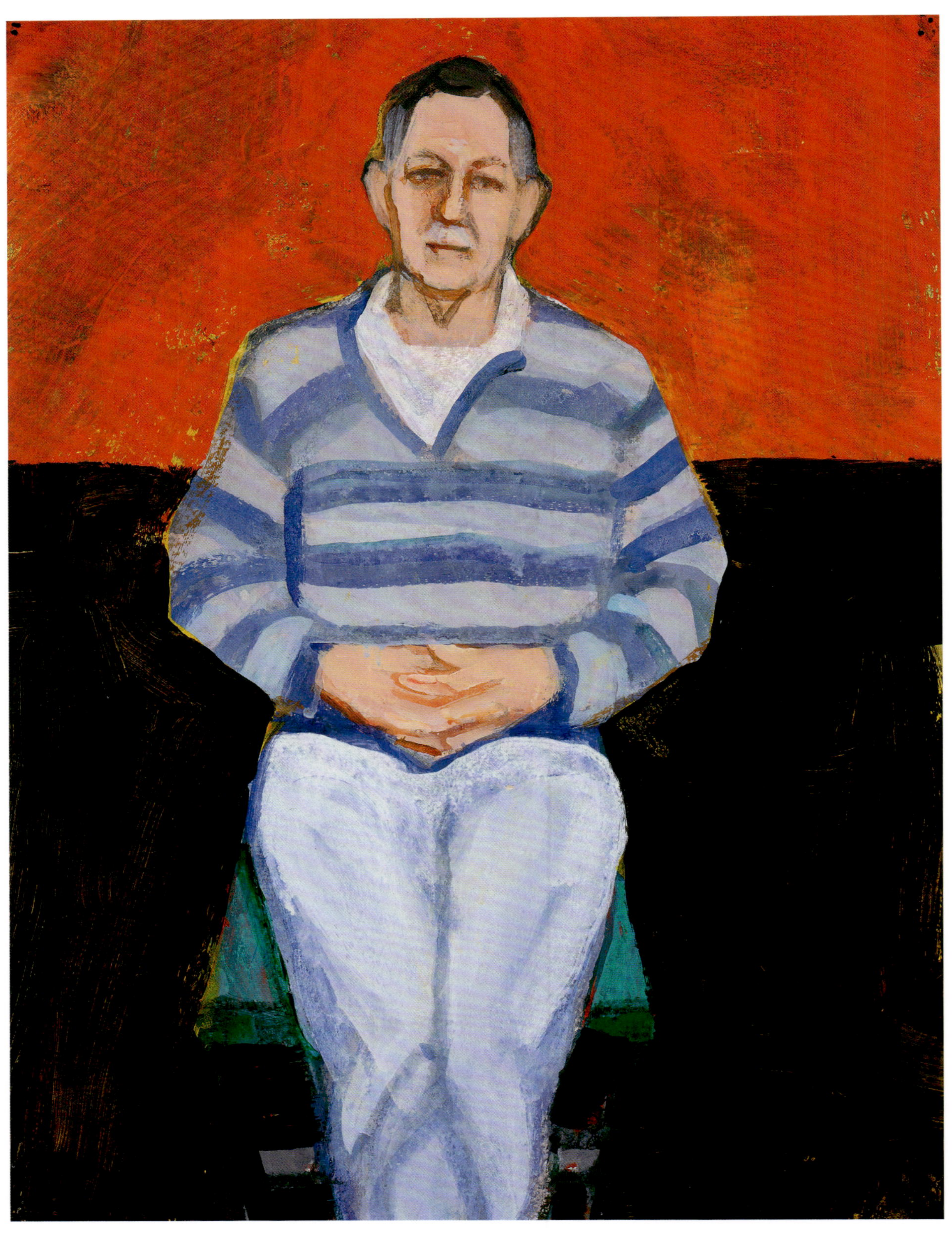

PAUL WONNER 1999, acrylic on paper, 12 x 8 1/2 inches. Collection of Glenna & Charles Campbell, San Francisco

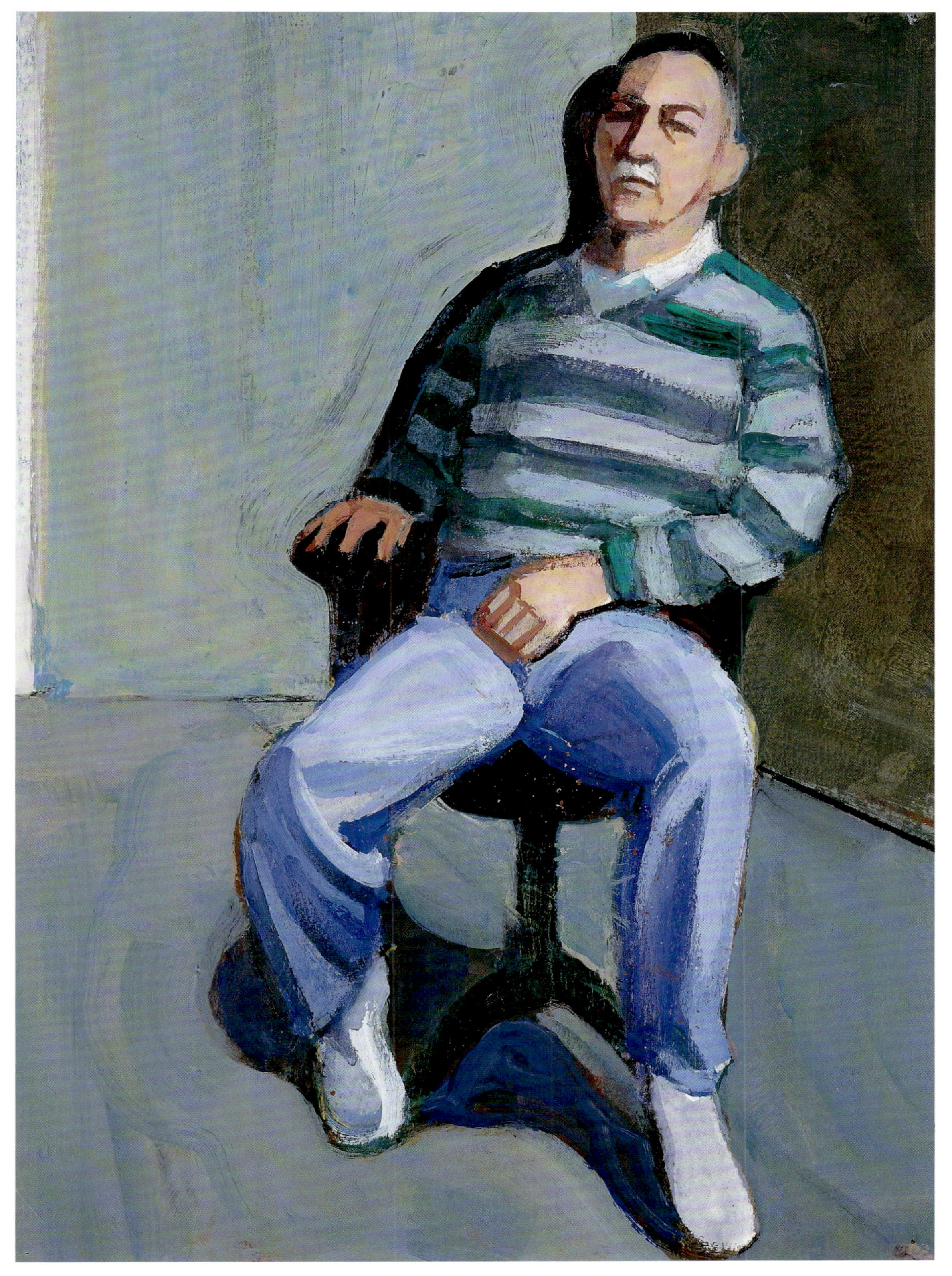

PAUL WONNER 1999, acrylic on paper, 12 x 8 5/8 inches. Private Collection

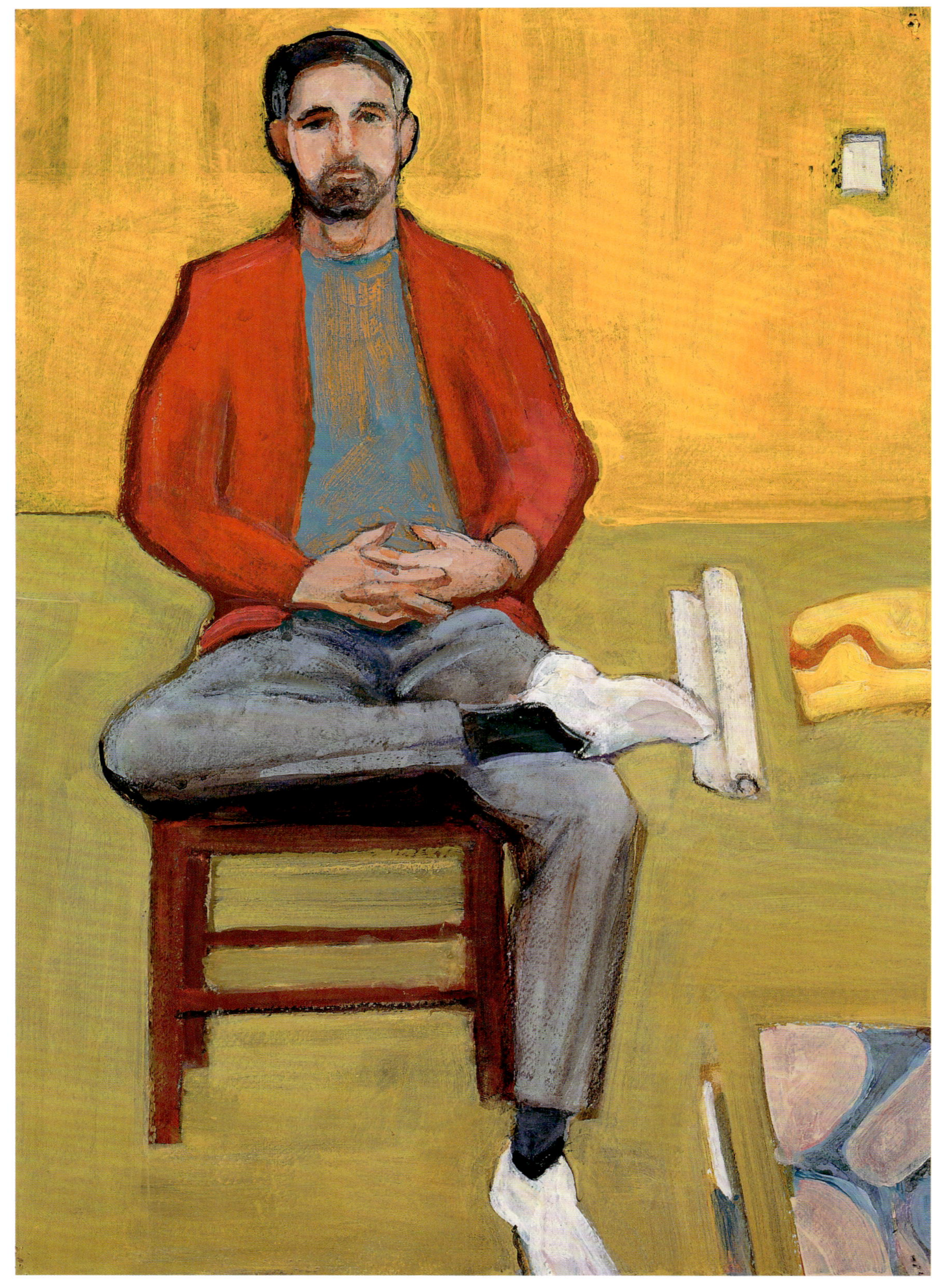

JAMIE 1998, acrylic on paper, 14 x 10 inches. Collection of John Knudsen, Carmel, California

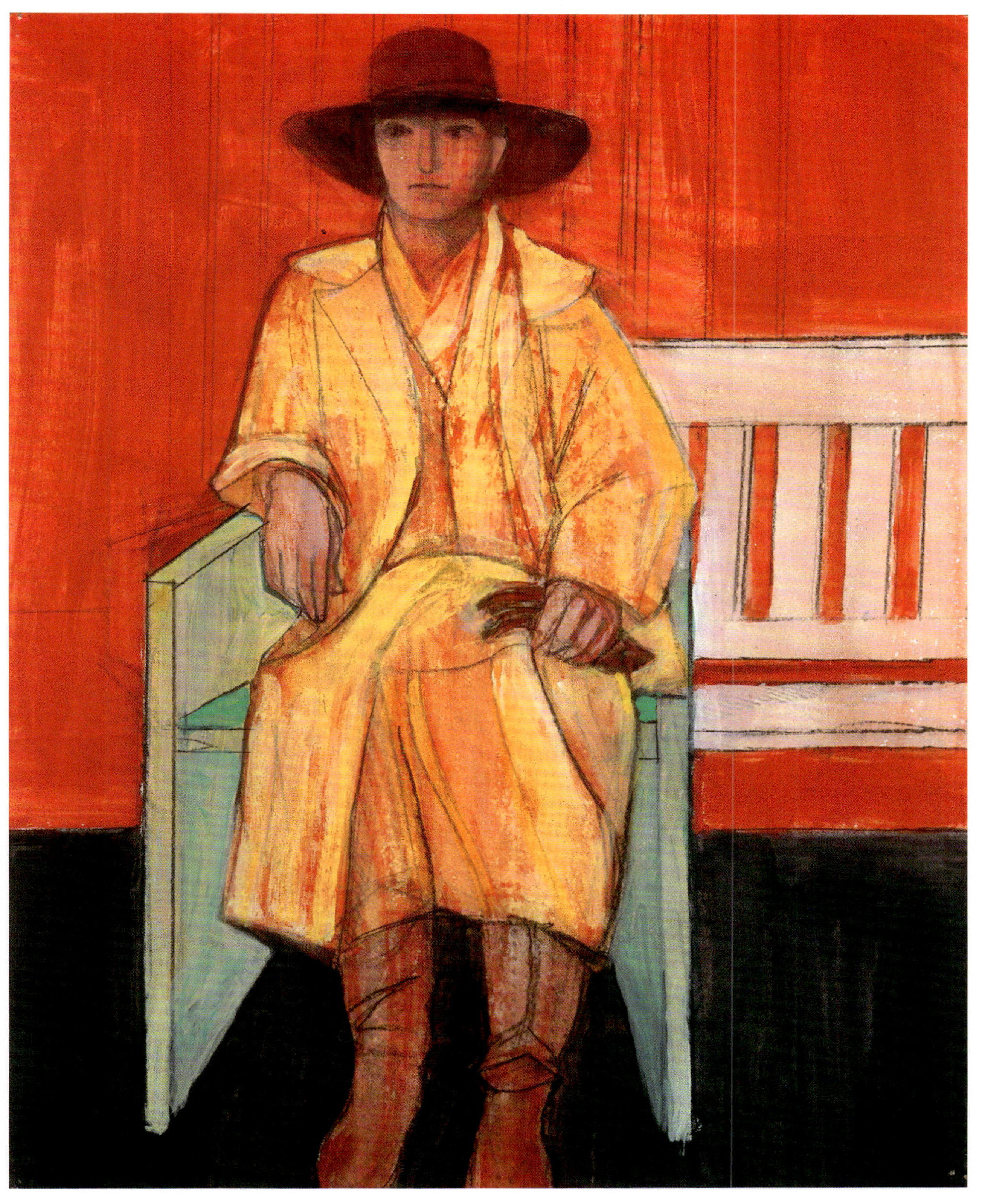

UNTITLED 1992, acrylic on paper, 14 x 17 1/2 inches. Private Collection

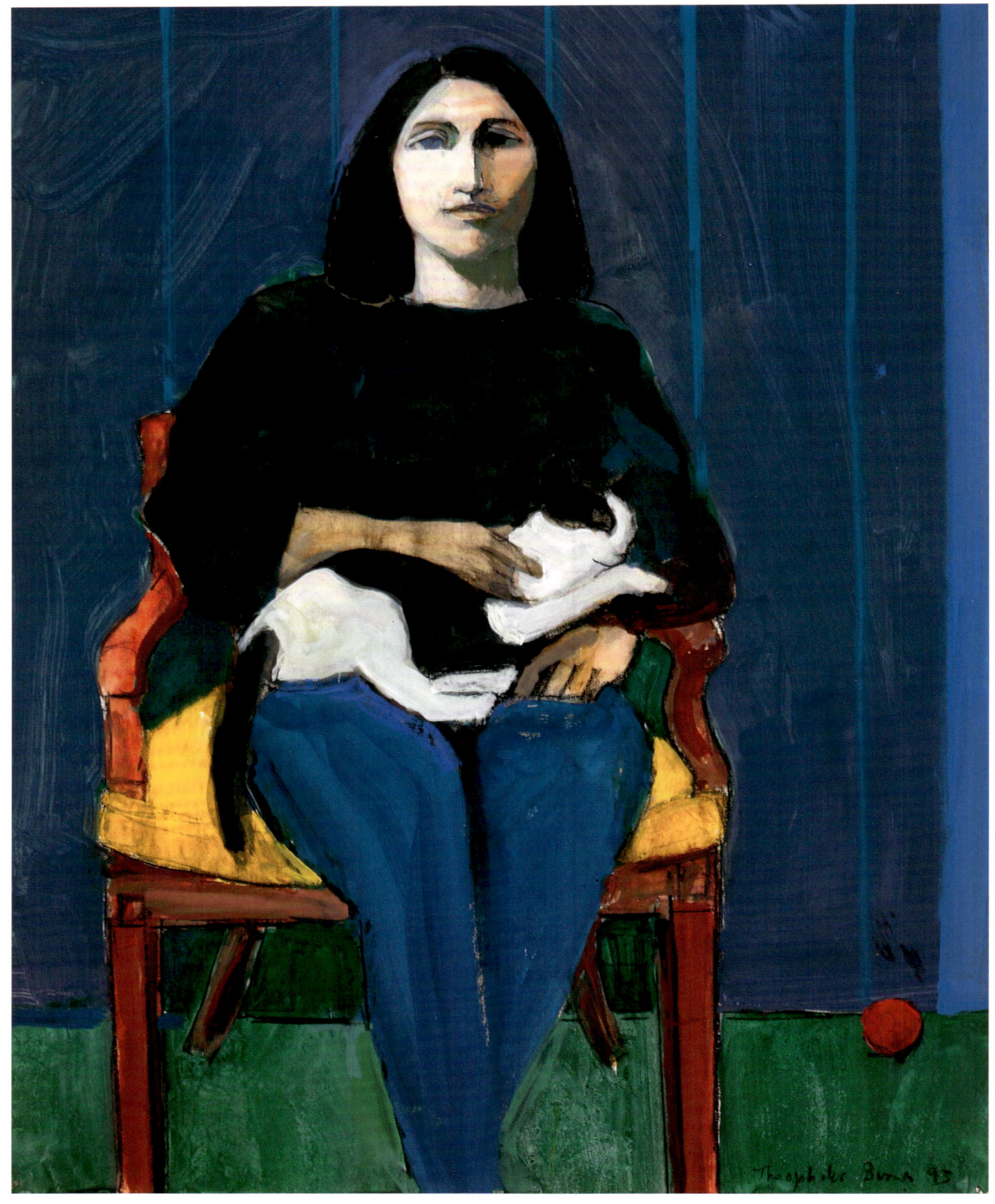

EVIE WITH CAT 1993, acrylic on paper, 14$\frac{1}{2}$ x 11$\frac{1}{2}$ inches. Private Collection

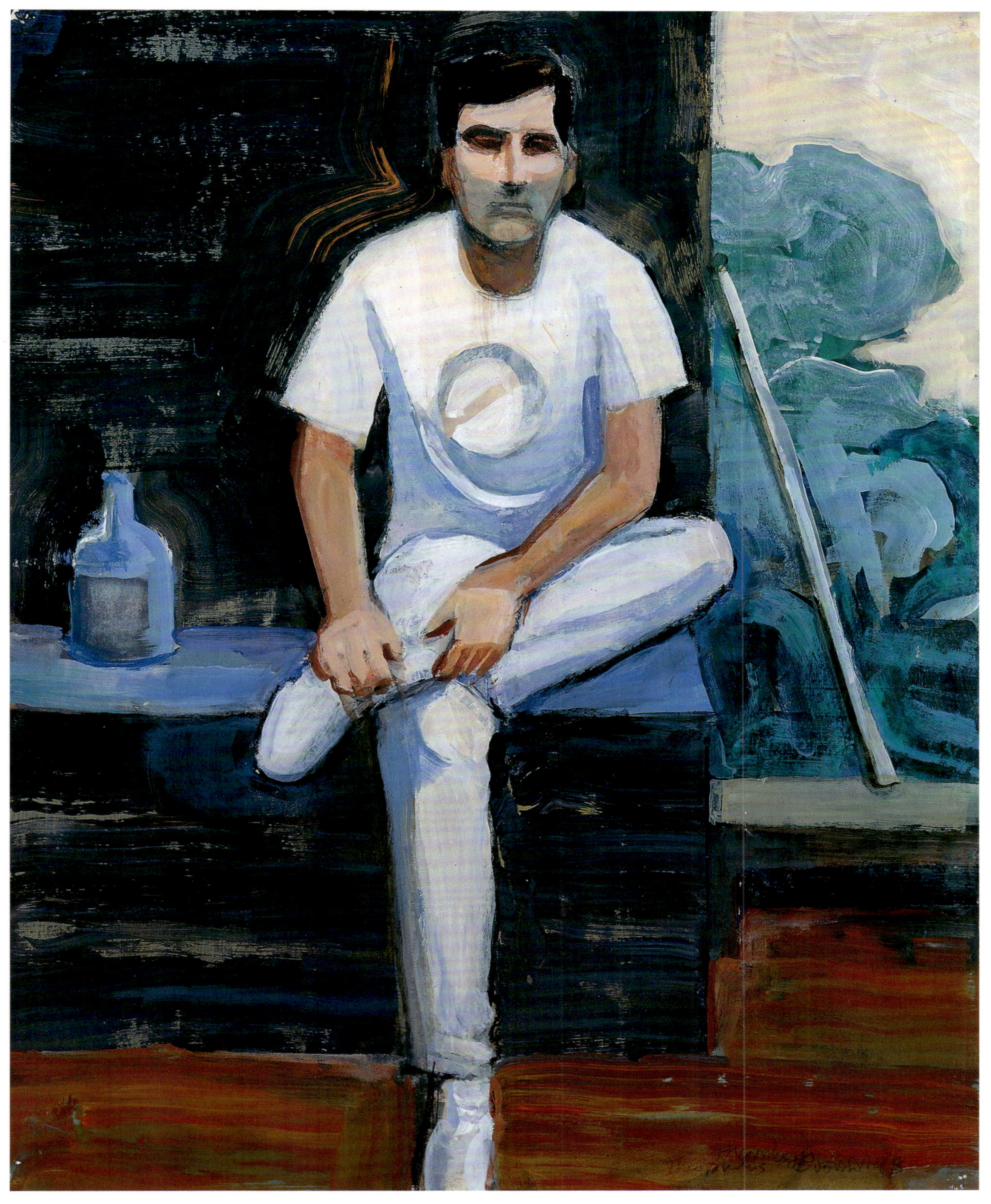

ROBERT SCHNEIDER 1998, acrylic on paper, 14⅜ x 11½ inches. Elins Eagles-Smith Gallery, San Francisco

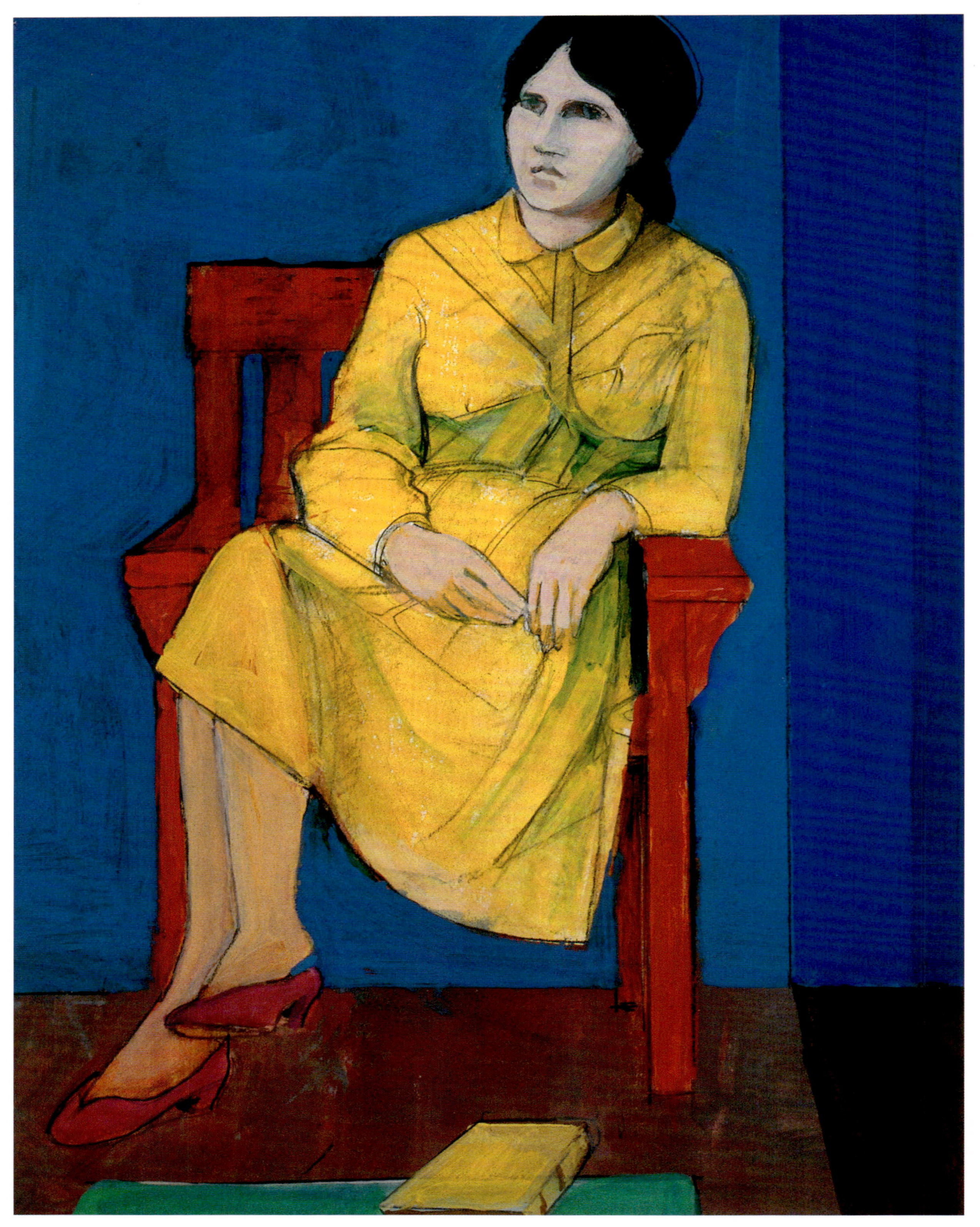

WOMAN IN A YELLOW DRESS 1990, acrylic on paper, 20 x 16 inches
Collection of Mr. & Mrs. Richard Segal, Rye, New York

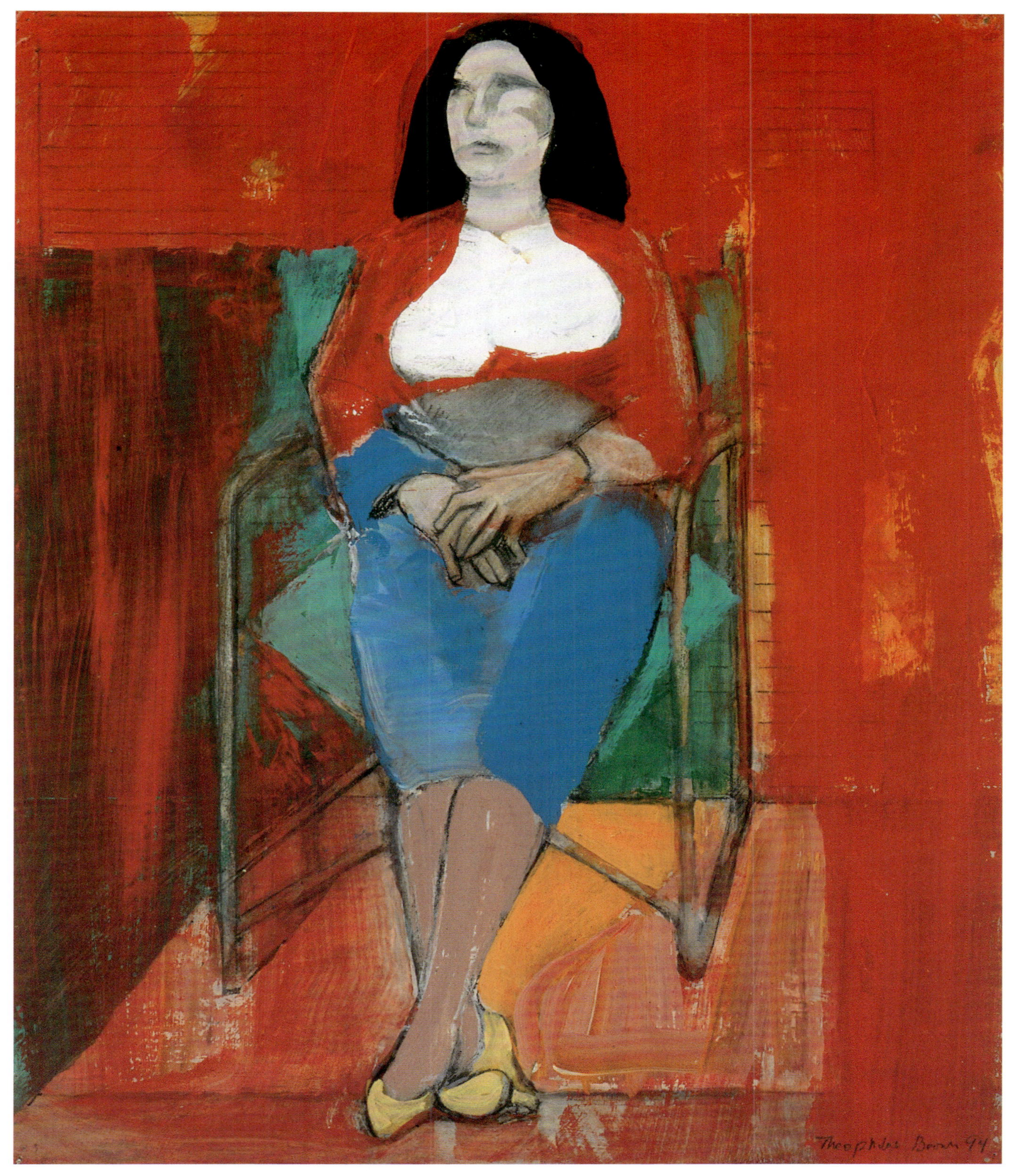

WOMAN IN RED AND BLUE 1987, acrylic on paper, 17 x 14½ inches. Private Collection

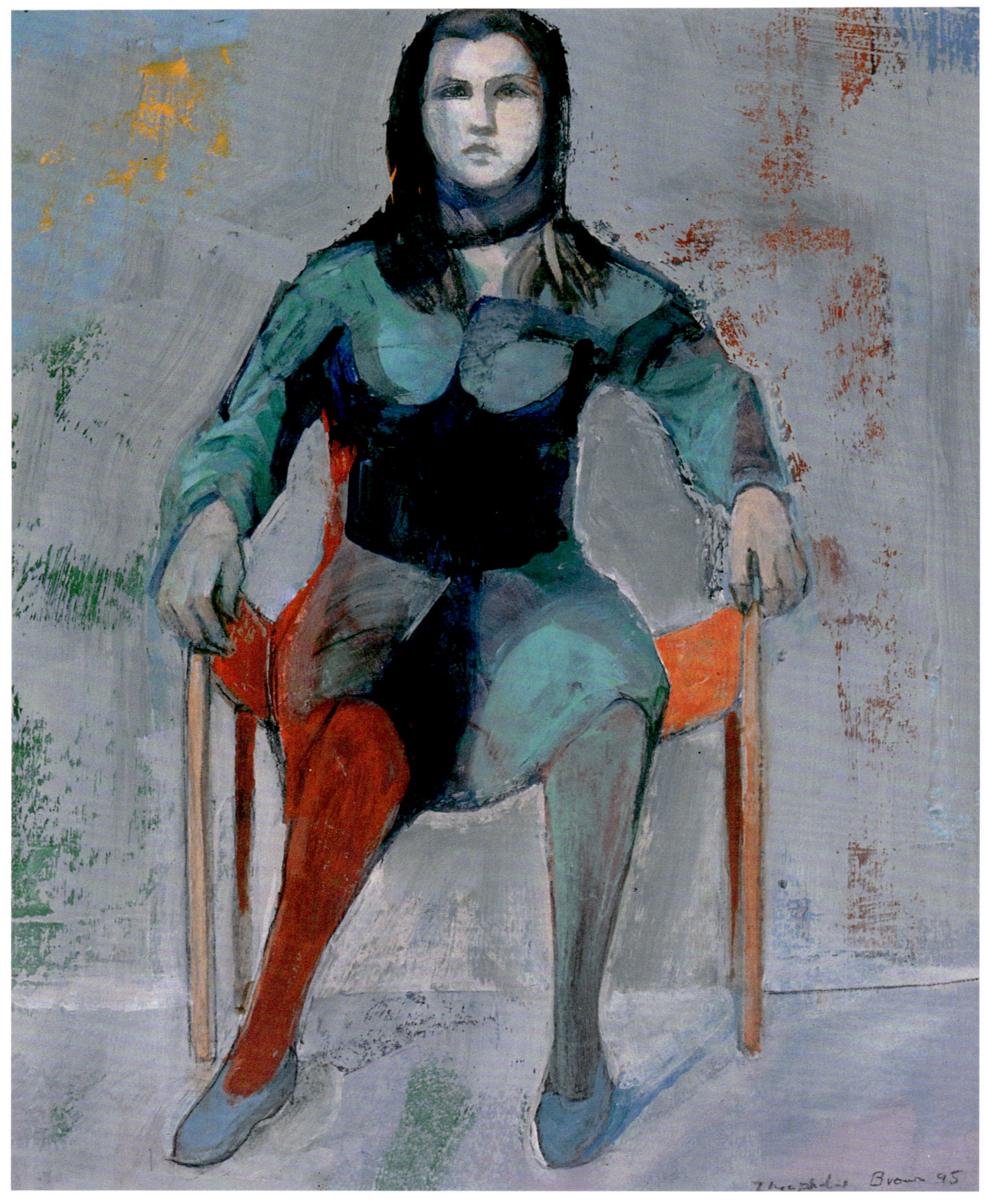

102   *WOMAN IN A RED CHAIR* 1985, acrylic on paper, 14 x 11 1/2 inches. Private Collection

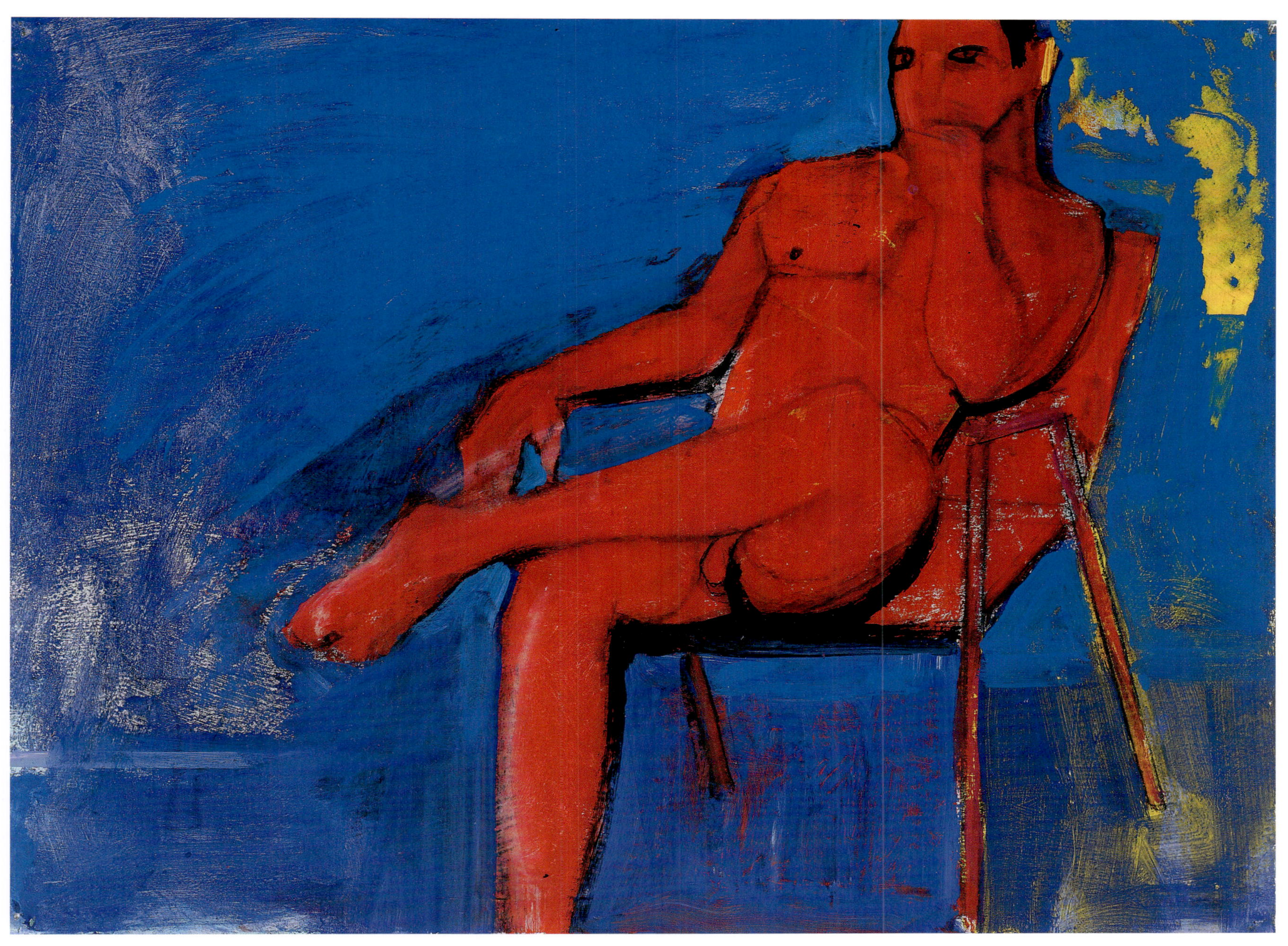

UNTITLED 1995, acrylic on paper, 12 x 85/8 inches. Collection of Glenna & Charles Campbell, San Francisco

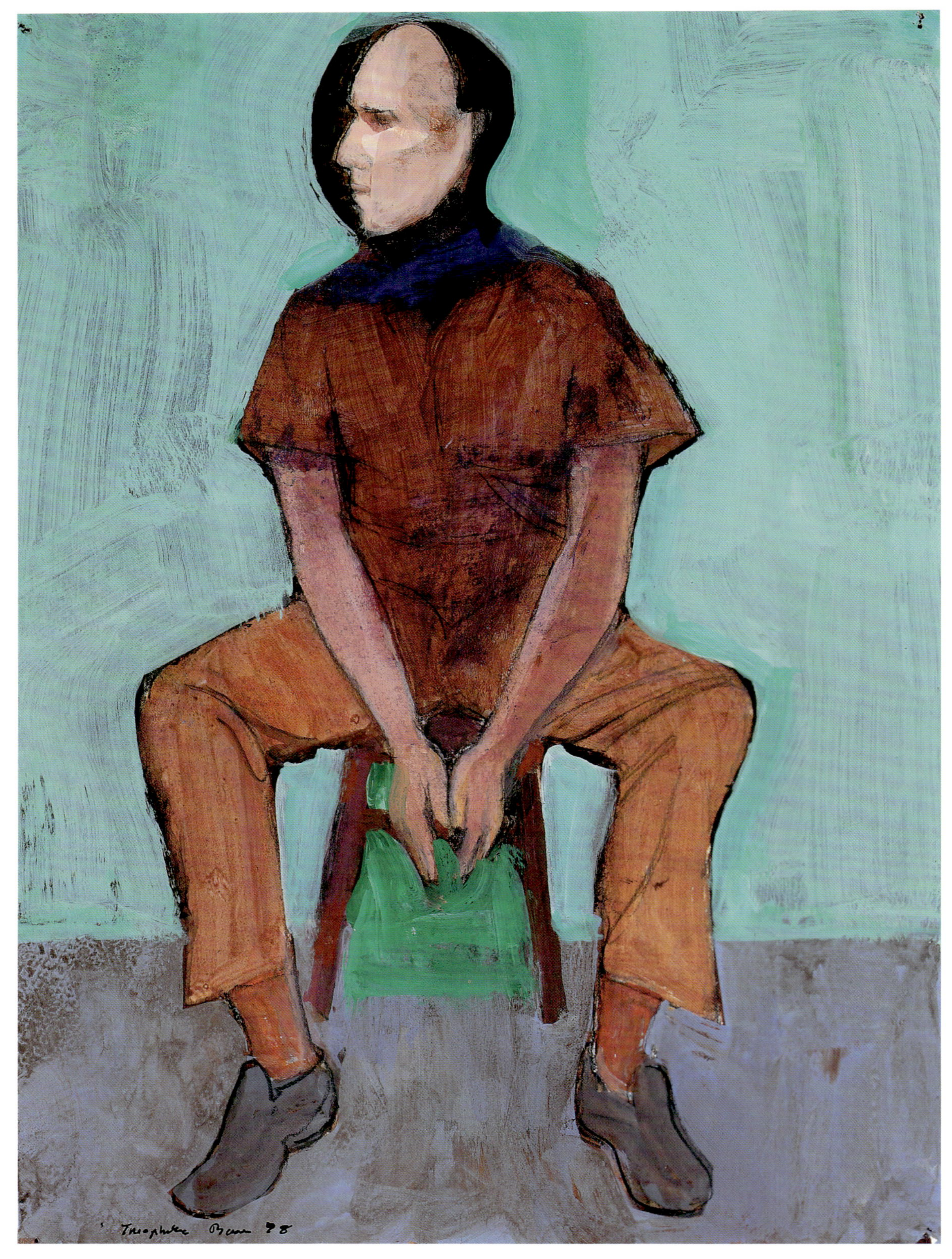

SELF-PORTRAIT 1998, acrylic on paper, 12 x 8 1/2 inches
Collection of Penny & Dewey Bunnell, Land O'Lakes, Wisconsin

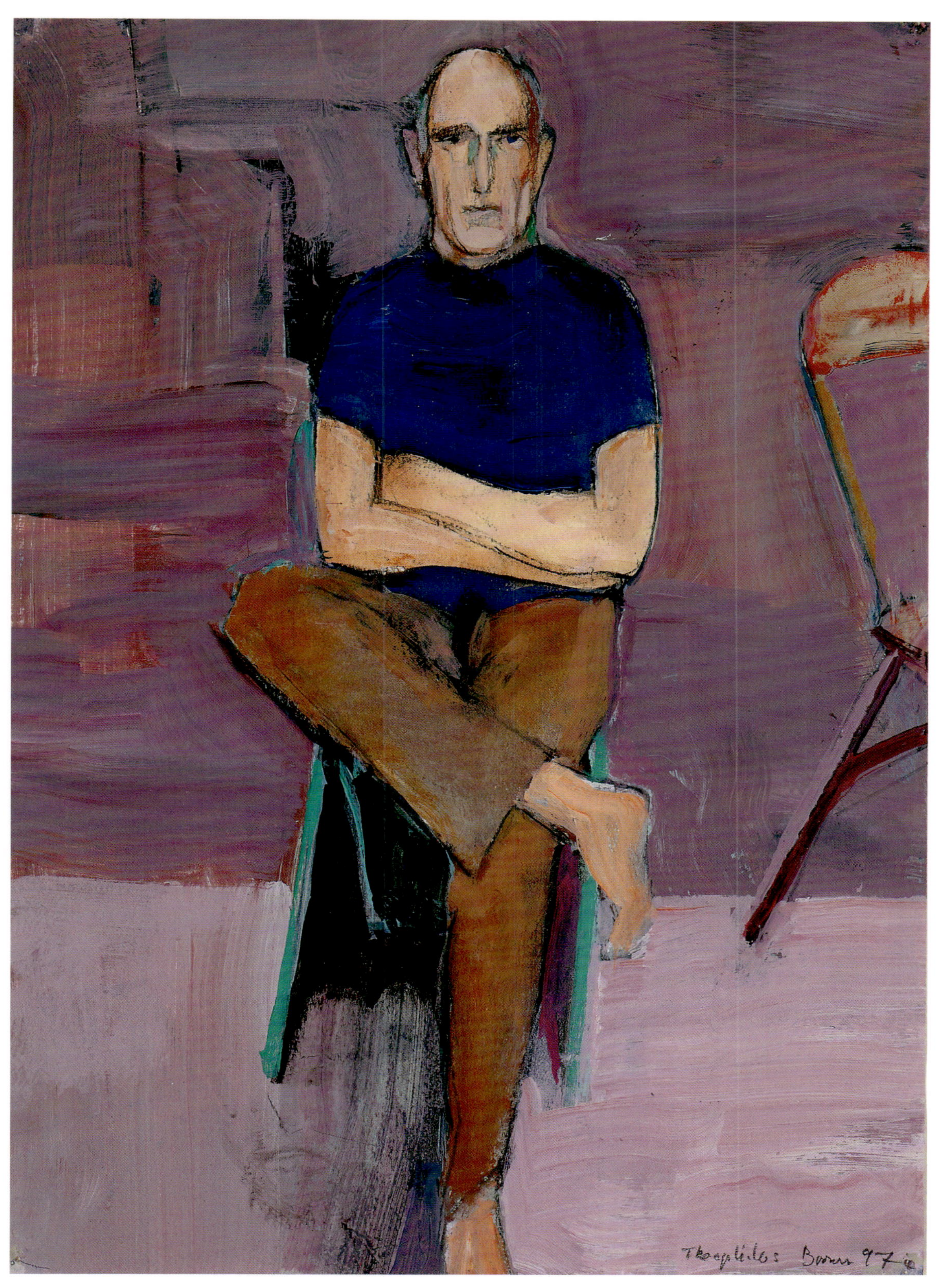

SELF-PORTRAIT 1997, acrylic on paper, 12 x 81/2 inches. Private Collection

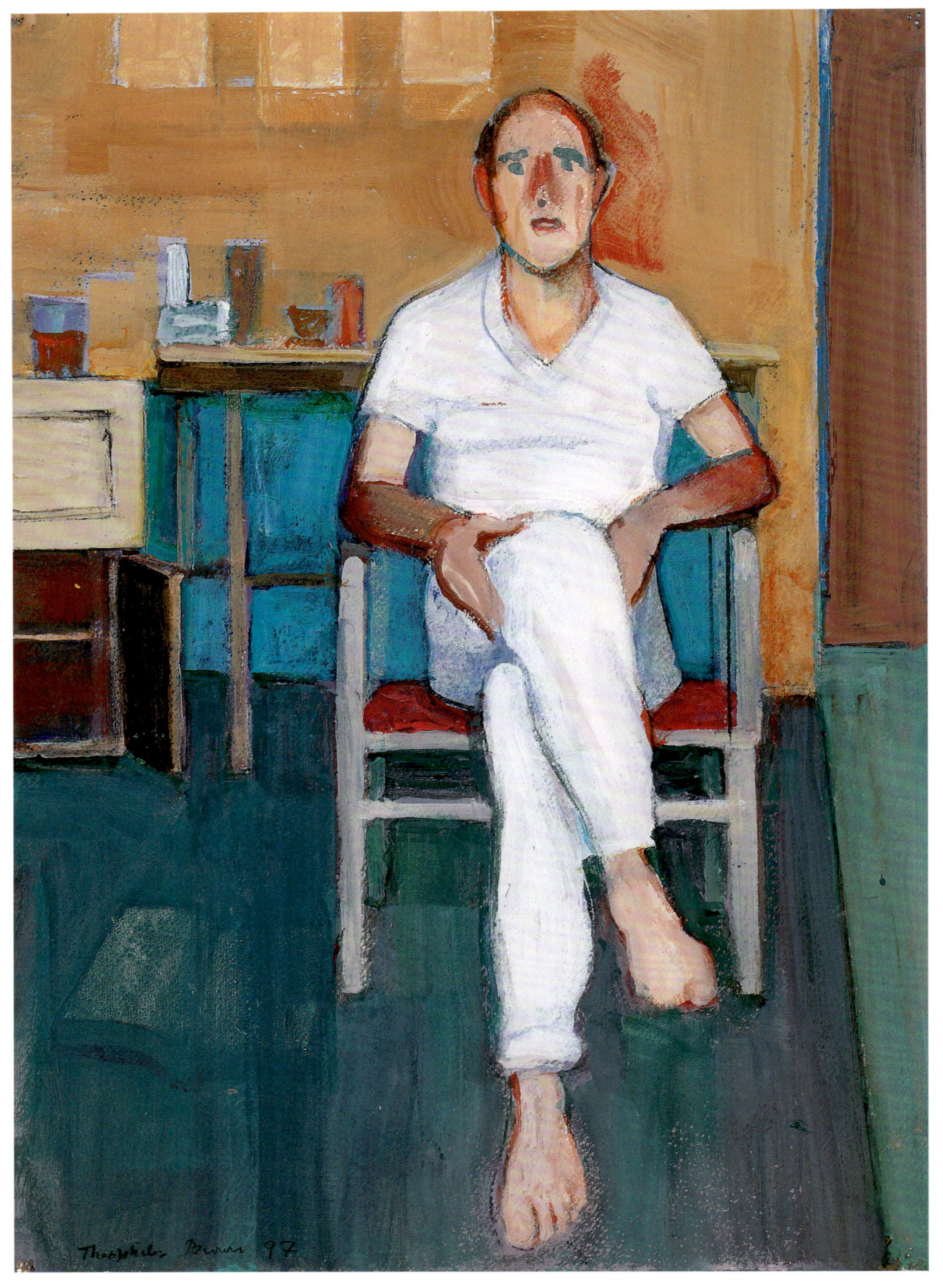

SELF-PORTRAIT 1997, acrylic on paper, 14 x 10 inches. Collection of Nancy & Jerry Barish, Pacifica, California

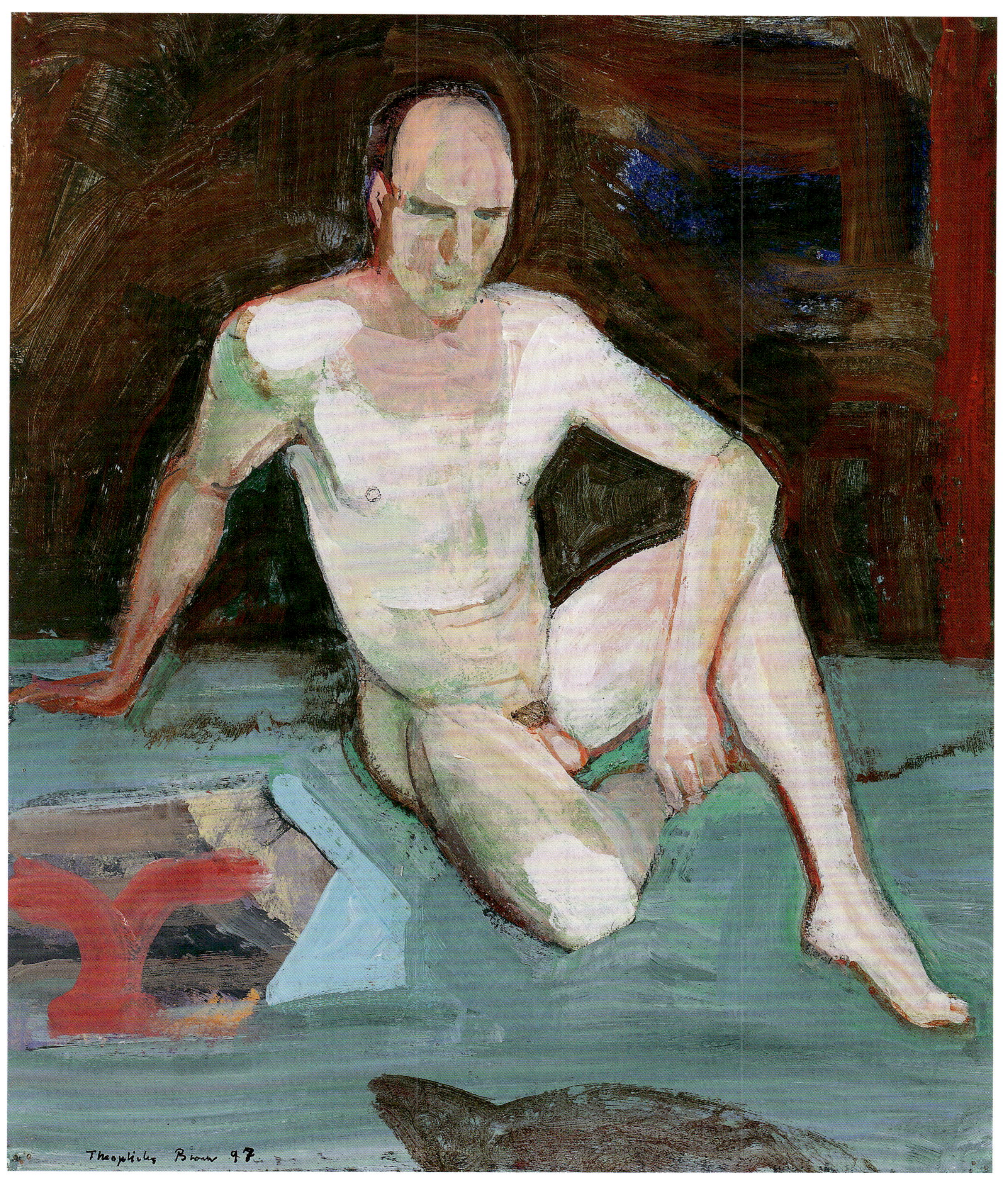

SELF-PORTRAIT 1998, acrylic on paper, 14 x 11 inches. Collection of Peter Linenthal, San Francisco

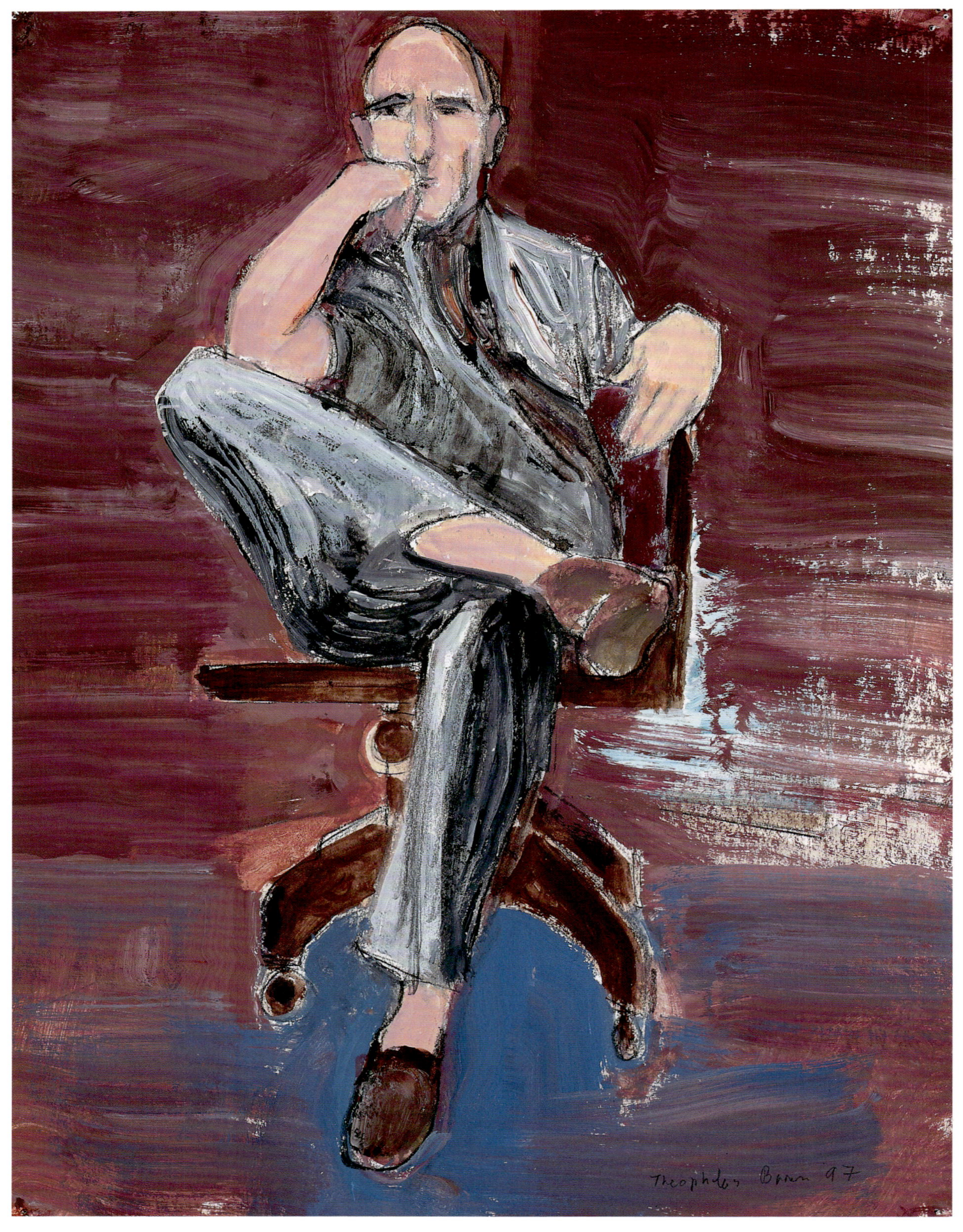

SELF-PORTRAIT 1998, acrylic on paper, 11 x 9 inches
Collection of Martha & Alan Armstrong, Hatfield, Massachusetts

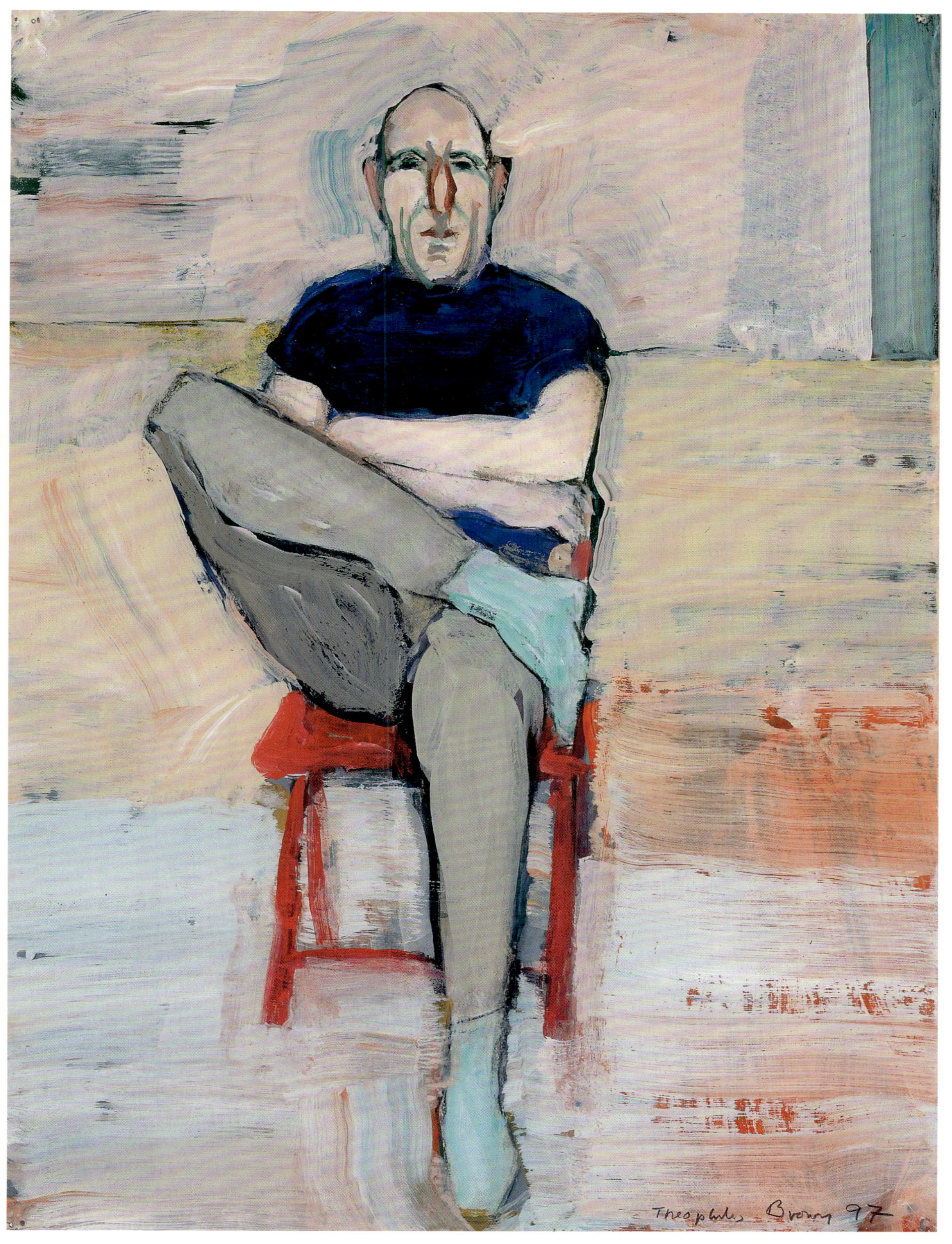

SELF-PORTRAIT 1997, acrylic on paper, 14 x 10 inches. Collection of Paul Wonner

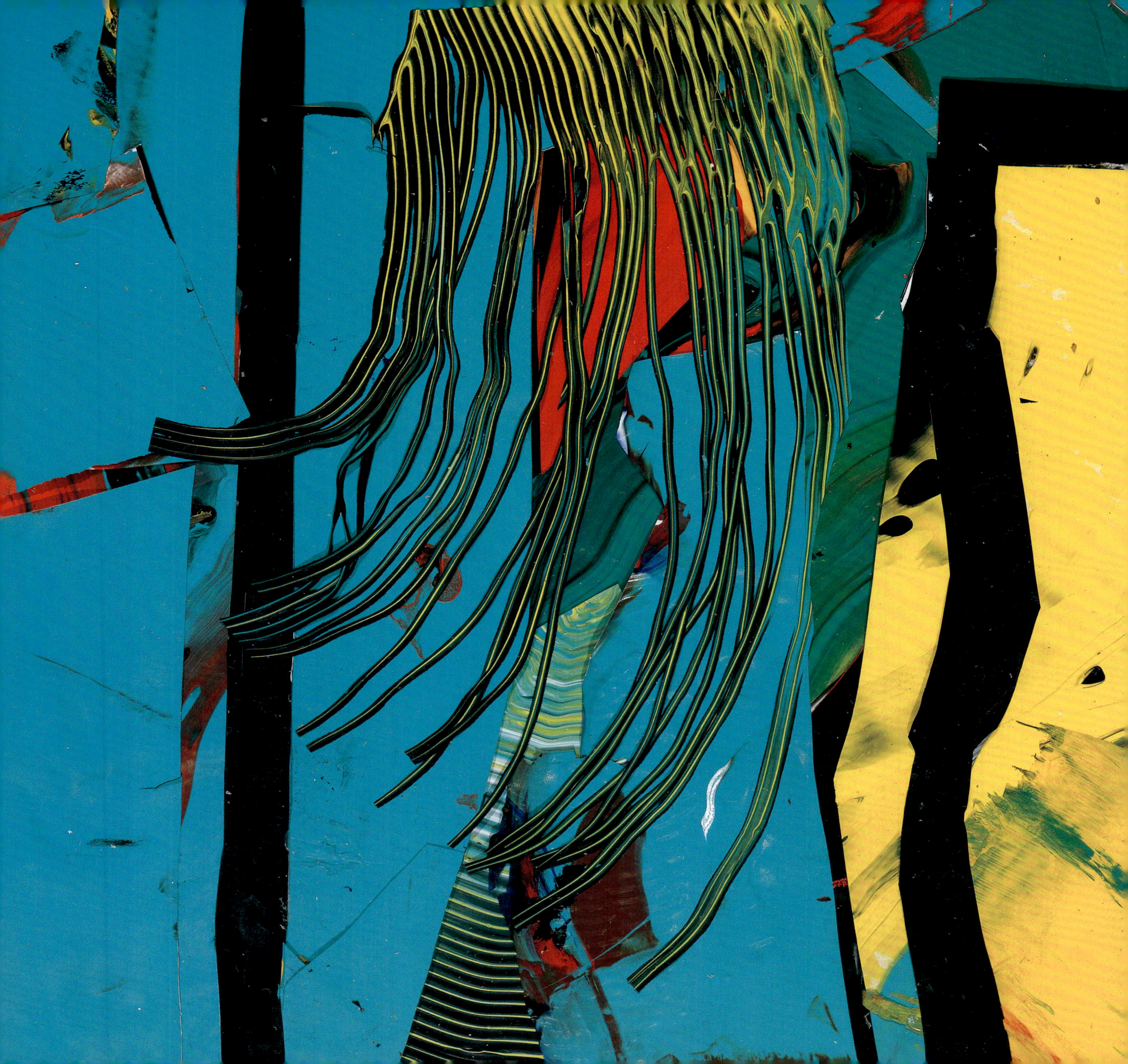

Chance and Confluence

They begin as an unknown adventure in an unknown space. It is at the moment of completion that in a flash of recognition they are seen to have the quantity and function which was intended. Ideas and plans that existed in the mind at the start were simply the doorway through which one left the world in which they occur.

The most important tool the artist fashions through constant practice is faith in his ability to produce miracles when they are needed. Pictures must be miraculous: the instant one is completed, the intimacy between the creation and the creator is ended. He is an outsider. The picture must be for him, as for anyone experiencing it later, a revelation, an unexpected resolution of an eternally familiar need.

—MARK ROTHKO

All growth is a leap in the dark, a spontaneous unpremeditated act without benefit of experience.

—HENRY MILLER

THE FIRST OF THEOPHILUS BROWN'S COLLAGES were done in 2001. They began with the remnants of acrylic paint peeled from his palette at the end of the day. At first there was no thought of these colorful little screeds being anything more than interesting residuals of his painting procedure. A few of the rubbery scraps were pinned to the wall. When he began assembling them into collages, their transition from studio detritus to non-objective compositions more closely paralleled Duchampian chance than the intellectual strategies of Formalist painting.

Like a Proustian sweet, the inherent beauty of these viscous snippets recalled the open-ended, improvisational traits of Willem de Kooning, the gestural physicality of Jackson Pollock, the encrusted layers of monochromatic lost-and-found forms in Franz Kline's collages, and the brooding elegance of Mark Rothko's canvases. In the early fifties, Brown—who has destroyed many of his drawings and paintings—cut up some of his earlier works on paper and reassembled the strips as abstract collages. A half century later, they are the only precedent in his oeuvre for these recent collages.

The spontaneous all-chips-on-the-table gamble of the literature, the audacious poetry, the painterly bravura of the Abstract Expressionists, and the strong sense of camaraderie that typifies the postwar years were not distant or vicarious experiences for Brown. He had joked with Pablo Picasso in Paris, spent time with Balthus and Giacometti, and received critiques from Willem de Kooning. He had watched Rothko, de Kooning, Park, and Diebenkorn paintings evolve, take false turns, and reach their final, hard-earned conclusions—an experience light-years away from our encounters with their canvases in the silent white interiors of our museums.

On the West Coast, from the mid-fifties through the sixties, David Park, Elmer Bischoff, and Richard Diebenkorn moved from complete abstraction to figuration and back. A few painters, such as Brown and James Weeks, never explored non-objective painting. Regarding their debt to de Kooning and others, Brown stated, "I felt we used Abstract Expressionism's language as a basis for our figurative painting." Whereas his canvases

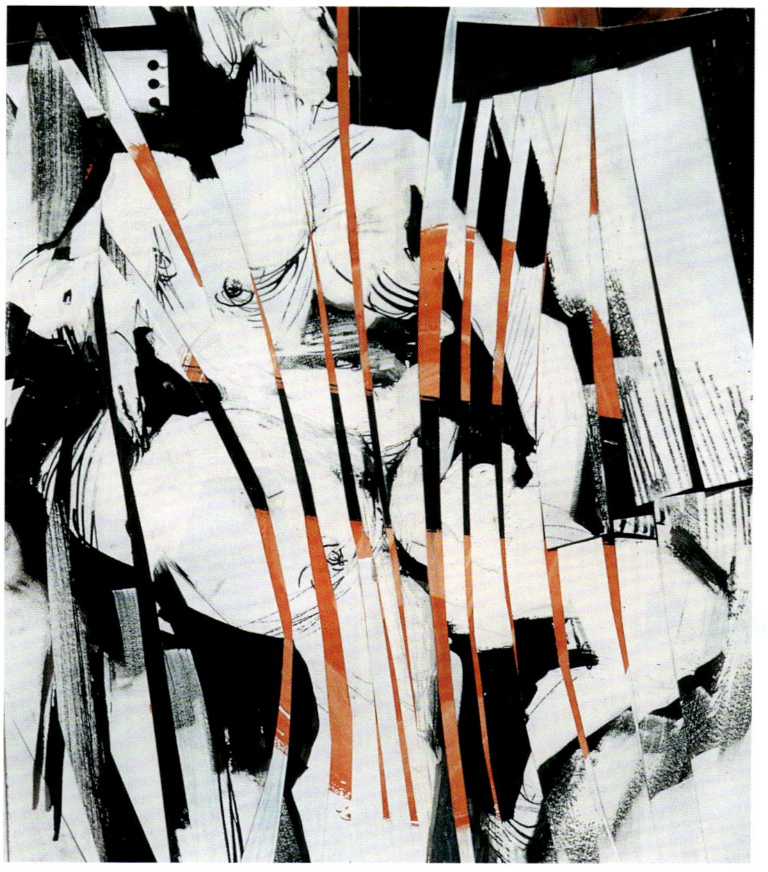

Collage constructed from cut-up drawings, 1972 (location unknown)

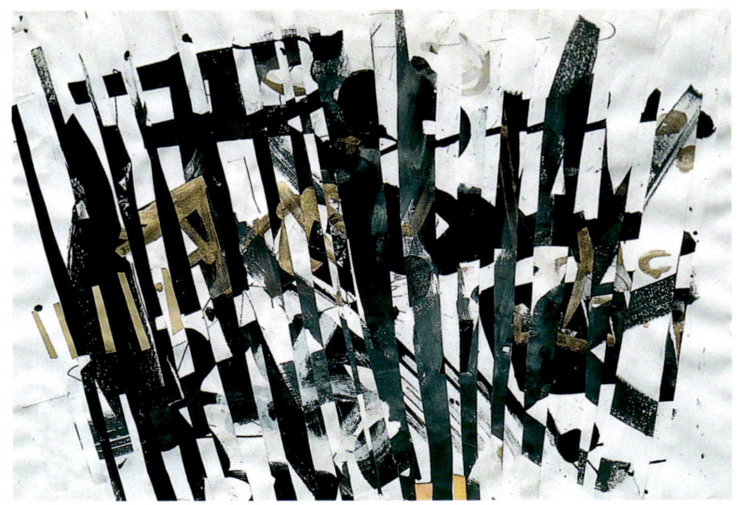

Collage constructed from cut-up drawings, 1972 (location unknown)

contained the gestural sensuality, compositional devices tracing back to Cézanne, the open-ended inventiveness of the Abstract Expressionists, and at times the compositional ploys of film noir, they never strayed into pure non-objective painting. Importantly, the figurative works of Brown, Weeks, Wonner, and Nathan Oliveira, while rendered with the loaded brush and physicality of Abstract Expressionism, centered on traditional subjects such as still lifes, interiors, and landscapes, as well as on the fleeting, incidental moments of their private worlds. In addition, their paintings, watercolors, and drawings were distinguished from those of Park, Bischoff, and Diebenkorn by their frequent use of narrative, cinematic, and allegorical imagery.

And so these bits and pieces of paint, assembled as colorful collages, are Brown's first non-objective works. Vigorously and without artifice they recall de Kooning's canvases of the fifties—those heavy-breasted harpies such as *Woman I*, the glossy monochrome of *Excavation,* and the rapacious, painterly daring of *Gotham News.* While a far cry from Rothko's somberness and vaporous forms, the boldness of these constructions recalls the pictographic and totemic character of his earlier paintings.

Also present are a bit of Dadaist unpredictability and the artlessness of objects made of castoffs, so beautifully demonstrated by Kurt Schwitters' elegant collages and *merz* constructions. It is easy to speculate on Brown's lingering memories of some of the Indian miniatures—so charmingly unsettling in their regal color, sense of scale, and pictorial daring—that he and Wonner collected decades ago. And last, in their refutation of preciousness they recall the wonderful abstractions painted on cigar box lids by their close friend Richard Diebenkorn in 1979.

The collages are untitled and abstain from all figurative references. Their chromatic richness and compositional solidity are unsettling, for they convey a sense of monumentality and their colors are electric in their boldness and simplicity—fire-engine reds set against a brilliant turquoise with small scraps of yellows, oranges, purples, and greens. Forms turn and twist organically, occasionally accentuated by the dark outlines of a Georges Rouault saint or a Max Beckmann sinner. Some remnants are grained with a trowel, either exposing the layers of colors beneath or turning the paint into stringy ribbons of pale blues, blacks, and yellows. The mellifluous and expressive range Brown is capable of conjuring in these opulent little eye dazzlers is endless. Some dance lightly on a field of color, while others take on the solidity and weight of a barge—plant-like in one and architectural in another. Some are as grounded and weighty as an elephant and others are gossamer light and wafting. While iconic or droll at times, they are always lyrical and deftly on target.

These paint/collages and Brown's recent turn to non-figurative abstraction mark one more facet in his long and surprisingly diverse oeuvre and demonstrate once again his ongoing intellectual and creative restlessness.

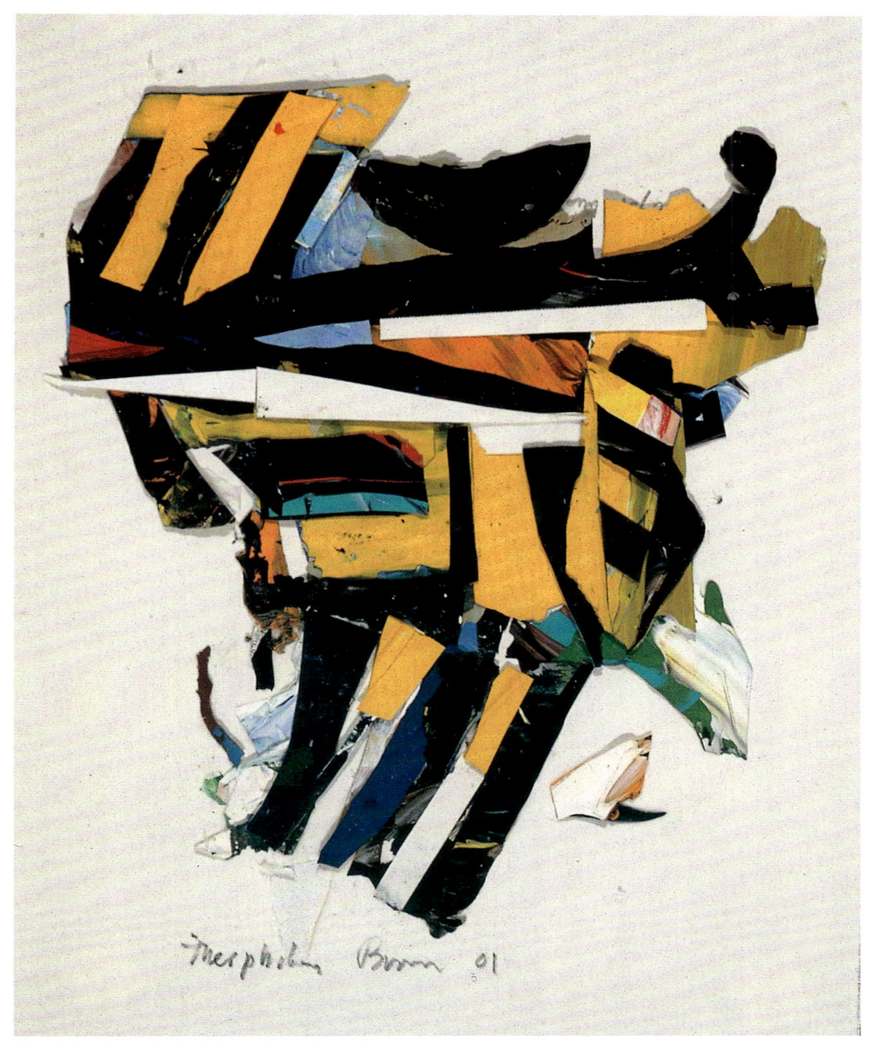

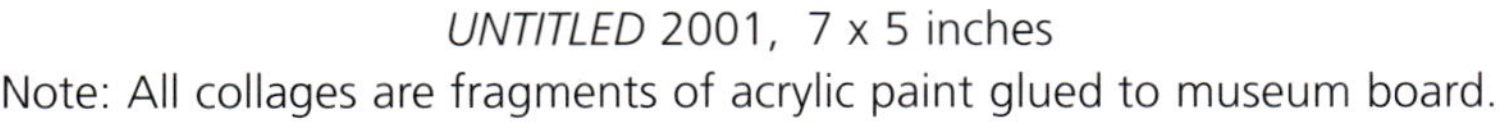

UNTITLED 2001, 7 x 5 inches
Note: All collages are fragments of acrylic paint glued to museum board.

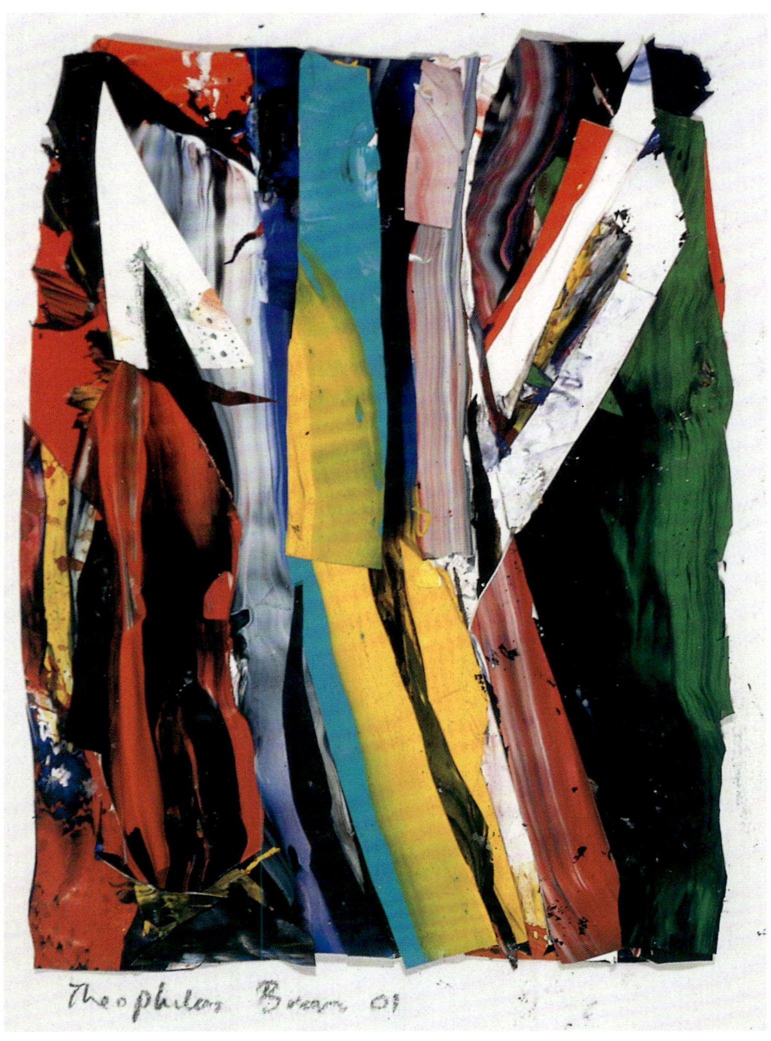

UNTITLED 2001, 11 x 8 1/4 inches
Collection of Mr. & Mrs. Ira Shrank, San Francisco

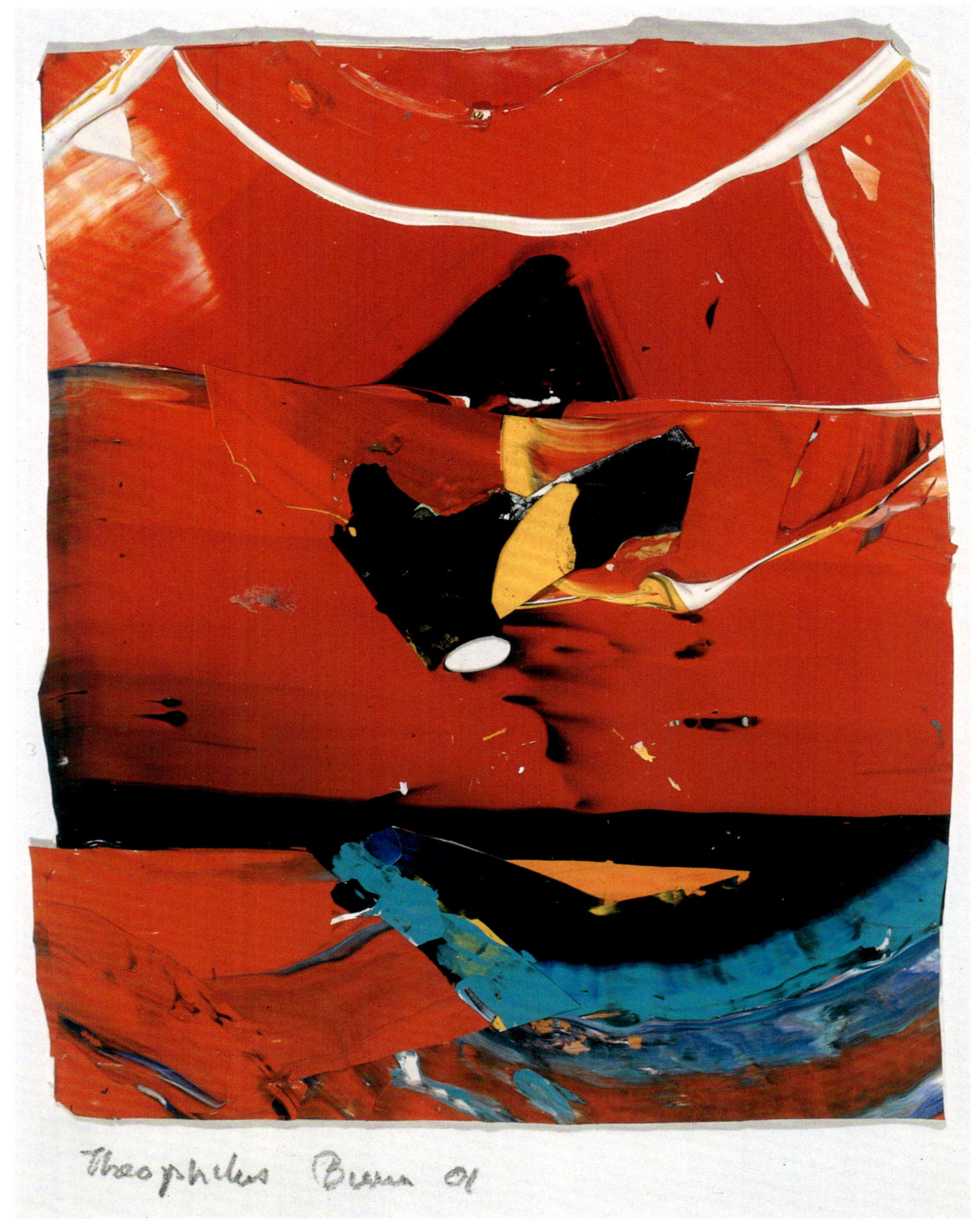

    UNTITLED 2001, 7 1/8 x 6 1/2 inches

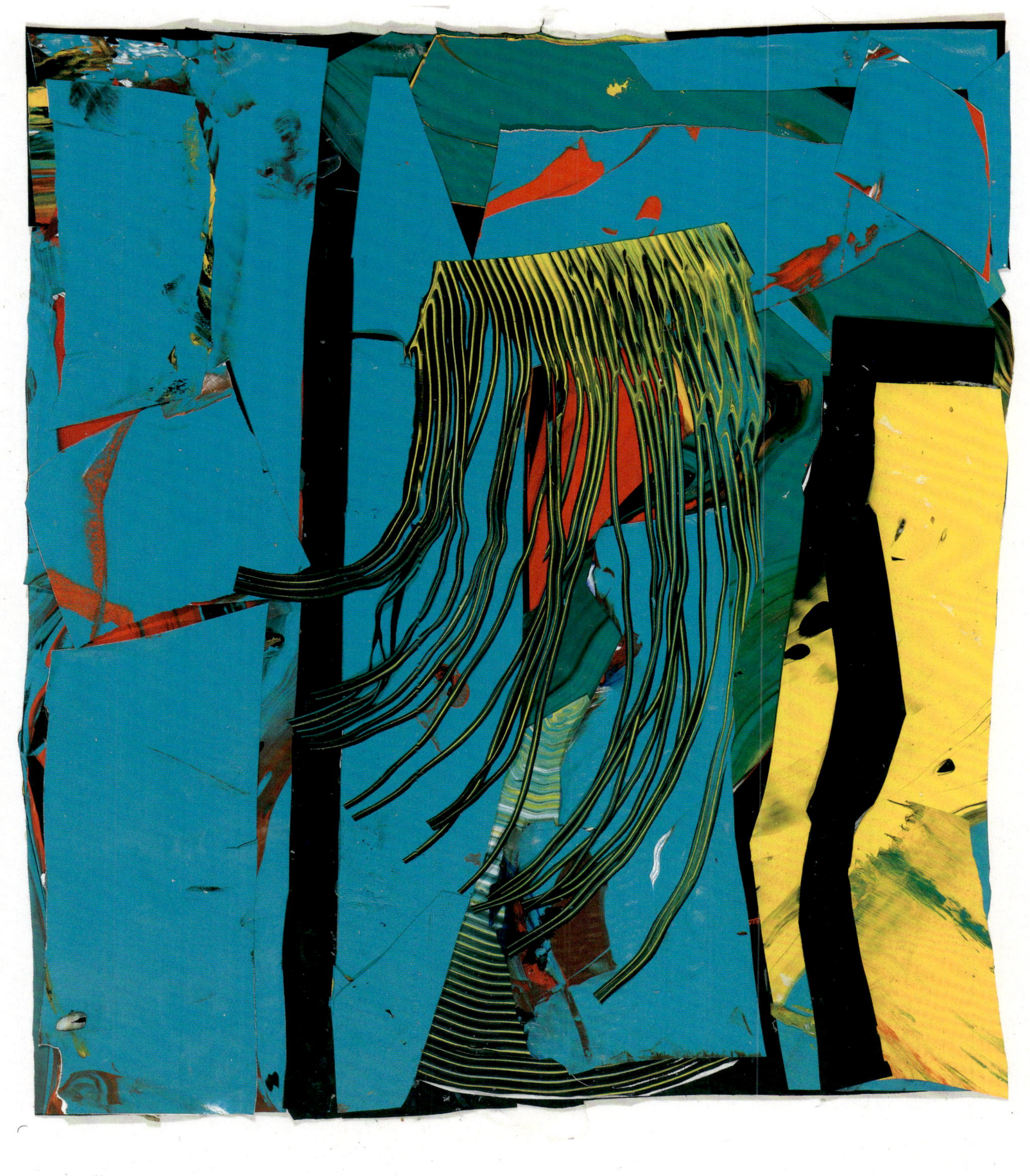

UNTITLED 2002, 7 1/8 x €3/4 inches. Elins Eagles-Smith Gallery, San Francisco

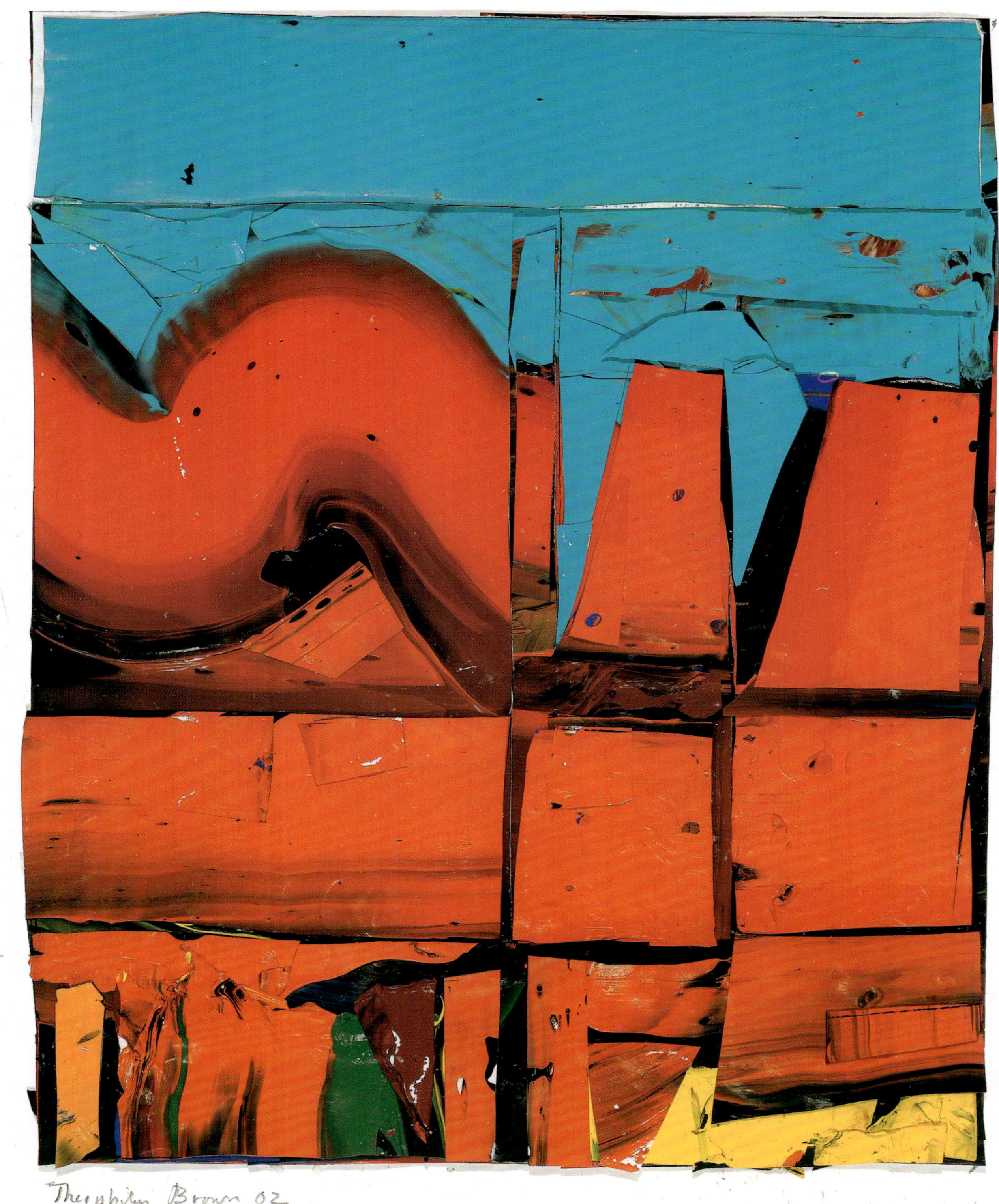

UNTITLED 2002, 10 x 8 inches

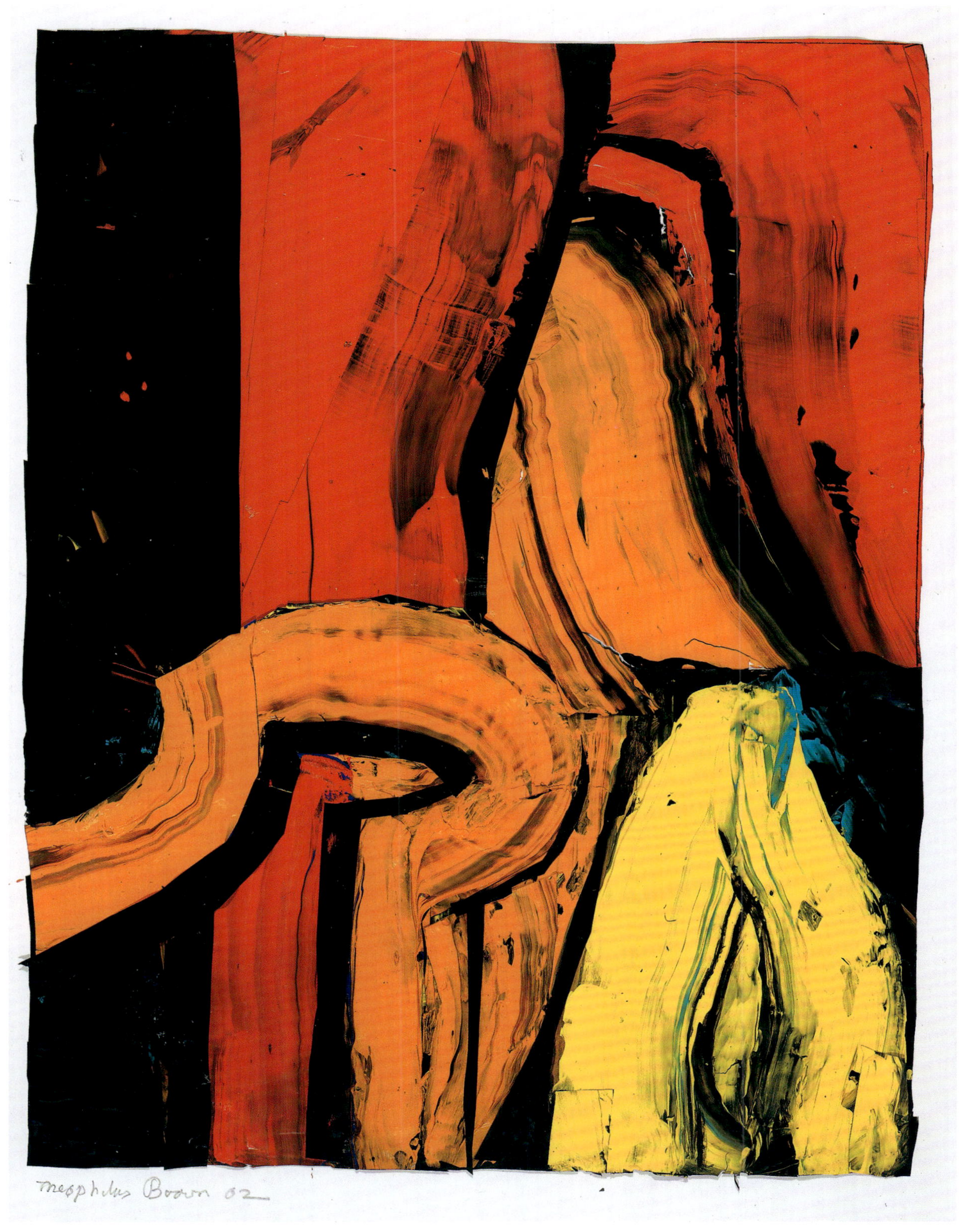

UNTITLED 2002, 13 x 10 inches. Private Collection

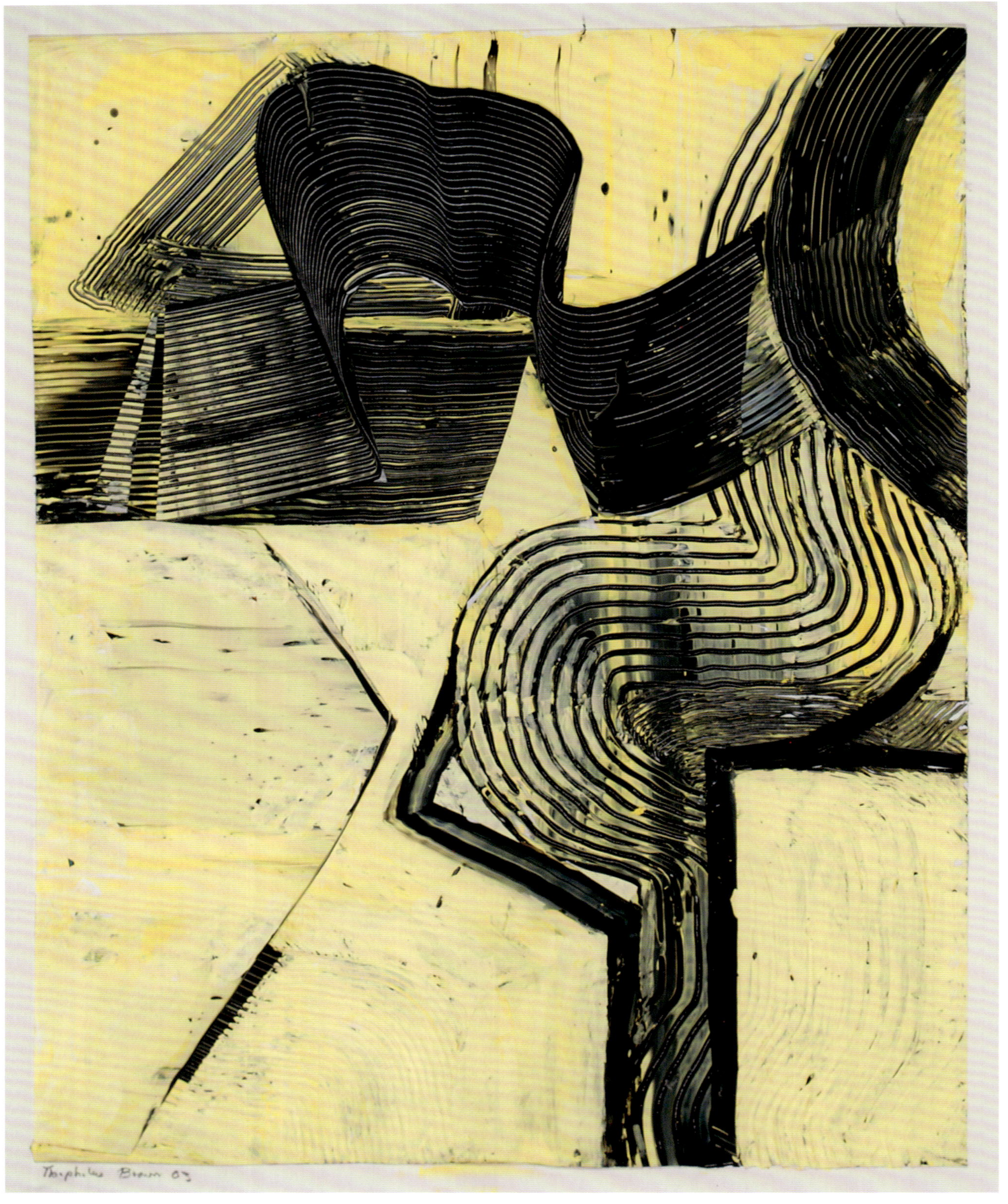

UNTITLED 2004, 20 x 18 inches. Elins Eagles-Smith Gallery, San Francisco

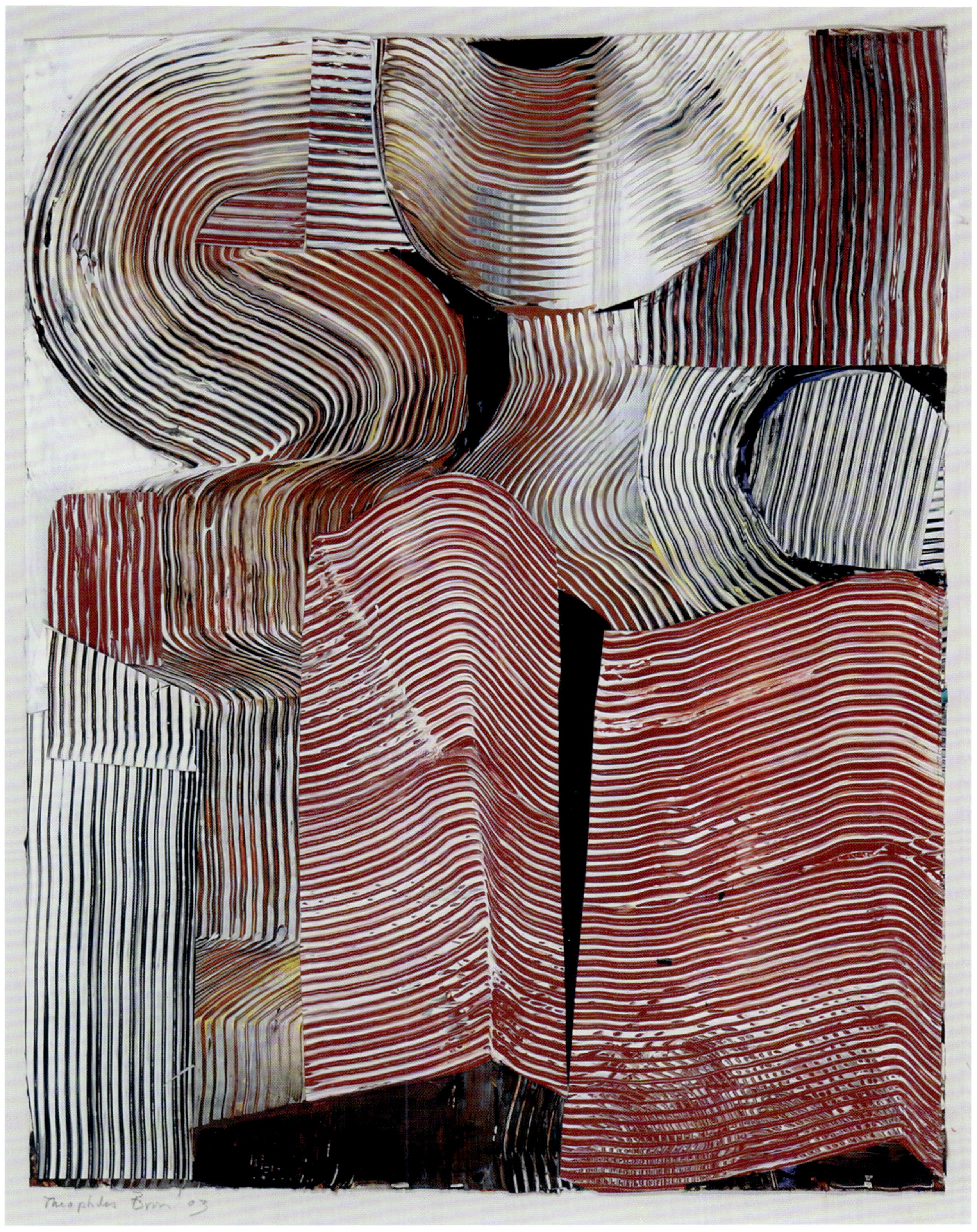

UNTITLED 2003, 15 1/2 x 12 inches. Elins Eagles-Smith Gallery, San Francisco

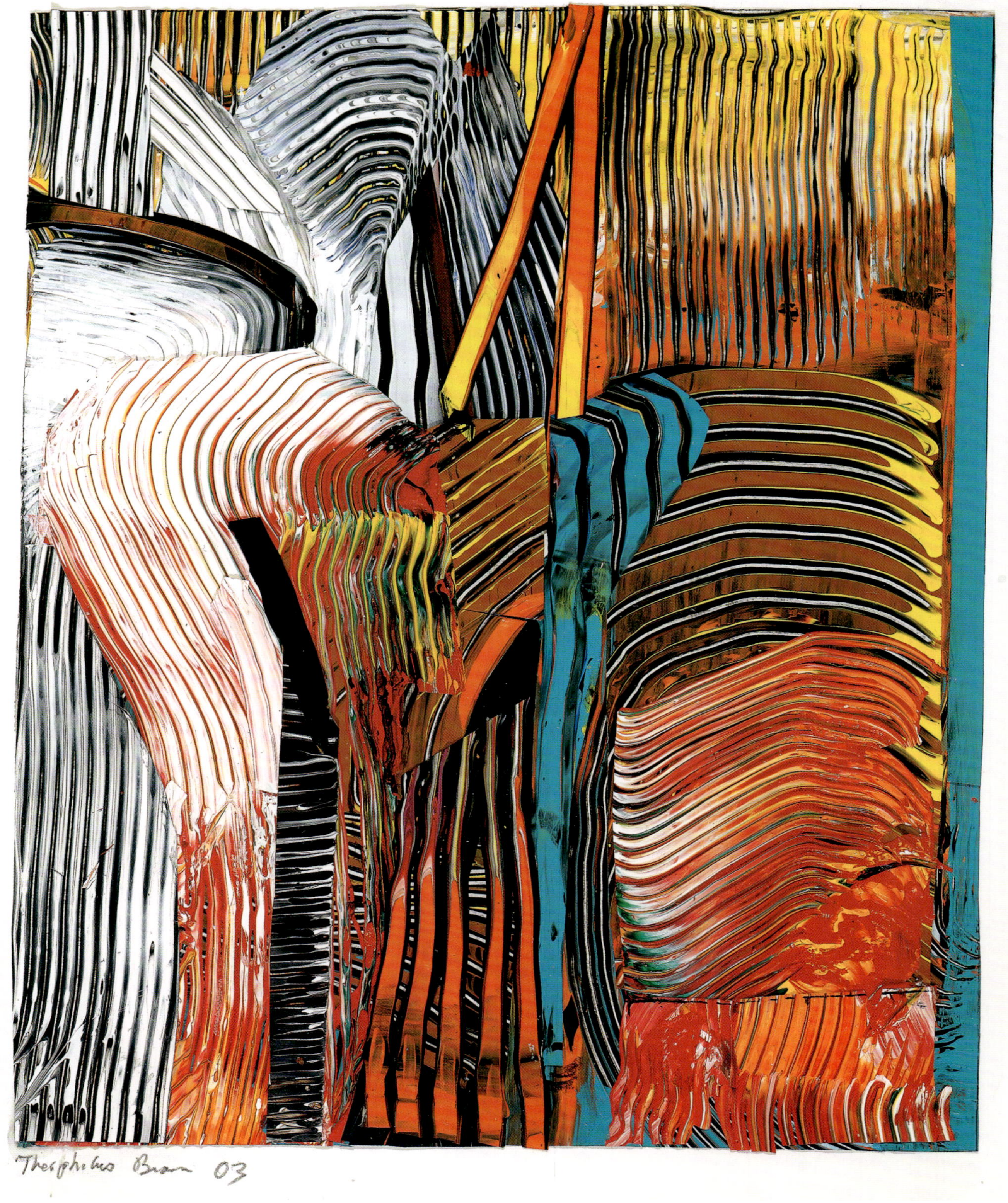

UNTITLED 2003, 19 3/4 by 15 3/4 inches. Collection of the Artist

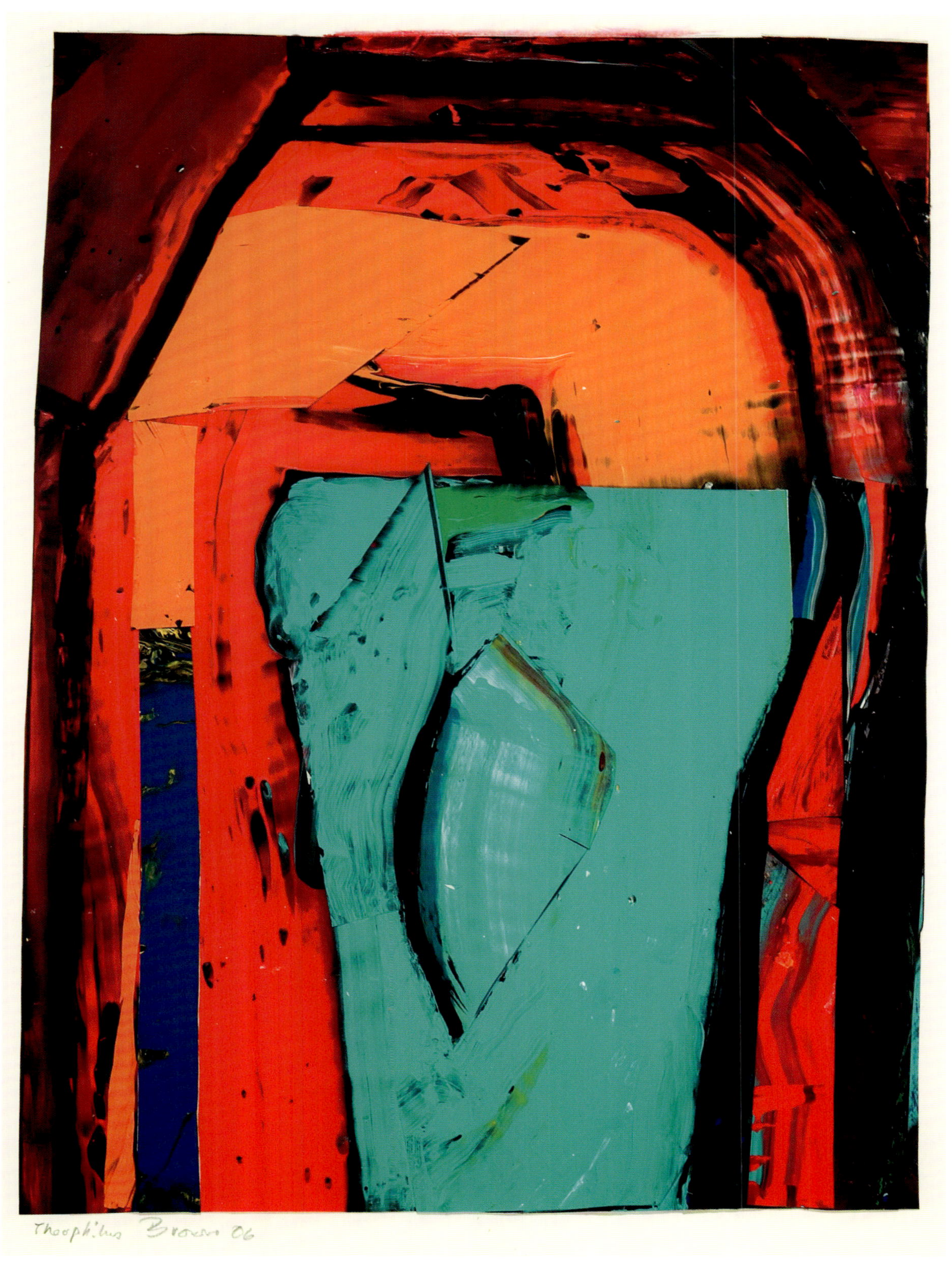

UNTITLED 2006, 11 x 8 inches. Collection of the Artist

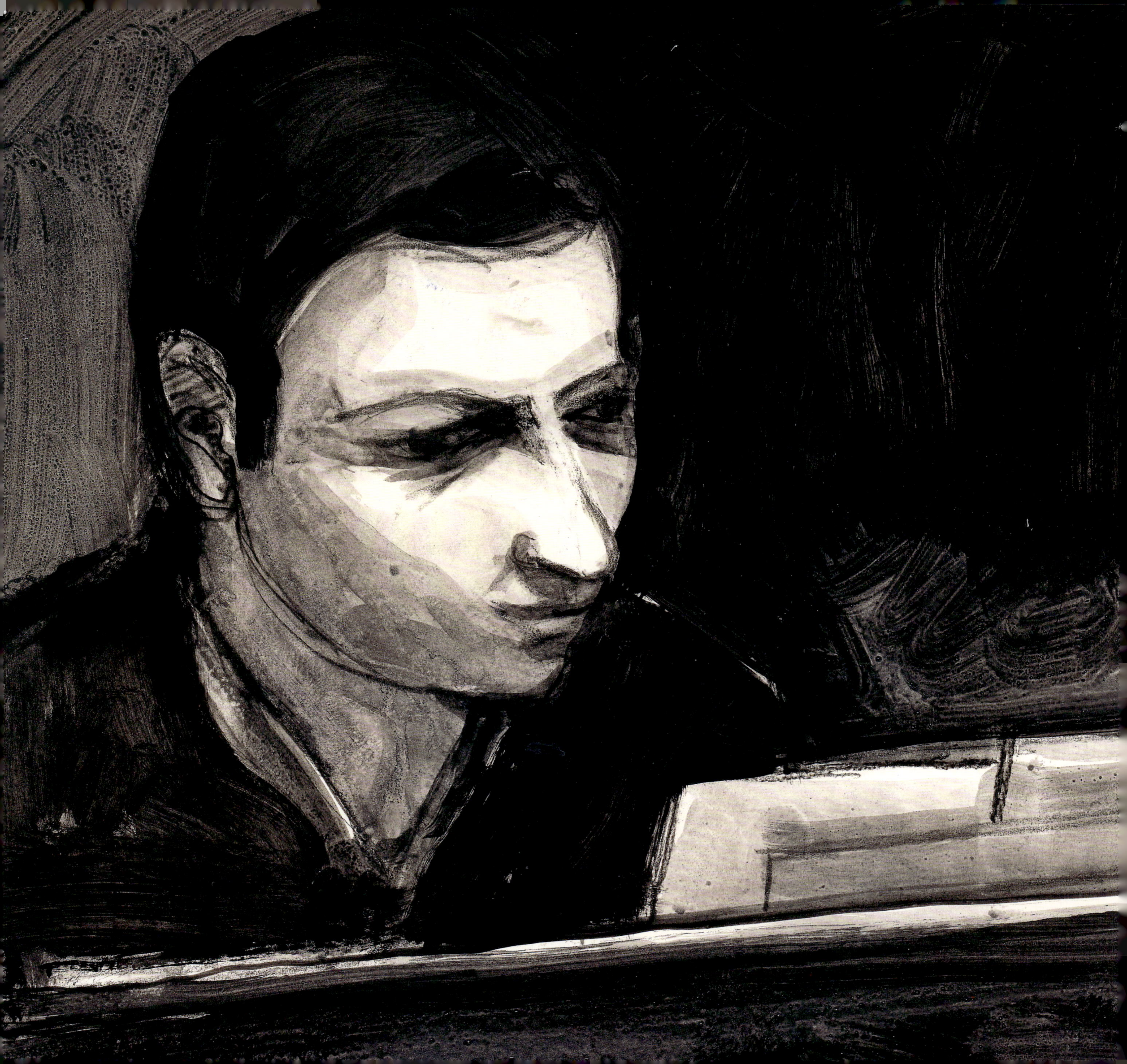

Drawings

The journey taken when making a drawing—unlike trips with known destinations—can take us, if we are lucky, to an unfamiliar, even a savage place. Armed with pencils, erasers, and a sheet of paper attached to a drawing board, we set out with optimism, even hopes. For there at the starting line, staring at the blank sheet of paper, we are still in the company of Rembrandt, Seurat or Degas. That blank sheet of paper with its seemingly limitless possibilities goads us on, like the carrot suspended before a donkey's nose. It scares us too.

—THEOPHILUS BROWN

THE ART OF DRAWING lies at the very center of Brown's work. Our belief in the veracity of his beach dwellers, figures, portraits, landscapes, and allegories—ranging from plein air sketches, figure studies, and metaphorical compositions—hinges on his ability to convince us of their truthfulness through this most basic act of observation and notation.

As a child William Theophilus Brown demonstrated a great precocity for both drawing and music. When he was twelve his father entered one of his drawings in a juried exhibition designated for adults only at the Davenport Museum of Art. The audience was quite surprised when Brown approached the podium to accept the drawing award from Grant Wood, who was then at the zenith of his career as an American Regionalist.

Upon entering Yale, Brown found that the school's art program held little appeal, so he switched his major to music and studied with the composer Paul Hindemith. During this period, he continued to draw and paint with a group of students, including Thomas Hess. Brown and Hess became close friends, with Hess playing an instrumental role in both Brown's career and his personal life. Over the years he introduced Brown to many influential American and European artists, from Marsden Hartley and Balthus to Willem and Elaine de Kooning.

During World War II, Brown served in the 99th Infantry Division's Signal Corps. Although he rarely discusses this period of his life, Brown took part in the Battle of the Bulge, from its first precarious days in the forest of Ardennes to its end. He crossed the bridge at Remagen, under fire and bombing runs by jet-powered planes—the first the Allies had seen in action. Taking the bridge was one of the most decisive events of the war, for it allowed the Americans to cross the Rhine and provided the Allies with their first foothold in Germany. Even

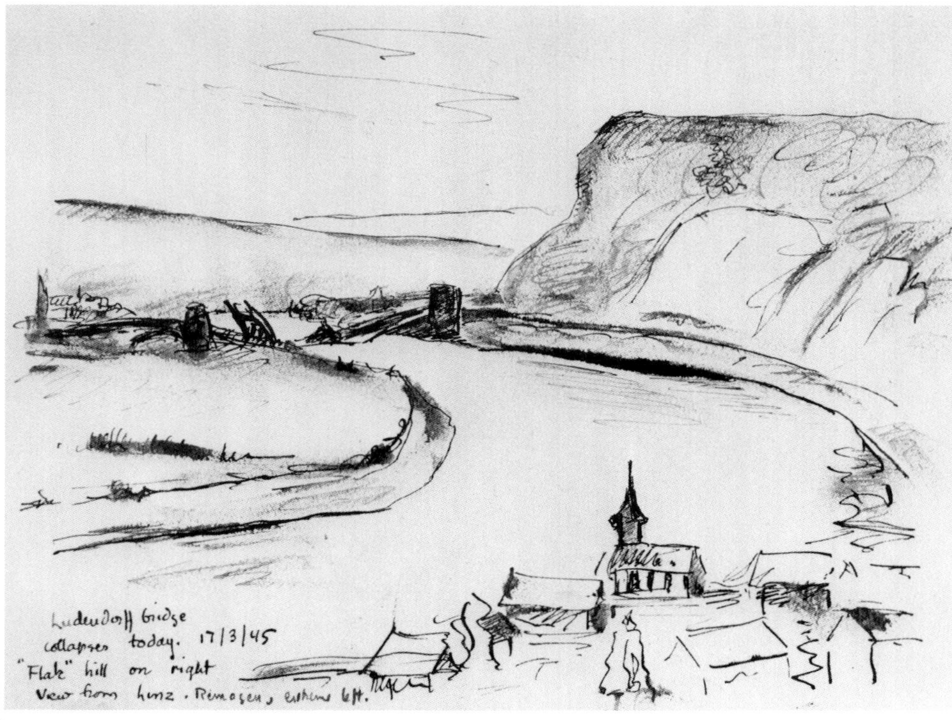

though the Americans had cut the wires to the Germans' explosives on the bridge, it was under continual attack by German artillery, grenades, and bombs, and it finally collapsed ten days after the crossing. Brown, like all of those fighting in the battle at Linz on the Rhine, was acutely aware of the monumental strategic importance of the bridge. Minutes after it crashed into the river he did a drawing to record and venerate the event. While all literature and art have autobiographical undertones and shadings, such a clear journalistic excursion is rare in Brown's work.

Brown's sketches and drawings are derived from a variety of sources and often follow the same themes as his paintings. His numerous figure studies provide the basis for his reveries of the beach and his commemorations of the painter's studio. Others celebrate a variety of erotic encounters, quirky incidents, and a rich assortment of allusive tales. The very act of drawing serves his voyeuristic and sensual delight through the process of watching and recording.

In his works on paper and in various paintings Brown has repeatedly displayed his great affection for an endless variety of creatures—the oddities of their forms, their traits, and their anthropomorphic behavior. There is a delightful procession of animals, from witty drawings of angry birds pursuing men, inexplicable appearances of elephants, and the perennial company of dogs.

These images are rendered with a variety of materials—pencil, charcoal, charcoal wash, stains of color, and washes of diluted acrylics—and vary from simple contour drawings to elaborate chiaroscuro compositions and richly colored paintings that recall the Indian miniatures he and Wonner collected. In addition, there is a handful of monotypes, etchings, and lithographs, but Brown's excursions in printmaking have been rare.

Regardless of the medium, Brown's works on paper serve as wonderful exemplars of Van Gogh's statement, "Drawing is everything."

Theophilus Brown has not only drawn and painted his friends, he has also sat for their drawings and paintings (pp. 138–139). The small studies by Diebenkorn and Park resulted from a day the model failed to show up, so they took turns sitting for each other. The Diebenkorn drawing is dated 1958, which was the year he gave it to Brown. There are remarkable portraits of Brown and Wonner by Don Bachardy that date from their years in Santa Monica and Malibu. While the Wonner gouache is a specific and recognizable portrait, Brown has also appeared in various paintings by Wonner.

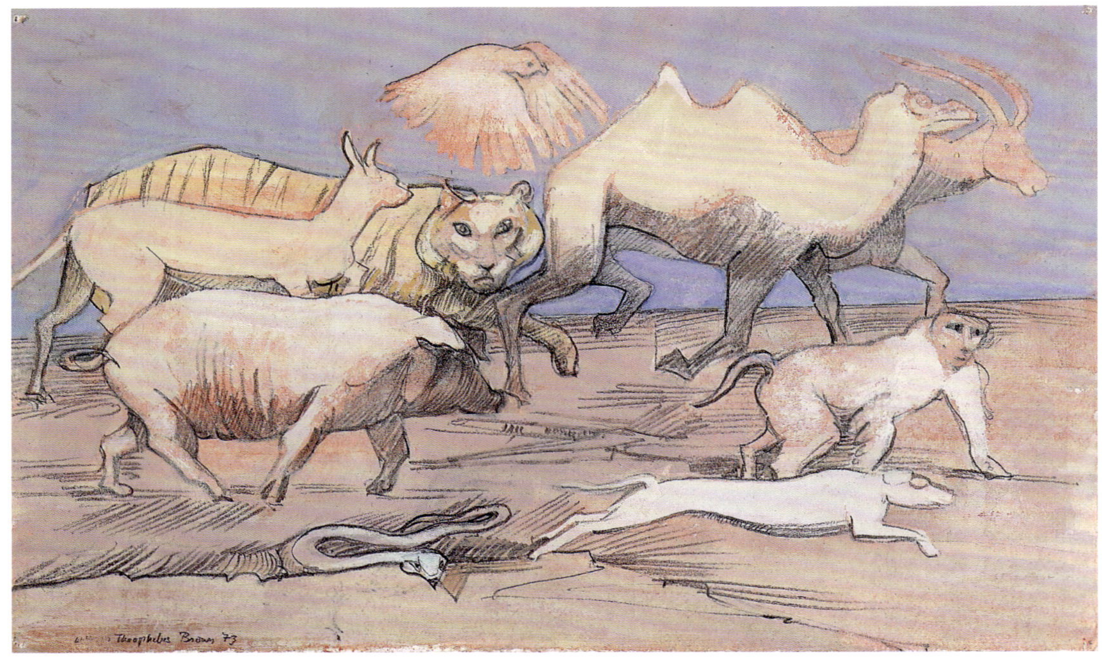

PEACEABLE KINGDOM 1973, pencil and casein on paper, 6¾ x 11 inches. Collection of Paul Wonner

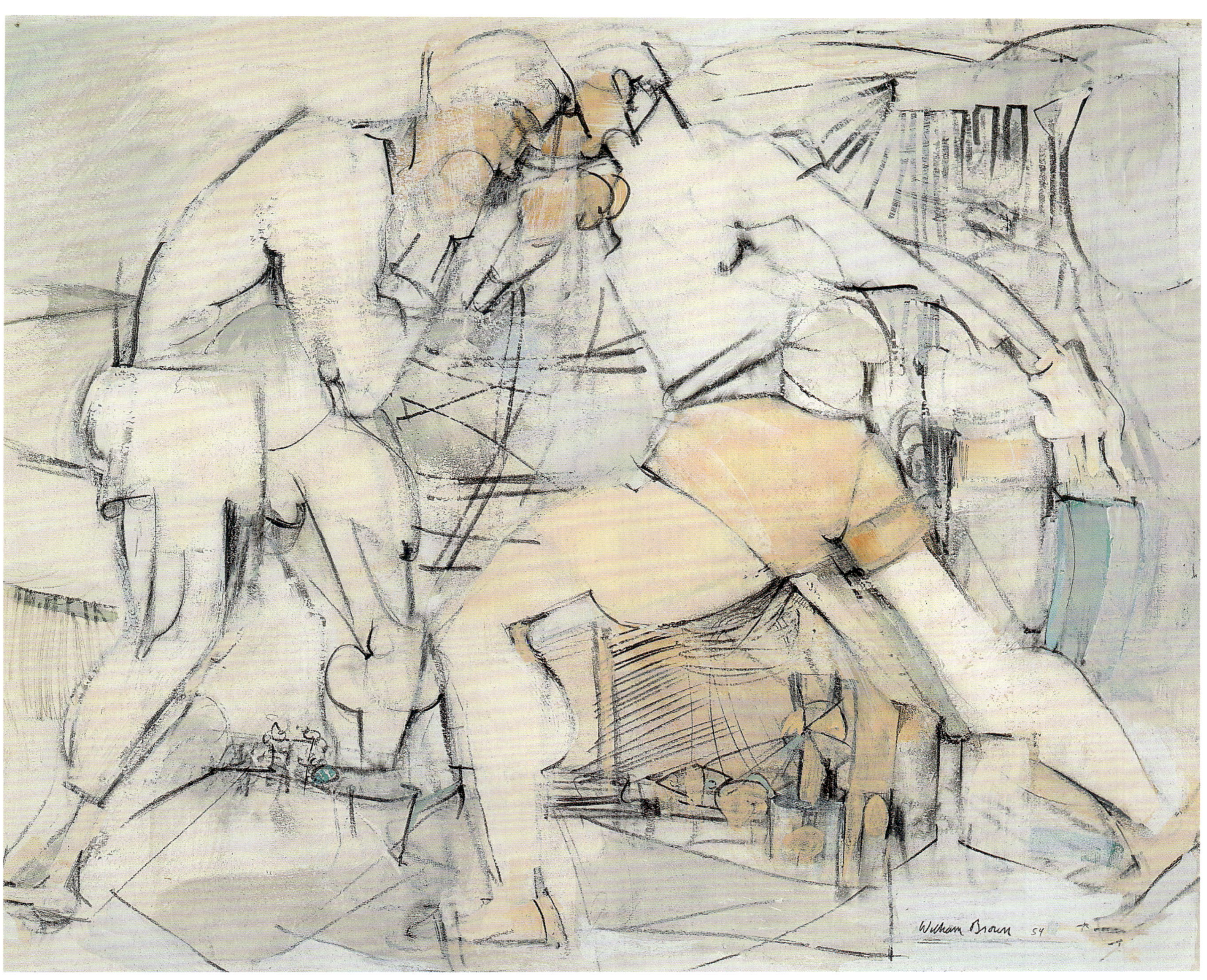

BOXERS 1952, pencil and casein on paper, 10½ x 11¾ inches. Collection of the Artist

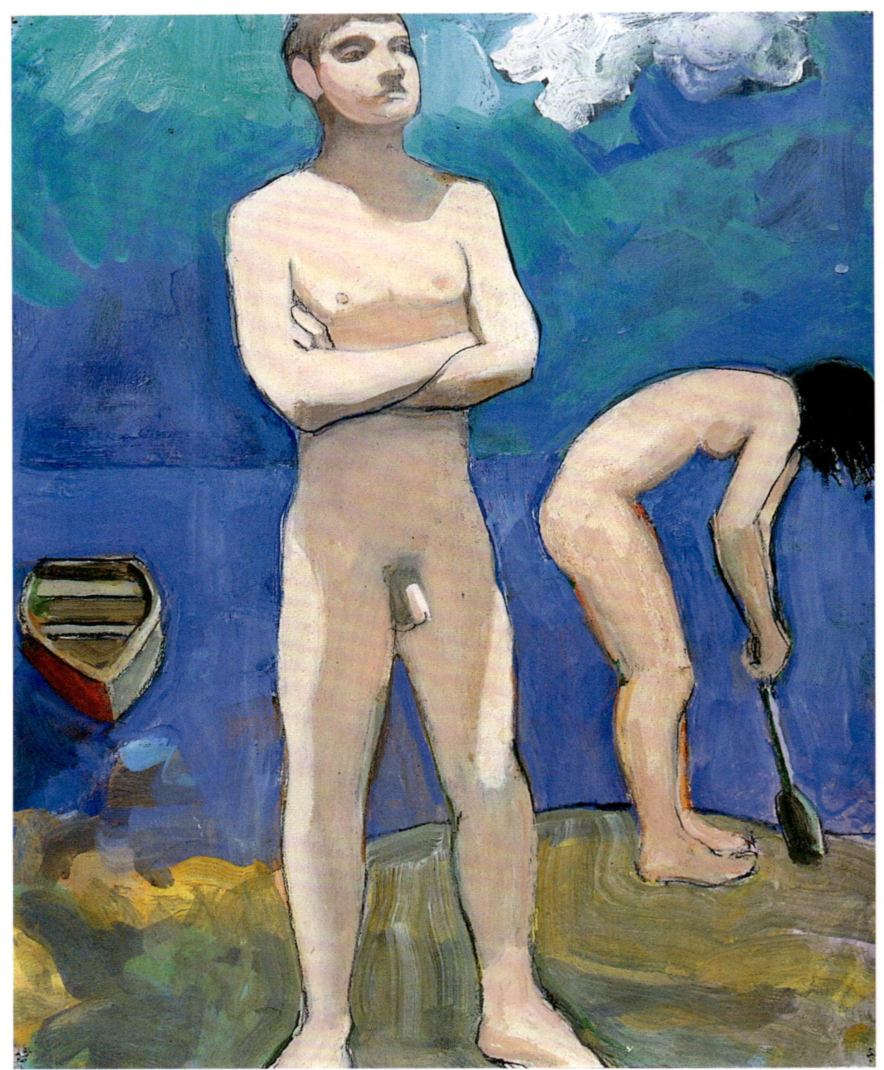 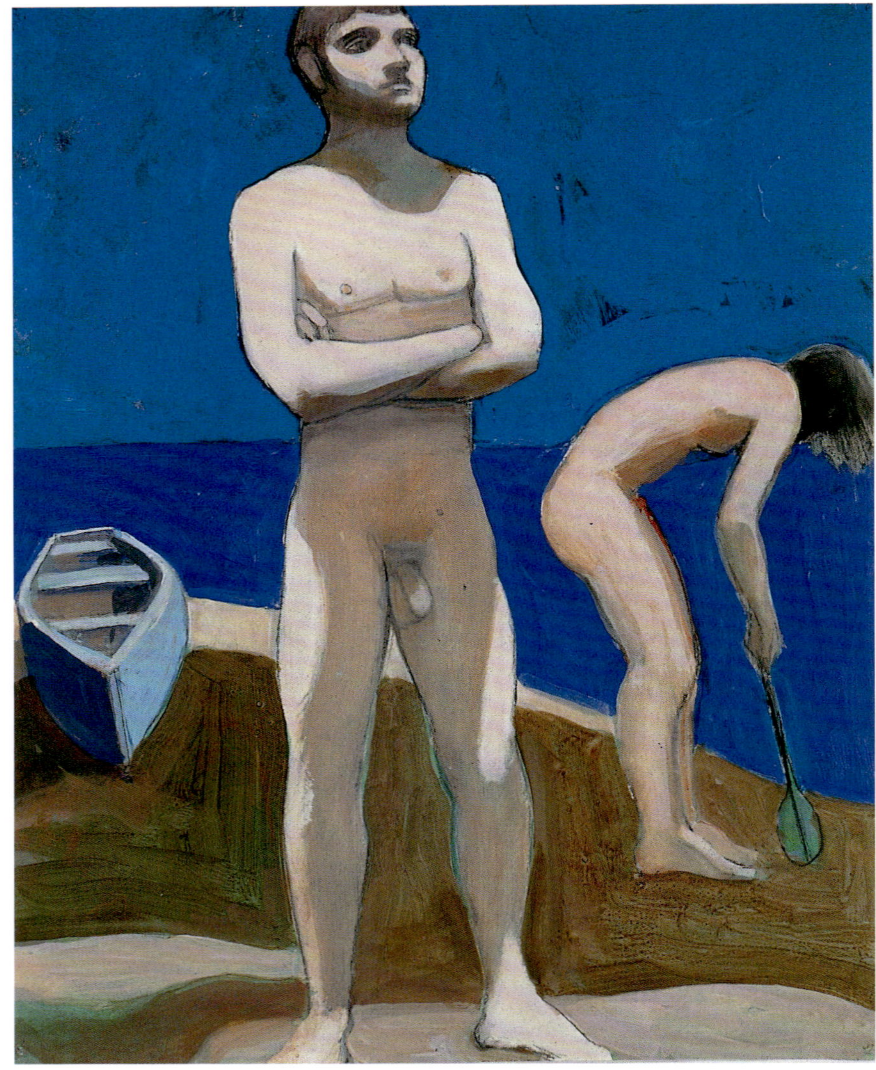

As has been mentioned earlier, Theophilus Brown often reworks his earlier paintings and drawings. This particular study of two nudes on a beach provides a few clues to his process of continual adjustments. Brown's modifications of the figures and the boat are subtle, but changes made to the foreground, water's edge, and sky are quite noticeable. It is an act of continual refinements.

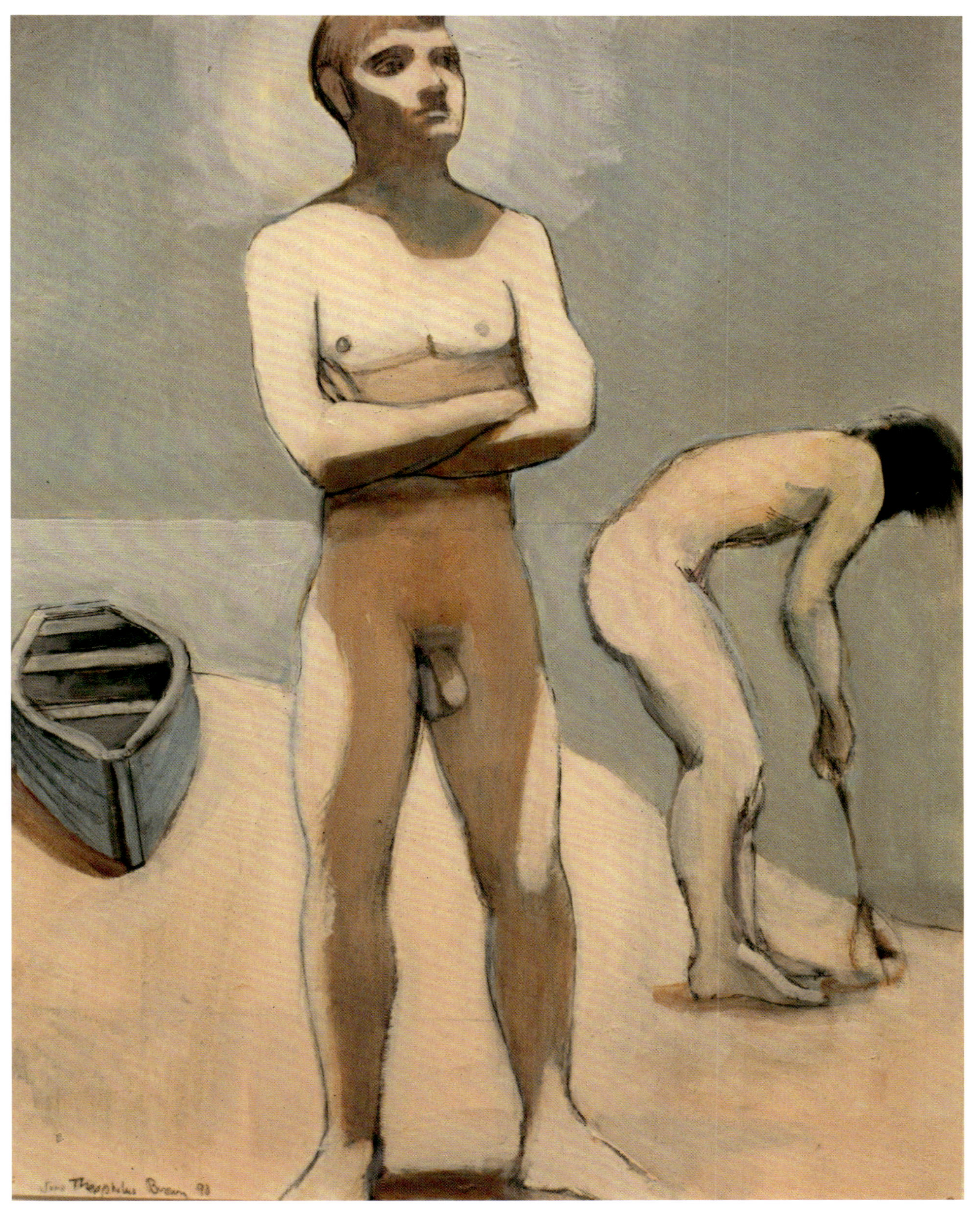

UNTITLED 1990, pencil and acrylic on paper, 11 1/2 x 14 1/2 inches. Collection of Ruth Gottlieb

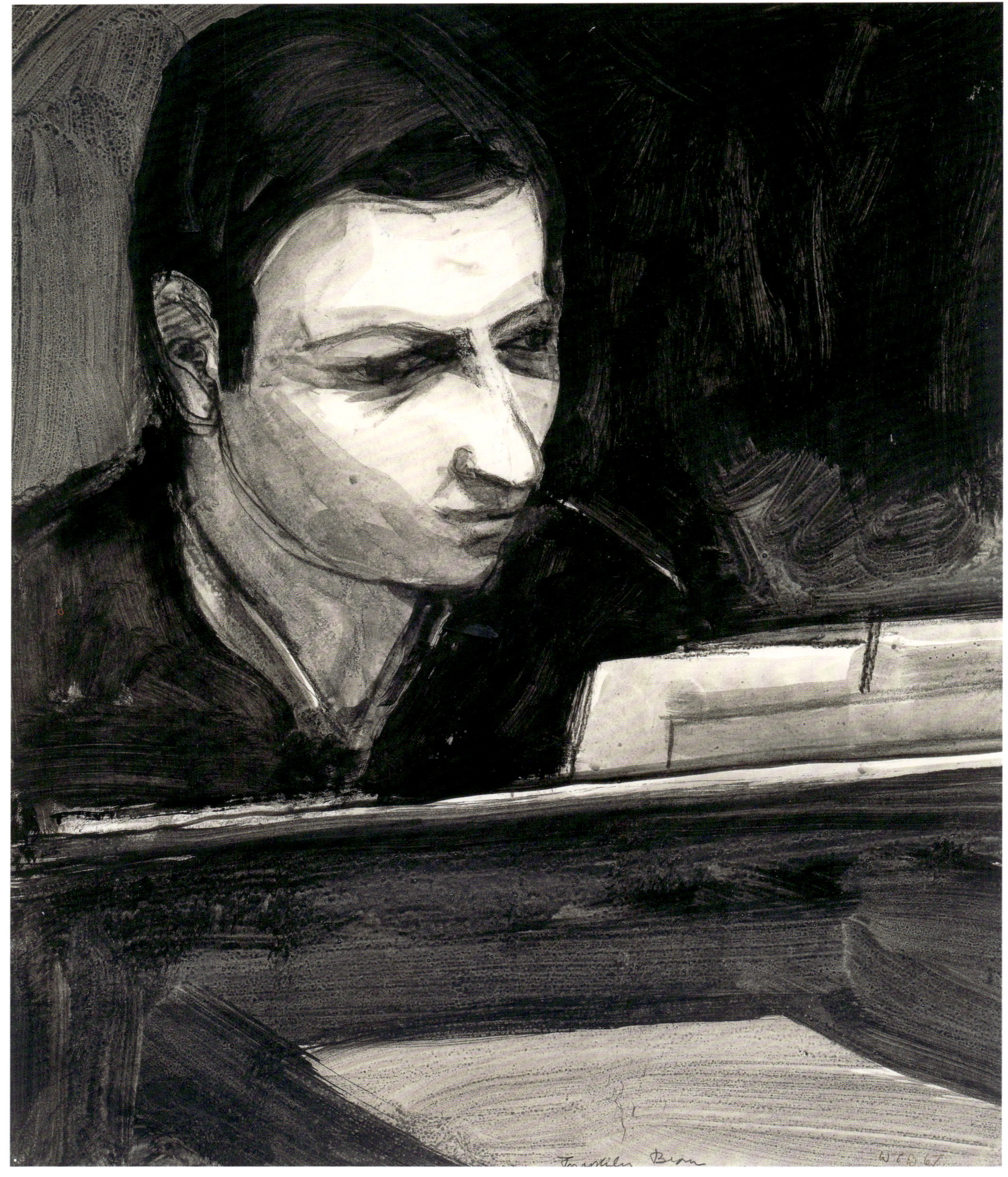

ANDRE PREVIN 1967, charcoal, pencil, and wash on paper, 17 x 14 inches. Collection of John Modell, San Francisco

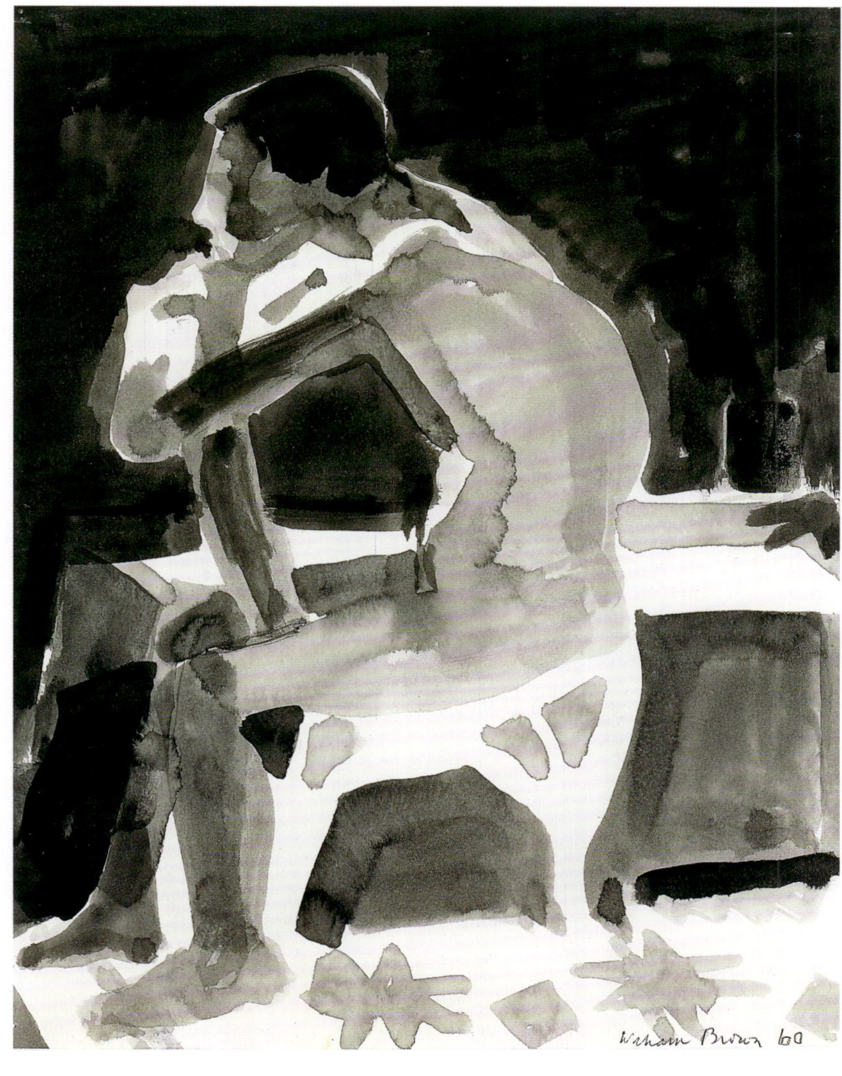

UNTITLED 1960, ink on paper, 11 x 8 1/2 inches. Private Collection

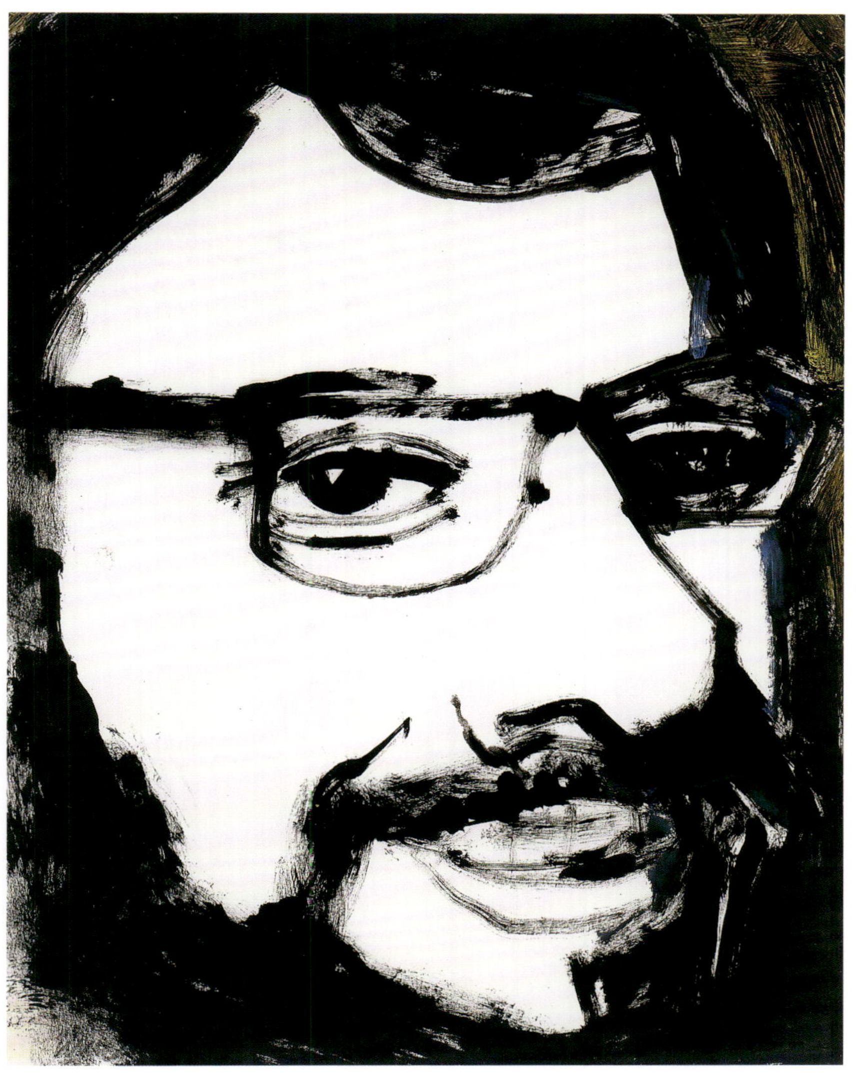

ALLAN GINSBERG 1961, brush and ink on paper, 11 x 8 1/2 inches. Private Collection

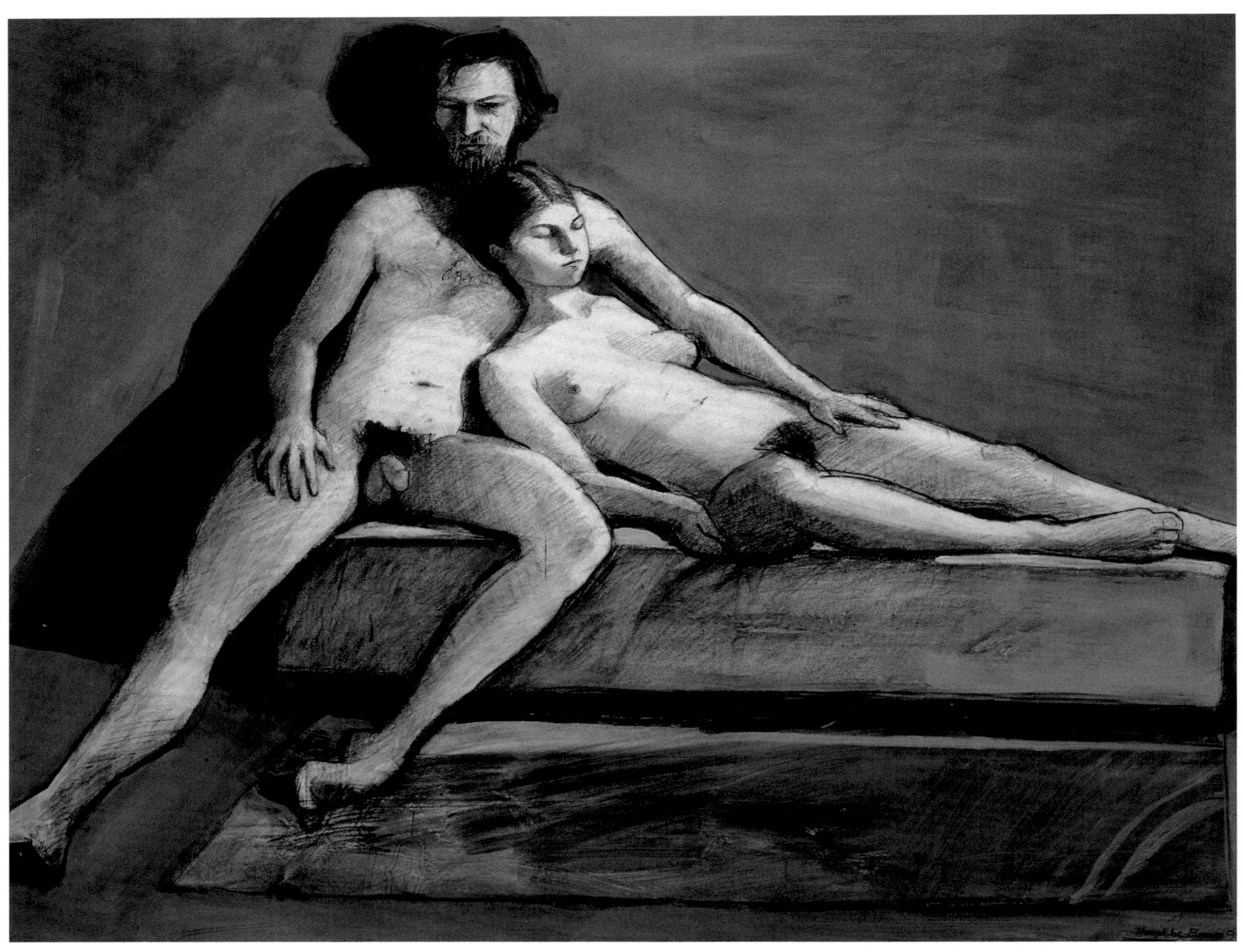

 UNTITLED 1990, charcoal and acrylic on paper, 22 x 28 inches. Collection of the Artist

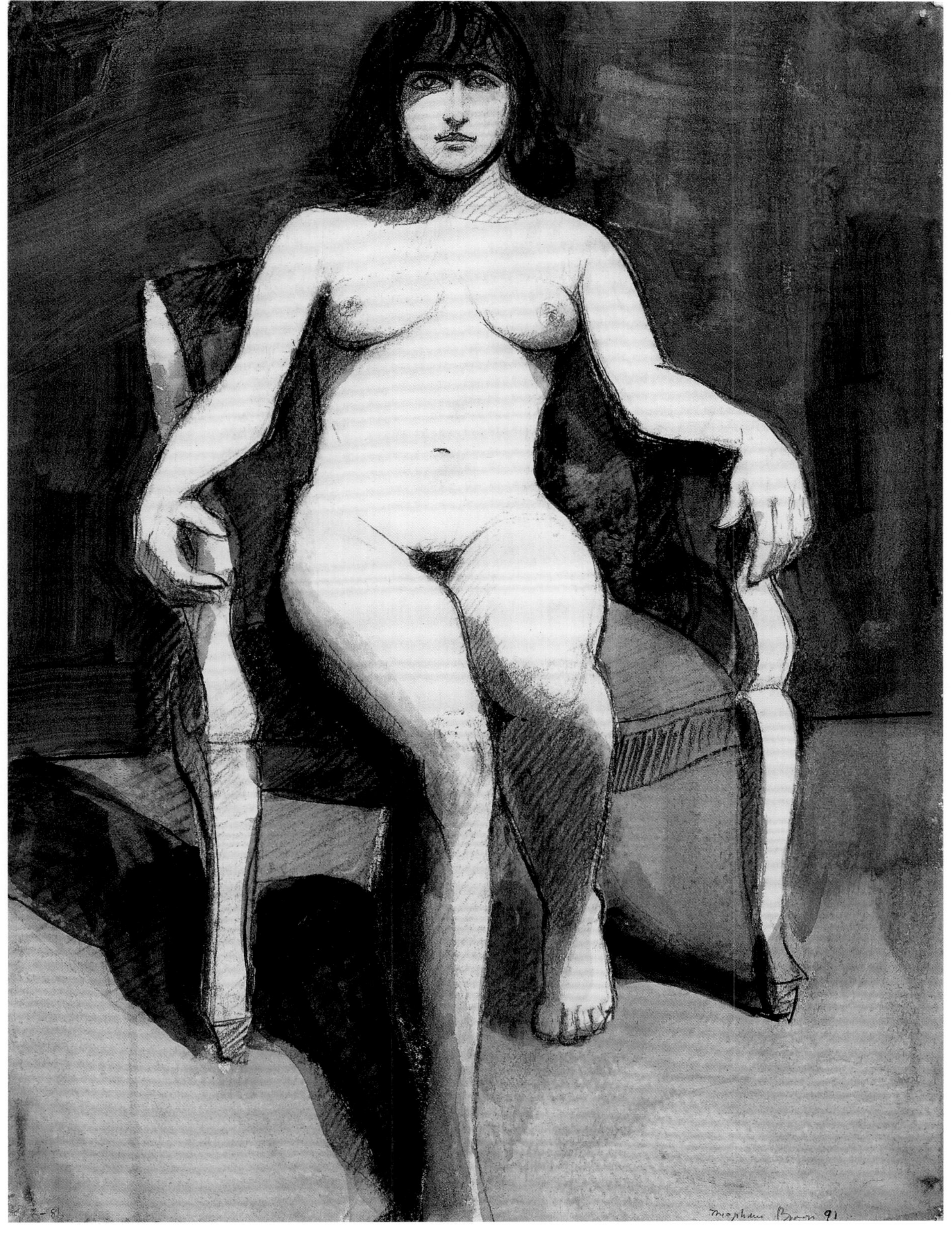

SEATED WOMAN 1991, pencil and ink on paper, 15 x 11 inches. Collection of Bill Scott, Philadelphia

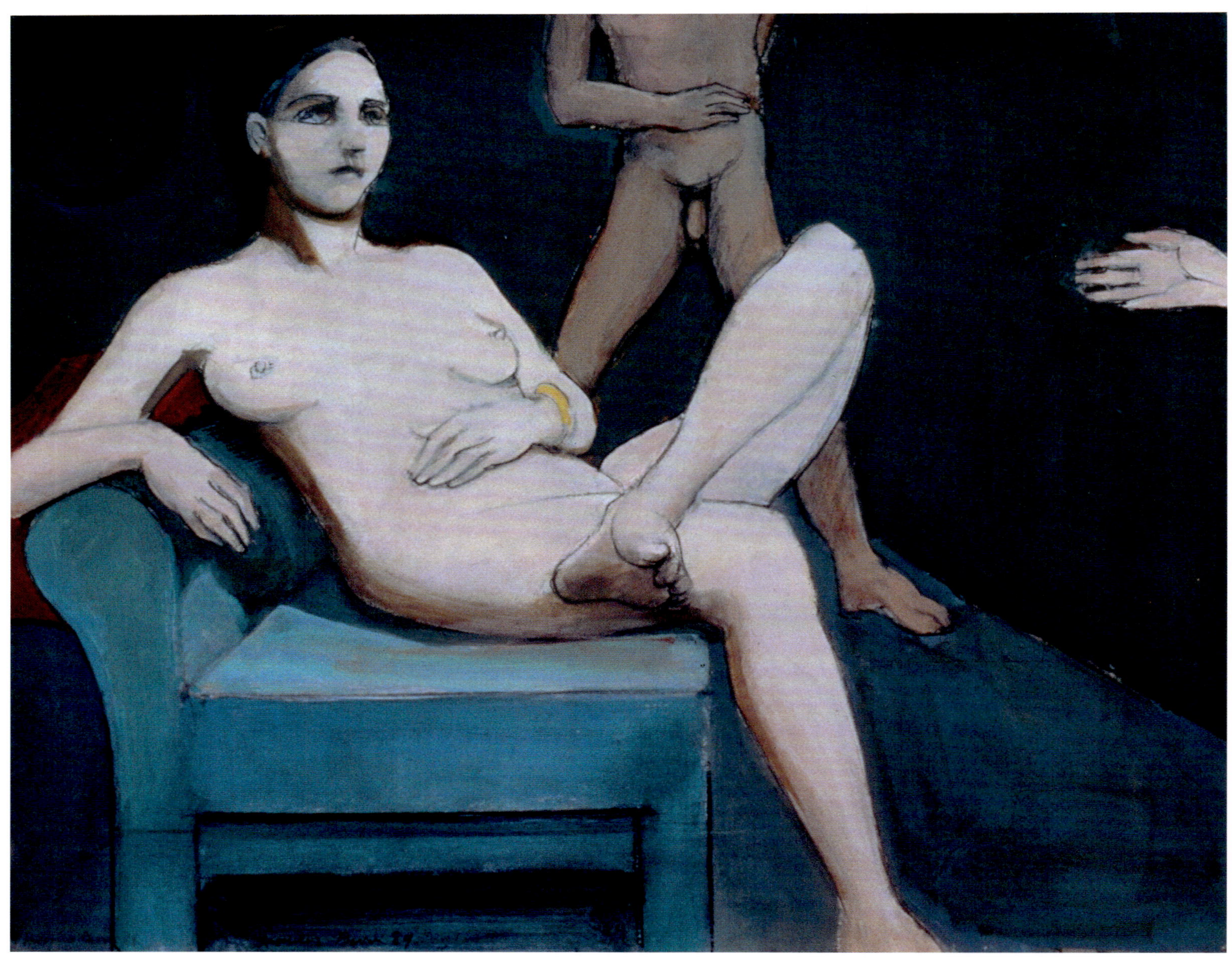

UNTITLED 1982, acrylic on board, 20 x 24 inches. Private Collection

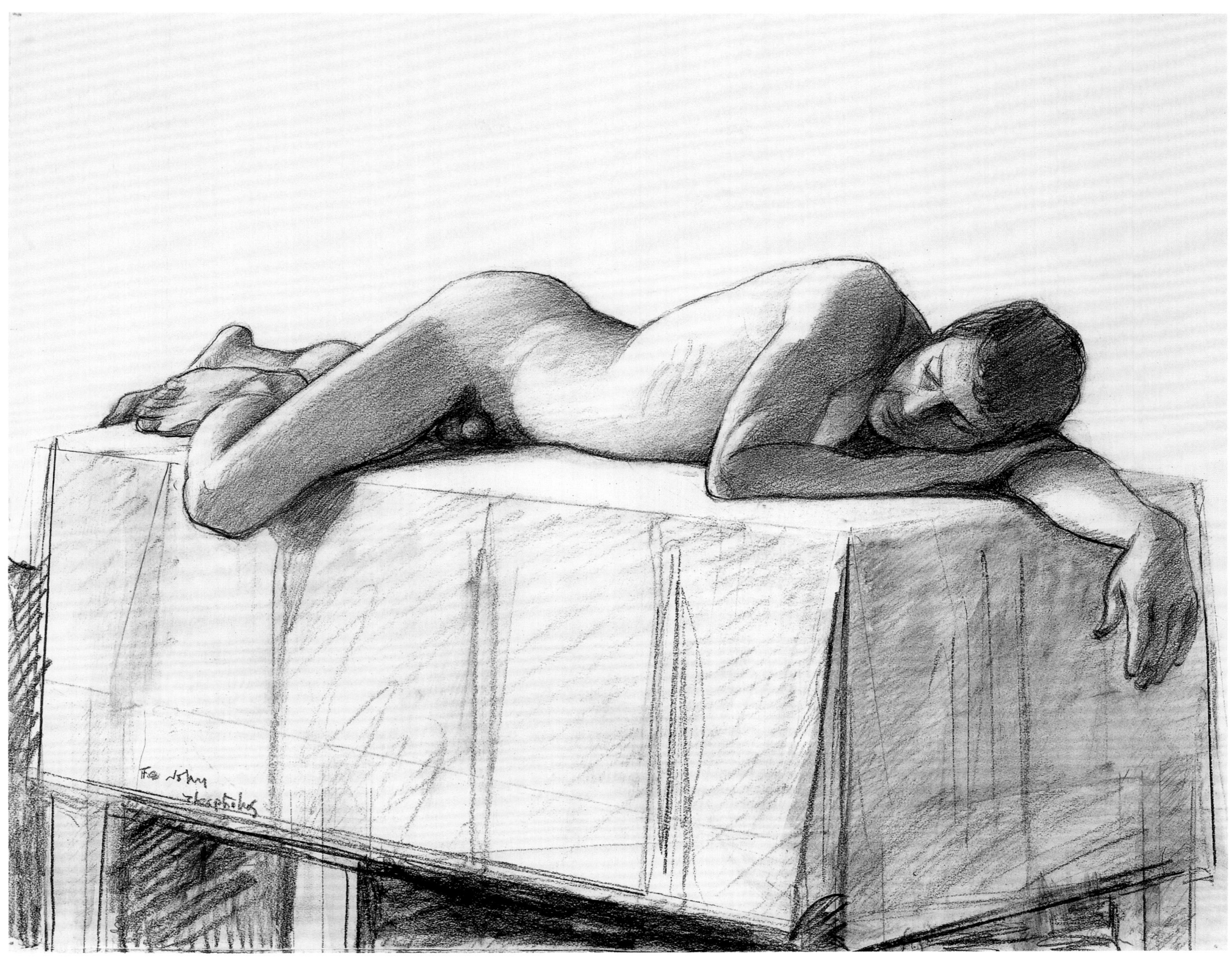

UNTITLED c. 1980, pencil and charcoal on paper, 11 1/2 x 14 1/2 inches. Private Collection

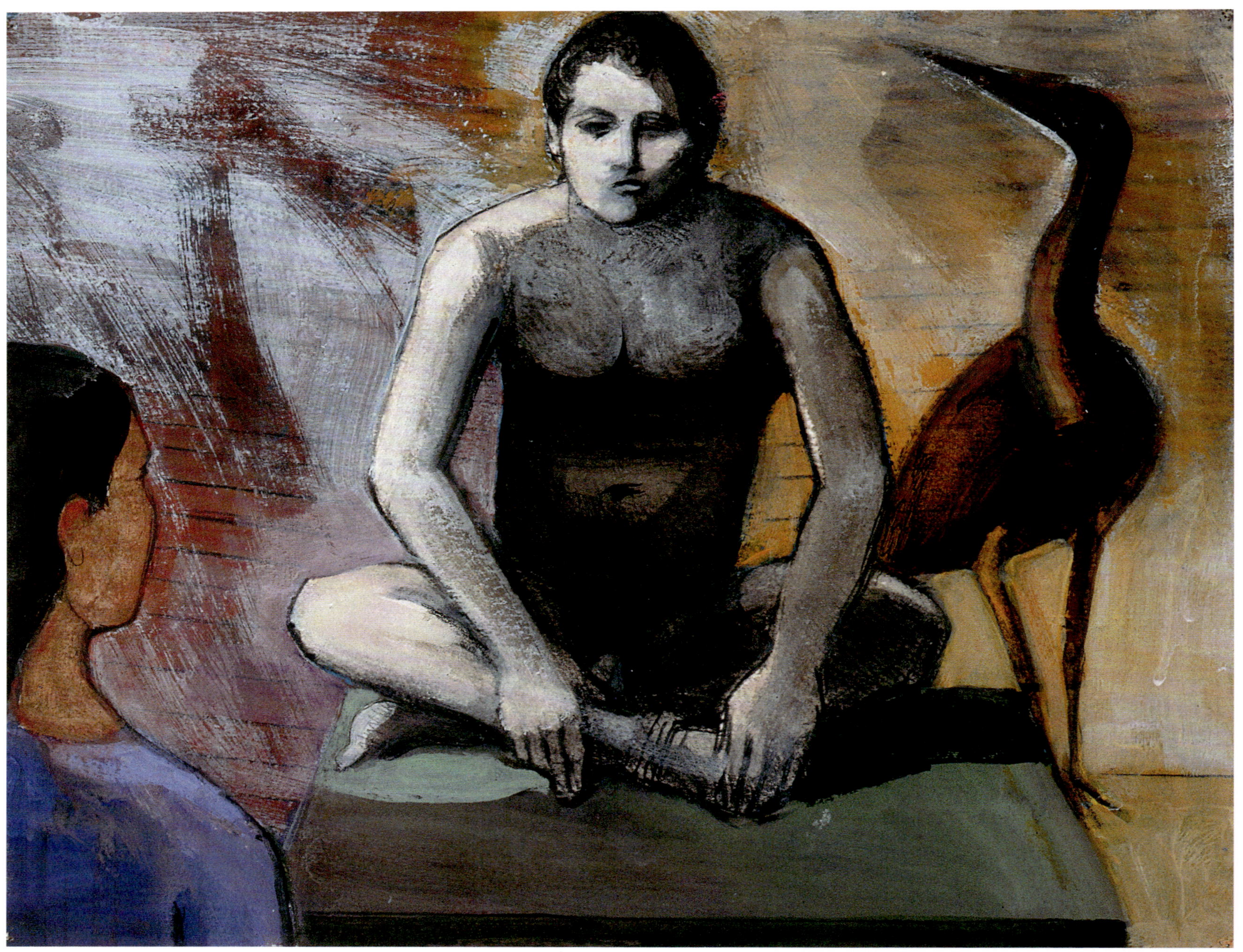

134 *UNTITLED* 1981, acrylic and charcoal on paper, 14 x 17 inches

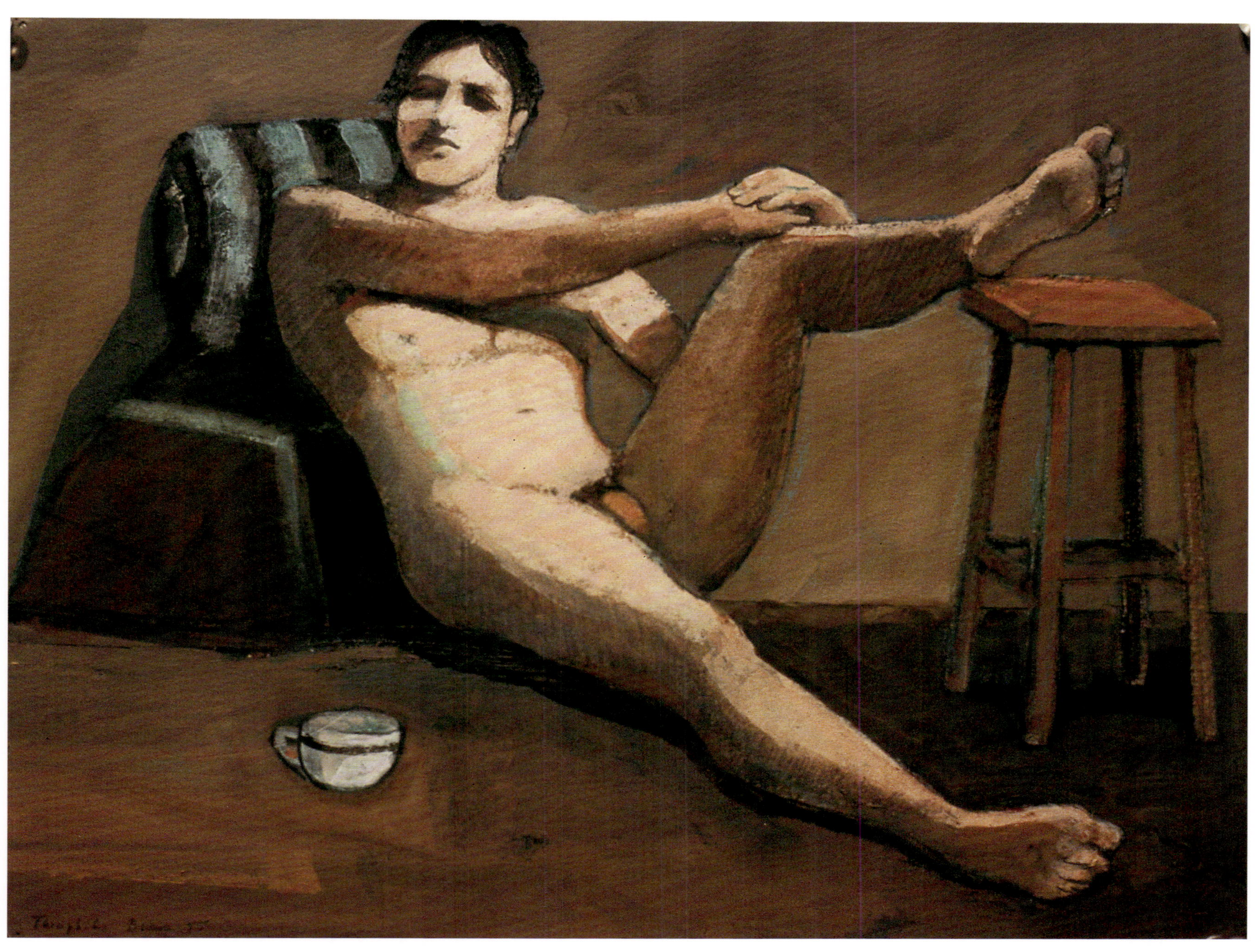

MALE FIGURE, LEG UP 1995, acrylic and charcoal on paper, 11 1/2 x 15 inches

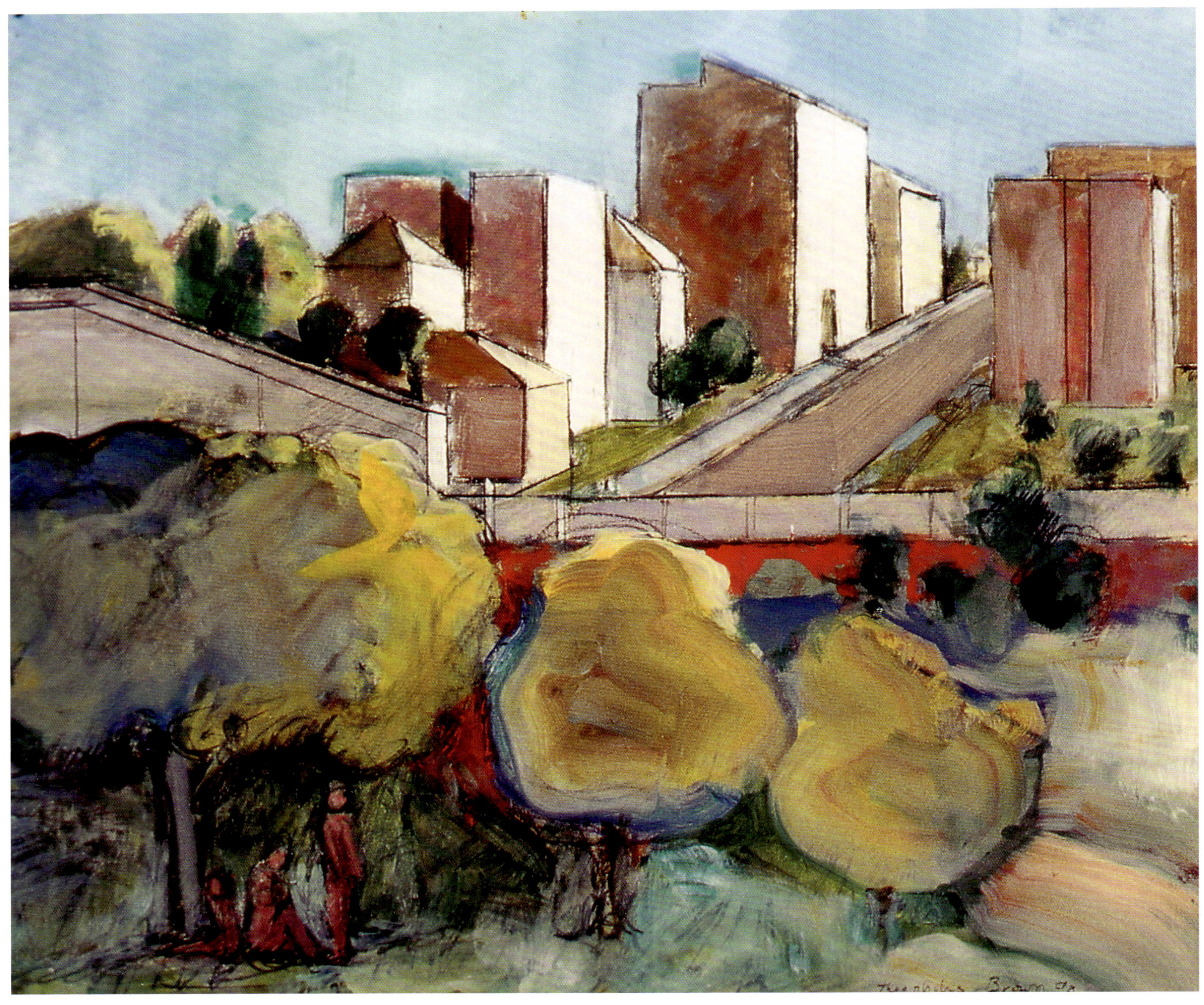

 UNTITLED 1990, pencil and acrylic on paper, 11 1/2 x 14 1/4 inches. Private Collection

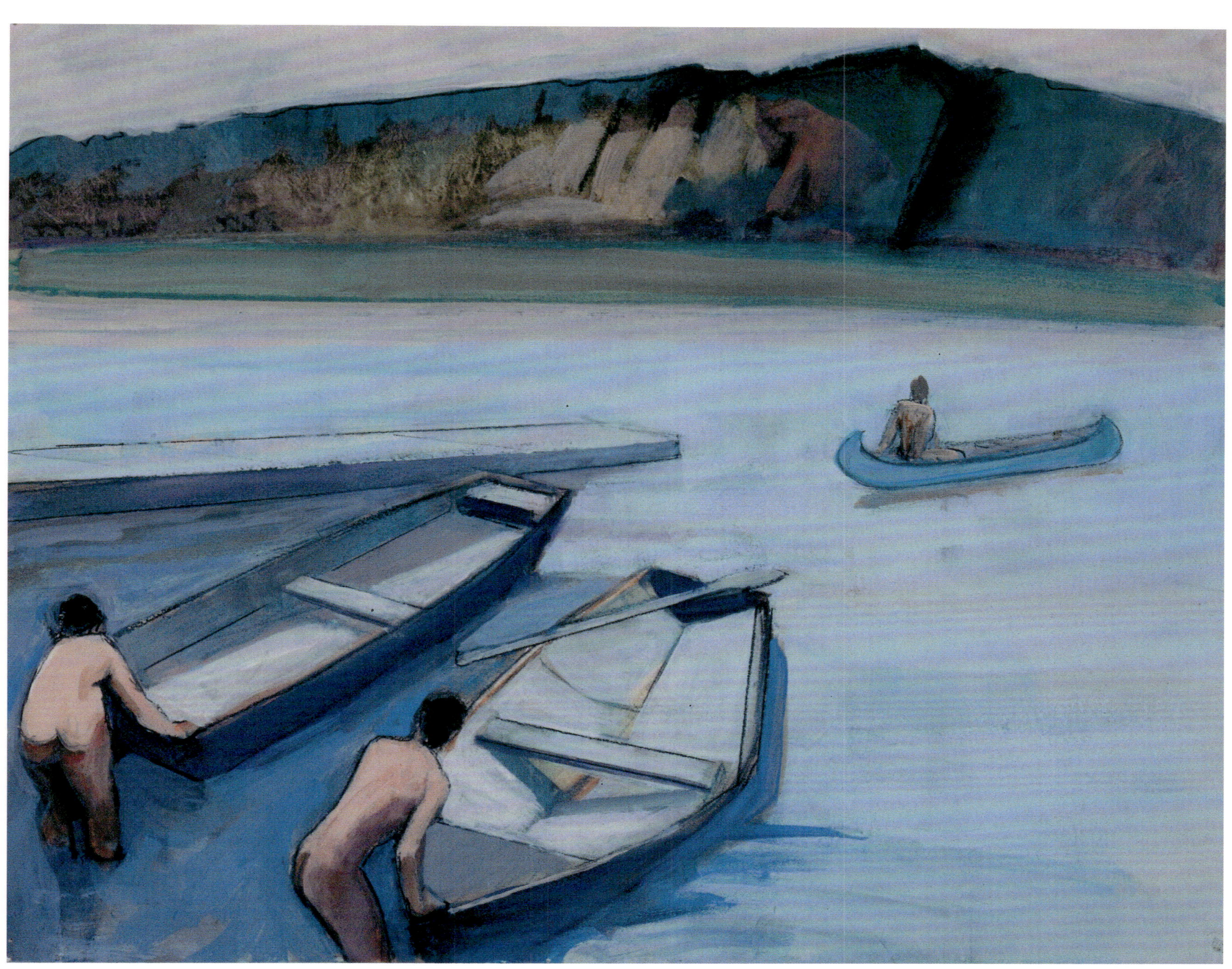

UNTITLED 1991, charcoal and acrylic on paper, 141/2 x 17 inches. Private Collection

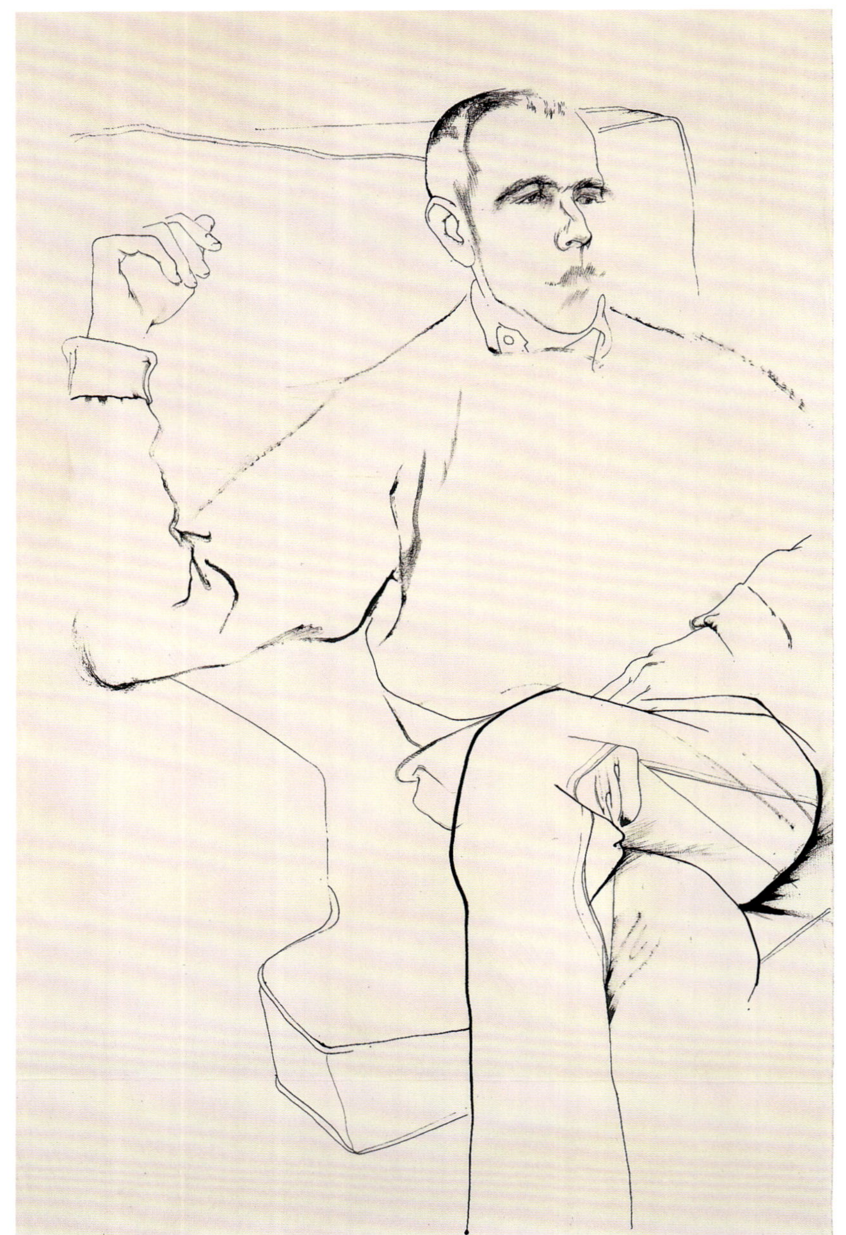

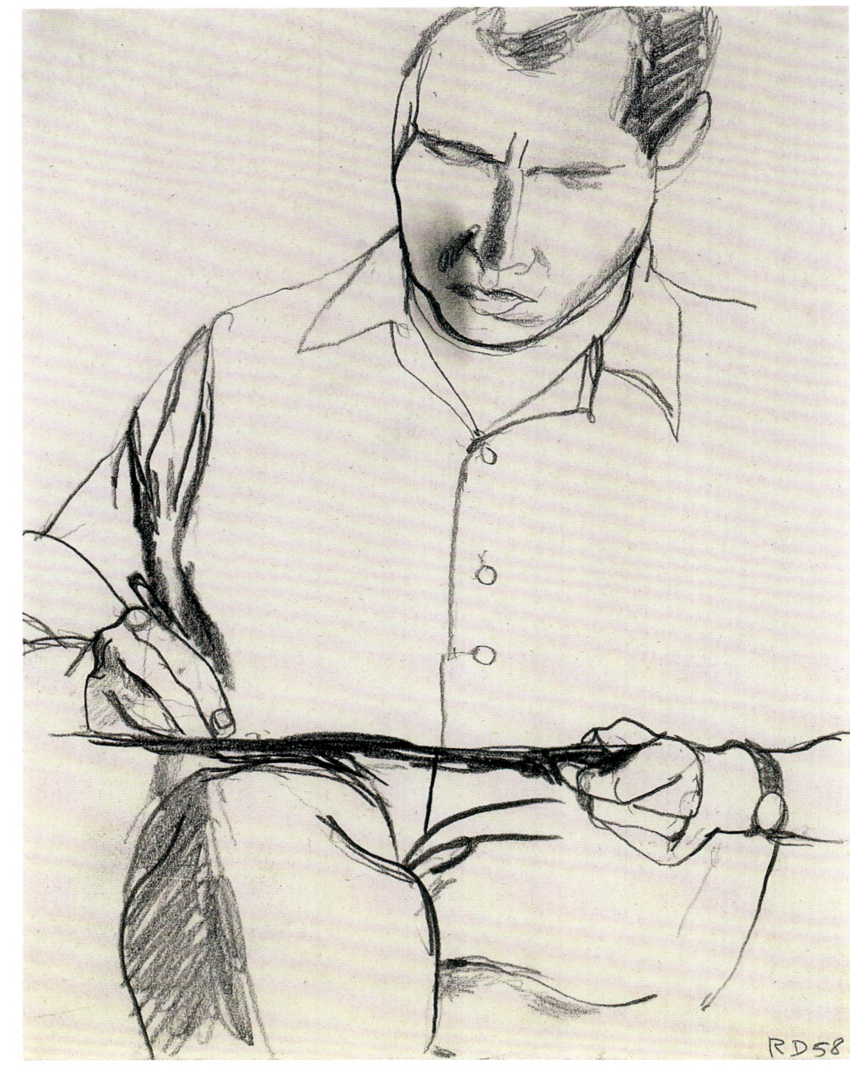

Four Portraits of William Theophilus Brown

Don Bachardy, 1963, ink on paper, 35 x 24 inches. Collection of Don Bachardy

Richard Diebenkorn, 1957, pencil on paper, 11 x 8 1/2 inches. Private Collection

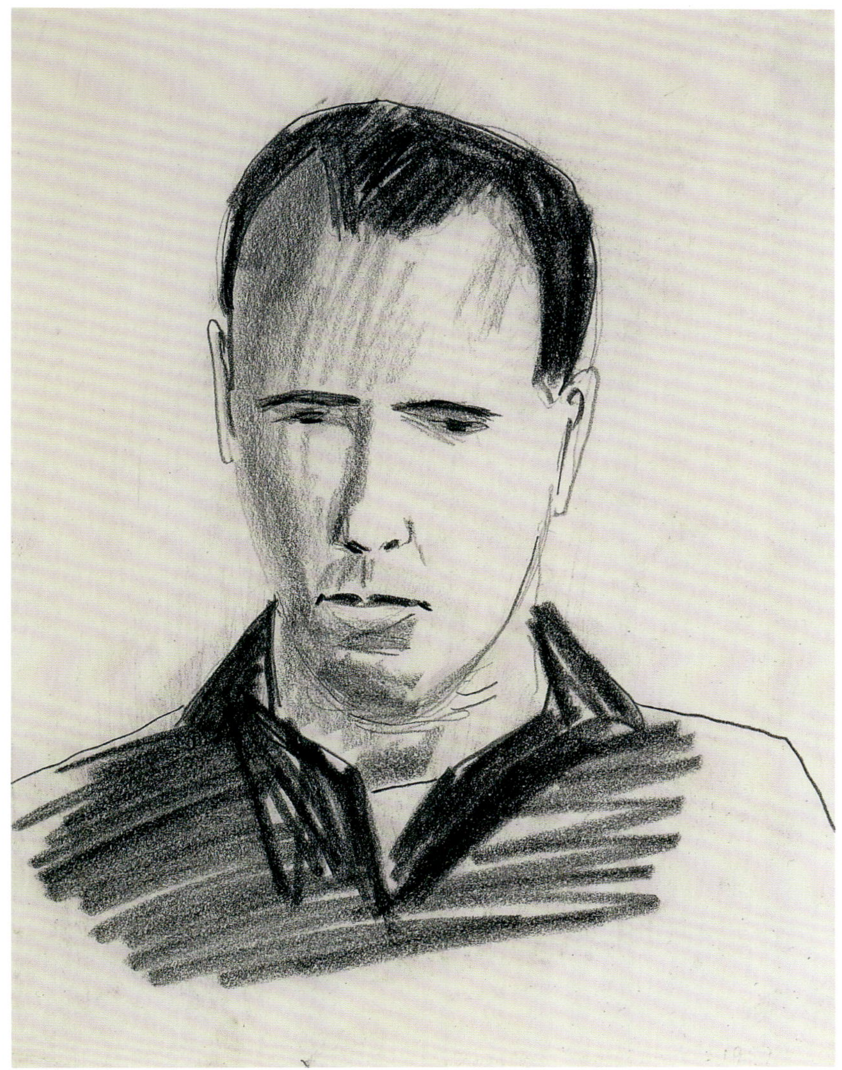

David Park, 1957, pencil and crayon on paper, 11 x 8 1/2 inches. Private Collection

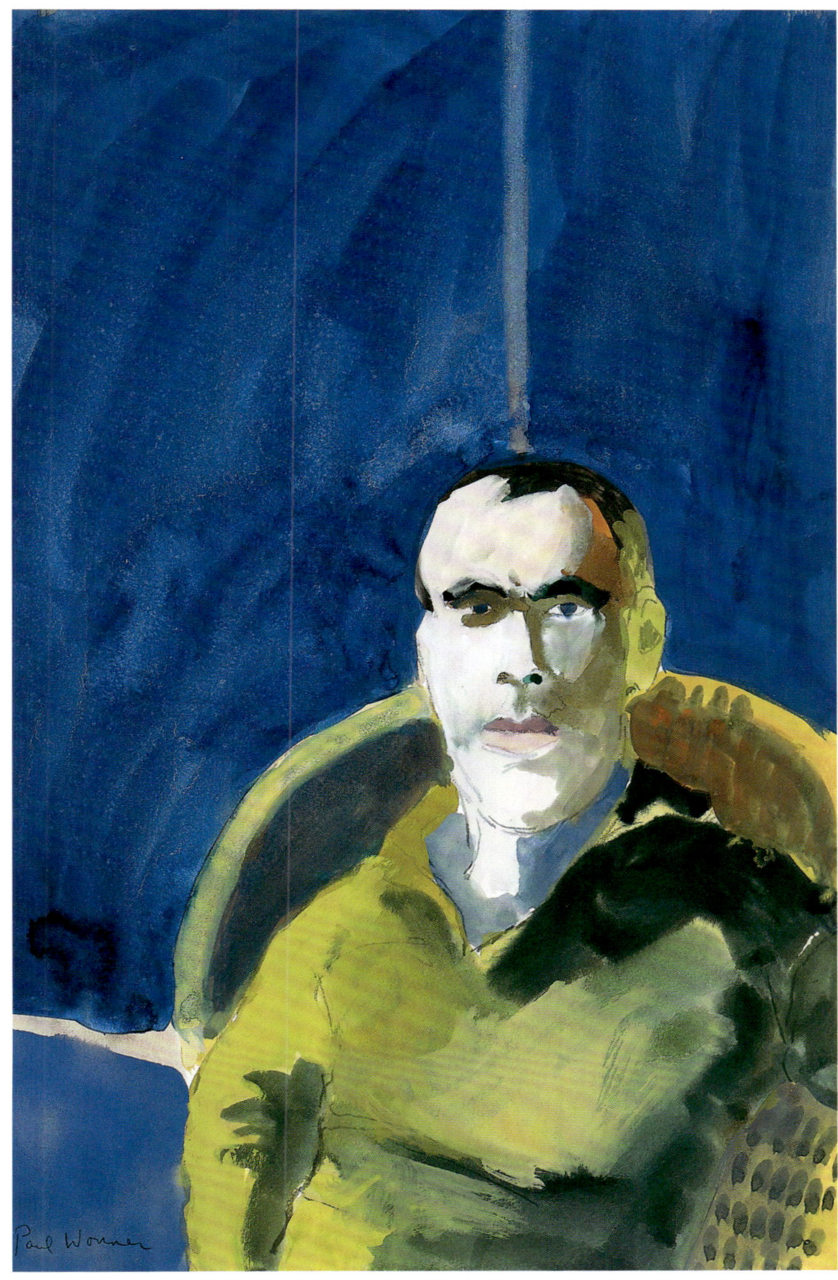

Paul Wonner, 1964, gouache on paper, 17 1/2 x 11 1/2 inches
Hackett-Freedman Gallery, San Francisco

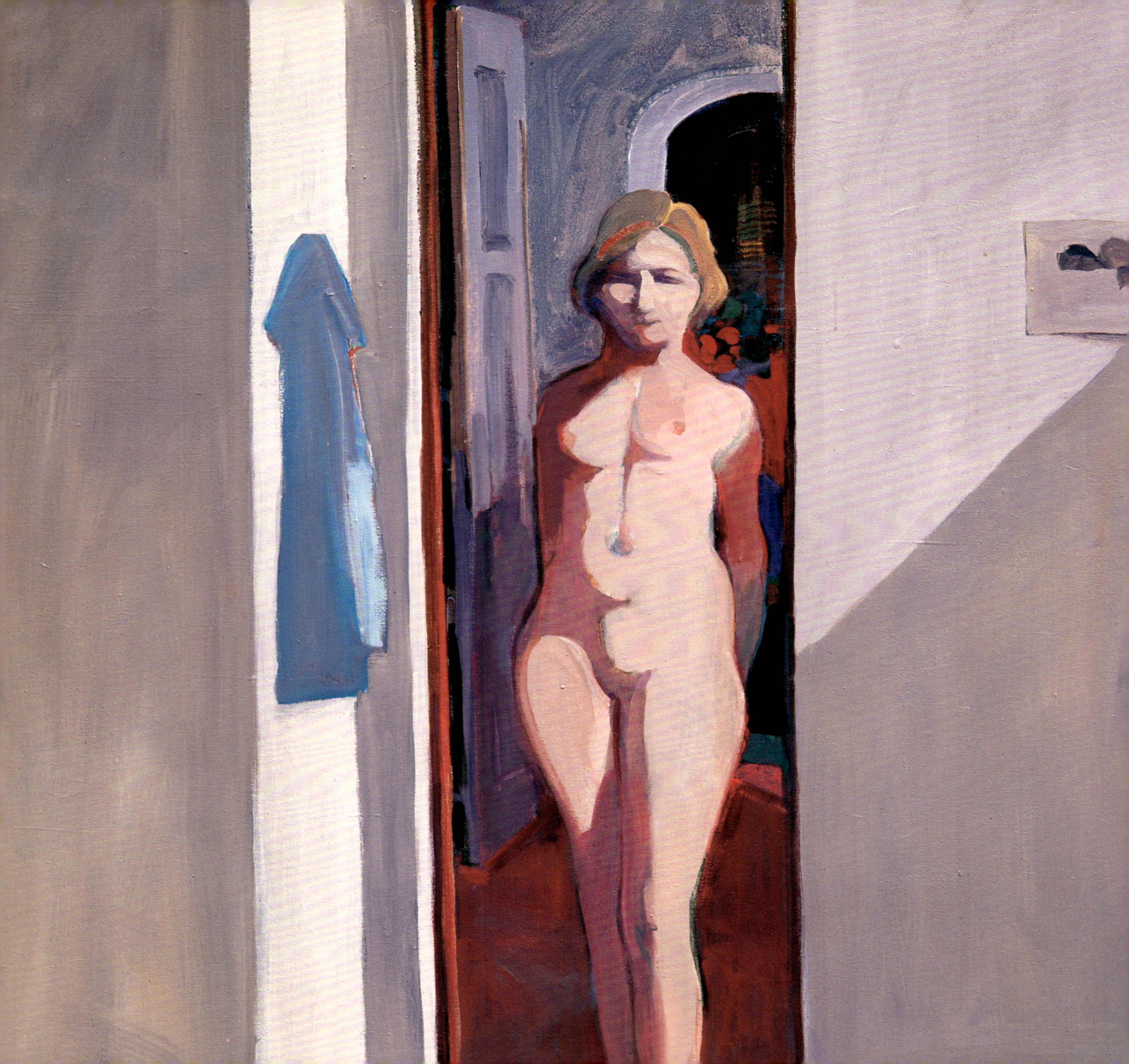

Epilogue

It is easy to identify William Theo Brown as a Western artist. His paintings appear to have grown out-of-doors, like plants. And there is a freedom of form and color that seems, like Western scenery, to know no boundaries. And the human figure takes its place as a natural part of the landscape, unseparated from it, as in the Matisse interiors. Man is not portraitured against a physical world that serves him as a mere background. He is an integral part of that world.

Other Western artists with whose work Brown's paintings have much in common are the late David Park, Richard Diebenkorn, Elmer Bischoff, and Paul Wonner. One might call them "the school of Western artists," for their paintings show marked similarities that must be the result of mutual influences upon one another; yet each of them has retained his identity. Most important of what they share is perhaps their common environment in which one is more aware of natural phenomena (the enormity of the sky, the mountains, the brightness of the sunlit world and the brilliance of its colors, the harmony to be found therein) than of the creations of man himself.

After the advent of Abstract Expressionism in this country, which produced in de Kooning, Pollock, Kline, Rothko, the first group of American painters to win high universal prestige and to cause European artists to look to this country for new visions (whereas American painters had before always looked to Europe, particularly to France), the American artist had to choose between two ways in which he could develop his contribution to plastic expression: he could return to the forms of nature with the new freedom he had found in the works of the abstract painters; or he could ignore the natural world and concern himself with the forms created by man. The Western painters chose the fist of these ways. One can not help feeling at times, studying he landscapes or the figures of Brown, or Wonner, or any of the other Western painters, that now the violence found in de Kooning and Pollock has been resolved, that peace and harmony can be found again, at least in the natural world; but he freedom remains to create dynamically in strong color and large, loose forms. Those who chose the second way to develop are known to us as Pop artists, and the Op. It is as much to be expected that their work would develop in the overpopulated East, where one is more conscious of man's created forms (skyscrapers, billboards, freeways) than of nature's. If at times their works appear "tricky," contrived, prankish, cerebral, these failings or attributes (depending on one's individual judgment) may also be attributed to an overpopulated, anxiety-ridden environment that has reduced the artist's pursuit to an almost primitive attempt to establish his personal identity, to become first a public figure, second an artist.

Easterners are often caught off-guard when they deign to visit the West. They admit the physical beauty of the land and its people, appreciate the temperate climate, and are a little surprised to find the tempo of the working day more leisurely than what they are accustomed to; for if one becomes inured to pandemonium, it takes a long adjustment to recognize the reality of a less strenuous world.

They become restless when they visit in California, they complain of the lack of intellectual stimulation, they distrust the physical freedom and the relaxed tempo, they seem to have no personal resources in dealing with time and environment and to be totally dependent upon the perhaps false stimulations of Eastern life and culture, the anxious status-seeking, the desperate scrabble for identity.

When reviewing an opening exhibition of one of the Western painters in a New York gallery, one of the city's newspaper critics summed up the response to the paintings as being "very comfortable to live with." The comment was not derogatory, but the critic had expressed this judgment, somehow, as if it had never before occurred to him that pictures could or should be comfortable to live with, and he did not seem to be convinced that this comfortableness was for certainty a virtue. Shock, sensation, repulsion have become such a fixed part of contemporary aesthetics, it is disarming to find a genuine artist who is not concerned with them.

The paintings of William Theo Brown are comfortable to live with. But one must not be deceived that this comfort is of blindness or indifference to the contemporary world. Rather, it is the comfort we feel in the presence of a sagacious friend who knows all the scandals and atrocities of the town's happenings, but who sees no reason to alarm his friends with shocking gossip and strives above all to retain humanness in all his relationships. And perhaps the harmony of these paintings is something that lies more deeply in the universe than its temporal eccentricities and conflicts. Perhaps to appreciate these paintings best, we must learn to accept the reality of harmony and oneness as surely as that of chaos.

—William Inge, 1967

STUDIO DOORWAY 1966, acrylic on canvas, 48 x 48 inches (on the cover of *RECENT PAINTINGS* published by the Felix Landau Gallery, 1968, Los Angeles, with essay by William Inge)

This statement was written for an exhibition of Theophilus Brown's paintings by one of America's greatest playwrights. William Inge's highly acclaimed dramas and their film adaptions, such as *Picnic, Bus Stop, Dark at the Top of the Stairs,* and *Splendor in the Grass,* illuminated the emotional undertow of the American psyche, framed by seemingly minor incidents of the Midwestern experience.

Like Theophilus Brown, Inge was raised in the middle of America and spent extended periods of time on both of its coasts. While it is not well known, Inge was a serious, knowledgeable, and discerning art collector. At the age of fifty he moved to Southern California where he wrote screenplays and several novels. It was during this period that he met Theophilus Brown, Paul Wonner, and other West Coast (described as "Western") artists.

For many who remember the predilections of the art world, particularly as they were manifested in the mainstream periodicals and by our major institutions during the fifties and sixties, Inge's statement remains very much on target. Considering the range of Brown's endeavor as it has evolved since the mid-sixties, William Inge's appraisal not only retains its astuteness as a summation of their character four decades ago, but quietly points us toward the continuous threads of his ambiguous imagery, the eroticism that haunts the inhabitants of his imagined terrains, and the lyricism of his reveries.

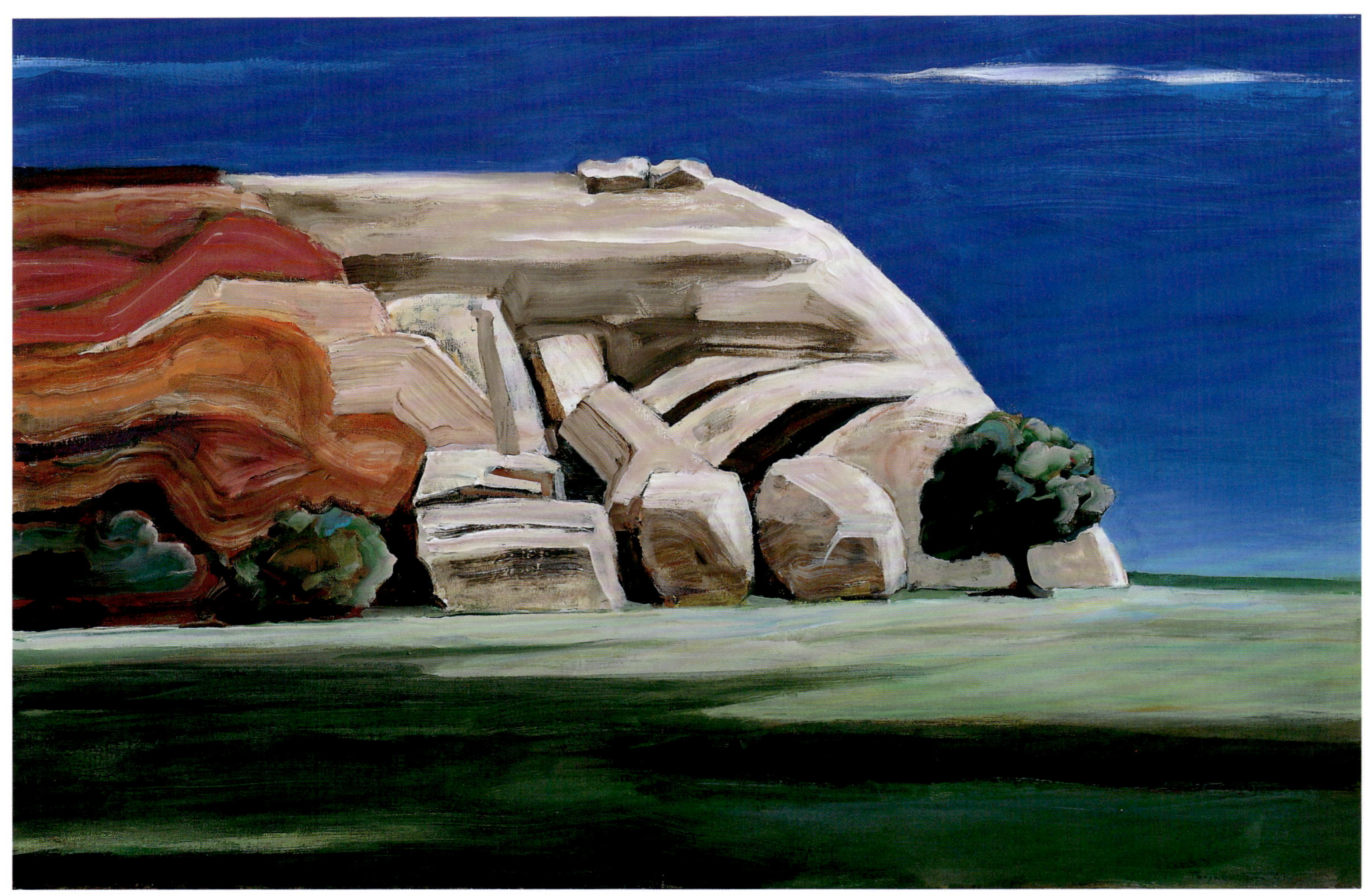

PETALUMA LANDSCAPE 2002, acrylic on canvas, 36 x 48 inches. Elins Eagles-Smith Gallery, San Francisco

THEOPHILUS BROWN

1919   Born on April 7 in Moline, Illinois
1941–45 United States Army, Stationed in United States and Europe

Education

1937   Lake Forest Academy, Lake Forest, Illinois
1941   Yale University, New Haven, CT, Bachelor of Arts Degree in Music
1948   Amédée Ozenfant Atelier, New York, New York
1949   Léger Atelier, Paris, France
1953   University of California, Berkeley, California, Master of Arts

Teaching

1954–56 University of California, Berkeley, California
1955–57 San Francisco Art Institute, San Francisco, California
1956–60,
1975–76 University of California, Davis, California
1968   Stanford University, Stanford, California
1968   University of Kansas, Lawrence, Kansas

SELECTED SOLO EXHIBITIONS

1957   San Francisco Museum of Art, California
1958   Felix Landau Gallery, Los Angeles, California
1960   Felix Landau Gallery
1961   Barone Gallery, New York, New York
1962   Kornblee Gallery, New York, New York
1963   Felix Landau Gallery
1965   E. B. Crocker Art Gallery, Sacramento, California
        Hollis Gallery, San Francisco, California
1965   Felix Landau Gallery
1967   University of Kansas Art Museum, Lawrence, KA
        Felix Landau Gallery
1968   Landau-Alan Gallery, New York, New York
1972   Charles Campbell Gallery, San Francisco, California
1975   Charles Campbell Gallery
1978   Charles Campbell Gallery
1982   Elizabeth Packard Smith Gallery, UC Santa Cruz, California
1983   John Berggruen Gallery, San Francisco, California
1987   Maxwell Davidson Gallery, New York, New York
        John Berggruen Gallery
1989   Maxwell Davidson Gallery
        Koplin Gallery, Los Angeles, California
1990   Tatistcheff Gallery, New York, New York
1991   Koplin Gallery
        John Natsoulas Gallery, Davis, California
1992   Tatistcheff Gallery
1994   Tatistcheff Gallery
1998   Dominican College, San Rafael, California
2000   Campbell-Thiebaud Gallery, San Francisco
2001   Robert Green Fine Art, Mill Valley, California
2002   Freddie Fong Gallery, San Francisco, California
2003   Elins Eagles-Smith Gallery, San Francisco, California

SELECTED GROUP EXHIBITIONS

1953   *Seventy-Second Annual Painting & Sculpture Exhibition of the San Francisco Art Association* (and numerous other Annuals). San Francisco, California

        Annual Exhibition: Paintings & Sculpture. Oakland Art Gallery, Oakland, California

        Seventeenth Annual Watercolor Exhibition of the San Francisco Art Association

1954   *Western Painters Annual Exhibition.* Oakland Art Museum

1955   *Fifth Annual Oil & Sculpture Exhibition.* Richmond Art Center, Richmond, California

1956   *San Francisco Art Association Members Show* (prize for Football). M. H. de Young Memorial Museum, San Francisco, California

1957   *Art of the Bay Region: Neil Sinton & William (Theophilus) Brown.* San Francisco Museum of Art

        American Paintings: 1947–57. Minneapolis Institute of Art, Minneapolis

1957–58 *Contemporary Bay Area Figurative Painting.* Oakland Art Museum, Los Angeles County Art Museum, and tour

1957   *Second Pacific Coast Biennial.* Santa Barbara Museum of Art, California

1957–59 *West Coast Artists.* San Francisco Museum of Modern Art, San Francisco, California and tour

1958   *Fresh Paint.* M. H. de Young Memorial Museum

        Tenth Anniversary Loan Exhibition. Felix Landau Gallery

        Twenty-Second Annual Drawing & Print Exhibition. San Francisco Museum of Art

        Third Pacific Coast Biennial. Santa Barbara Museum and tour

1959   *East-West (with Paul Wonner and John Paul Jones).* Zabriskie Gallery, New York, New York

        Bay Area Printmakers' Society Sixth National Exhibition. Oakland Art Museum

1960   *Winter Invitational Exhibit.* California Palace of the Legion of Honor, San Francisco, California

1960   *Twentieth Century Drawing.* Art Center, La Jolla, California

1960   *Sixty-Fourth American Exhibition: Painting & Sculpture.* The Art Institute of Chicago, Illinois

1961   *Third Winter Invitational.* California Palace of the Legion of Honor

1961   *Lithographs from the Tamarind Workshop.* Art Galleries, University of California, LA, and tour

1962   *Painters West of the Mississippi: The Realist Image.* Colorado Springs Fine Arts Center, Colorado

1963   *Paul Wonner: Watercolors & Drawings; Theo William Brown: Paintings & Drawings.* Esther Bear Gallery, Santa Barbara, California

1964   *Paintings & Constructions of the 1960's: Selections from the Richard Brown Baker Collection.* Museum of Art, Rhode Island School of Art, Providence, Rhode Island

1964   *The Painter and the Photograph.* The Art Gallery, University of New Mexico, Albuquerque, New Mexico, and tour

1964–65 *Theophilus Brown & Paul Wonner.* Esther Bear Gallery, Santa Barbara, California

1965   *American Painting 1966.* Virginia Museum, Richmond, Virginia

1966   *Drawings from the Figure: Mark Adams, Theophilus Brown,
        Gordon Cook, Wayne Thiebaud, and Beth Van Hoesen.*
        California State University Gallery, Hayward, California

1981   *Contemporary Landscapes.* Art Museum of South Texas,
        Corpus Christi, Texas

1982   *California Contemporary.* Monterey Peninsula
        Museum of Art, Monterey, California

1983   *Figure Drawings: Mark Adams, Theophilus Brown, Cordon Cook,
        Wayne Thiebaud, Beth Van Hoesen.* Charles Campbell Gallery

1983   *Bay Area Figurative Art: 1950–1965.* San Francisco Museum of
        Modern Art, California; Hirshhorn Museum and Sculpture
        Garden, Washington, DC; and Pennsylvania Academy of Fine
        Arts, Philadelphia, Pennsylvania

1990   *American Realism & Figurative Art: 1952–1990.* Miyagi Museum
        of Art, Sendai; Sogo Museum of Art, Yokohama; Tokushima
        Modern Art Museum; Tokushima; Museum of Modern Art, Shiga
        and Kochi Prefectural Museum, Kochi, Japan.

1991–92 *Still Life.* Gerald Peters Gallery, Santa Fe, New Mexico

1993   *American Realism & Figurative Painting.* Cline Fine Art Gallery,
        Santa Fe, New Mexico

1999   *Green Woods & Crystal Waters: The American Landscape
        Tradition.* Philbrook Museum of Art, Tulsa, OK; John and Mable
        Ringling Museum, Sarasota, FL; and Davenport Museum of Art,
        Davenport, Iowa

        Theophilus Brown and Paul Wonner, Wiegand Gallery, College
        of Notre Dame, Belmont, California

SELECTED MUSEUM AND CORPORATE COLLECTIONS

Achenbach Foundation for Graphic Arts, Legion of Honor,
San Francisco, California
Berkeley Museum, University of California Berkeley, California
Cantor Center for the Arts, Stanford University, Palo Alto, California
Capital Records, Los Angeles, California
Crocker Art Museum, Sacramento, California
Commerce Trust Company, Kansas City, Kansas
Davenport Museum of Art, Iowa
Hirshhorn Museum and Sculpture Garden, Washington, DC
Metropolitan Museum of Art, New York, New York
Oakland Museum of Art, California
Readers Digest Association, New York, New York
San Francisco Museum of Modern Art, San Francisco, California
Sheldon Memorial Art Gallery, University of Nebraska, Lincoln, Nebraska
University of Kansas Art Museum, Lawrence, Kansas

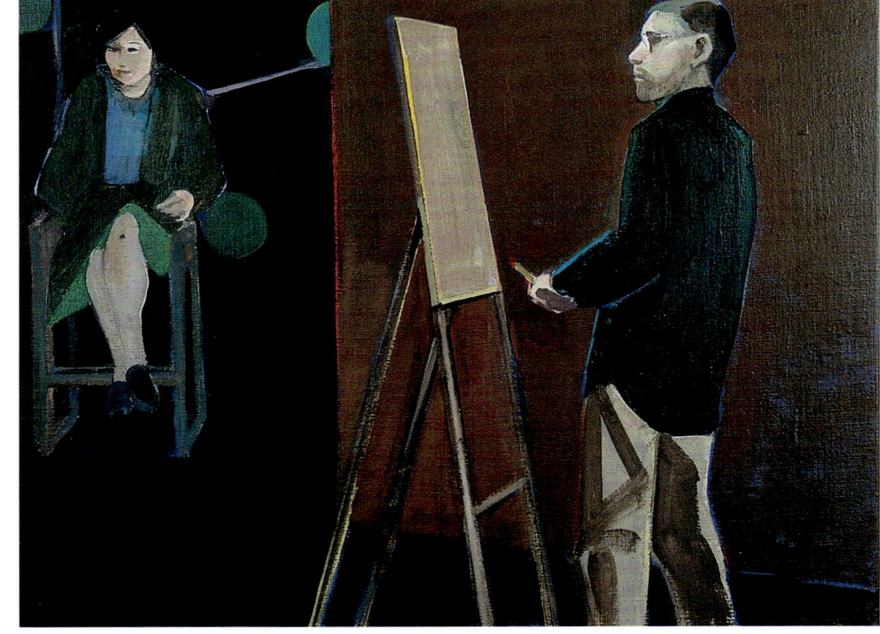

MARK DRAWING 1985, acrylic on board 18 x 24 inches
Collection of Beth Van Hoesen, San Francisco

PHOTOGRAPHY CREDITS:

John White, Lee Fatherree, Phocasso, Scott McClaine,
Sixth Street Studio, Joseph Painter, Gini Stoll

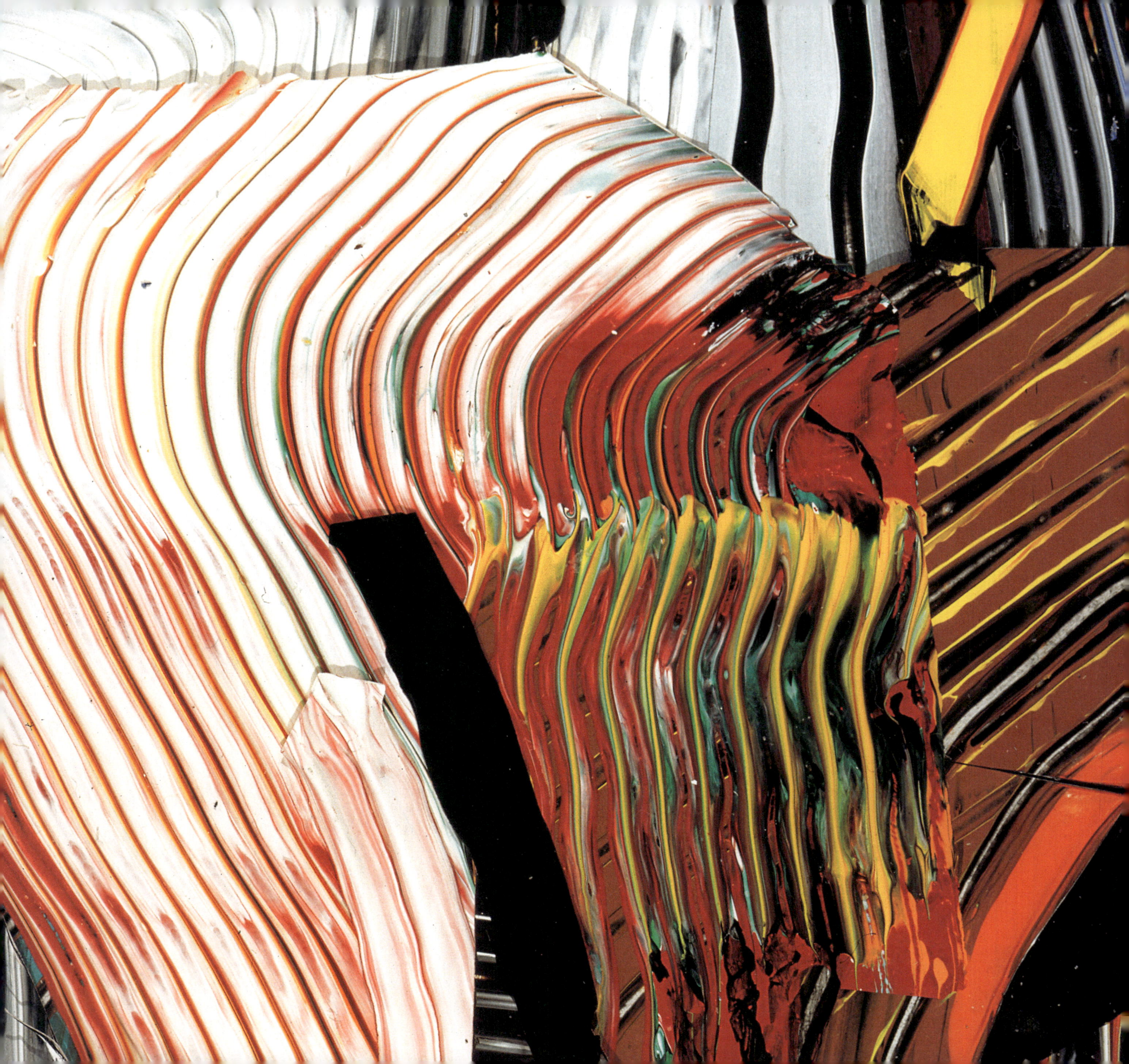